Penguin Book 2012
The Shocking History of Advertising

Ernest Sackville Turner was born in Liverpool in 1909
and was educated at the Priory School, Shrewsbury,
and Orme School, Newcastle-under-Lyme. He was a
journalist in the 1930s working on the *Glasgow
Evening Times*, the *Glasgow Evening Citizen*, and the
Scottish Daily Express. During the Second World War
he served in the Royal Artillery, joining the staff of
the army magazine, *Soldier*, in Brussels in 1945. He
became editor in 1946 and held the position until
1957, when he resigned to concentrate on writing.
He was awarded the O.B.E. in 1953.

E. S. Turner's work as a freelance writer has appeared
in some fifty newspapers and magazines and he has
written a great deal of light verse, on the profits of
which he visited America four times before the war,
once on the maiden voyage of the *Queen Mary*. He
has also written *Boys Will Be Boys*, a light-hearted
study of boys' magazines and 'penny dreadfuls',
Roads to Ruin (or *The Shocking History of Social
Reform*), *A History of Courting*, *Gallant Gentlemen*,
Call the Doctor, *The Court of St James's*, and many
others. His latest book is *Taking the Cure*. In 1964 he
was appointed to the *Punch* Table.

Ernest Turner has an American wife and two
daughters. His home is at Orpington, in Kent.

D1513348

E. S. Turner

The Shocking
History of
Advertising

Penguin Books
in association with Michael Joseph

Penguin Books Ltd, Harmondsworth,
Middlesex, England
Penguin Books Inc., 7110 Ambassador Court,
Baltimore, Maryland 21207, U.S.A.
Penguin Books Australia Ltd, Ringwood,
Victoria, Australia

First published by Michael Joseph 1952
This revised edition published in Penguin Books 1965
Reprinted 1968

World Copyright © E. S. Turner, 1952, 1965

Made and printed in Great Britain by
Butler & Tanner Ltd, Frome and London
Set in Monotype Times

This book is sold subject to the condition
that it shall not, by way of trade, be lent,
re-sold, hired out, or otherwise
disposed of without the publisher's consent,
in any form of binding or cover other
than that in which it is published

Contents

Author's Note

This revised edition of a book first published in 1952 takes note of some subsequent developments in the story of advertising. Among these are the introduction of commercial television in Britain, the rage for motivational research in America, the controversy over 'subliminal' advertising, and the ban on sky-writing and similar activities in Britain. The opportunity has also been taken to include other new material in various chapters.

The scope of the book is confined to commercial advertising in newspapers and magazines, on hoardings, in the streets, in the sky, and on radio and television. It does not touch on advertising in the ancient world (gladiatorial shows were placarded on the walls of Rome) or in the Middle Ages. This is partly for reasons of space, partly because all that can usefully be written about advertising in those days has already been written at length. Nor does the book touch on the history of shop and inn signs, on bellmen, or on old playbills, all of which have been adequately dealt with elsewhere.

State propaganda is mentioned only in so far as it influenced commercial advertising. Such extensions of advertising as public relations, fairs, and exhibitions are not treated here, nor are specialized fields like window-dressing and direct mail advertising. The book does take in its stride many unorthodox forms of advertising, as for instance on the coin of the realm or on the sails of yachts, but it does not set out specifically to deal with 'publicity' – of the kind which takes the form of hanging an elephant (as once described by Mr H. L. Mencken) or swimming the English Channel for commerce.

The field is limited to Britain and America. To avoid repetition, the chapters on America are designed to be complementary to those on Britain.

Henry Sampson's much-quoted *History of Advertising* was published in 1874, before modern advertising began. Frank Presbrey's *History and Development of Advertising*, published in 1929, was devoted more to American than to British advertising, especially in its latter stages. Both these books contain a good deal more about the early origins of advertising than the present one. Sampson found much material in the long articles on advertising which appeared in the *Edinburgh Review* in 1843 and the *Quarterly Review* in 1855, to which the present writer is also indebted.

Introduction

Advertising is the whip which hustles humanity up the road to the Better Mousetrap. It is the vision which reproaches man for the paucity of his desires. The *New Yorker* calls it 'our industrial chinook – keeping the fires of trade stirred up, keeping the Press defiant'.

No one doubts that advertising has done much to raise the standards of physical well-being. The catalogue of its benefactions, real and claimed, is a long one. It has speeded the introduction of useful inventions to a wide as distinct from a select circle. It has brought prosperity to communities which did not know how to sell their rotting crops. By widening markets, it has enabled costs of raw materials to be cut, accelerated turnover, lowered selling prices. It has spread seasonal trade and kept people in employment. It has given a guarantee of dependability – for who (as that advertisement used to ask) would buy a nameless motor-car put together in a back-street workshop? Its defenders claim that advertising has abolished heavy underwear, made people clean their teeth (which was more than the dentists could persuade them to do), and made them Nice to be Near. These gratifying results have been achieved, not only by informative, but by persuasive and indeed by intimidating advertisements. The prime object of the exercise was not, of course, to benefit humanity but to sell more fabrics, more toothpaste, more disinfectant.

Not least important, advertising is also the buttress of a free and cheap press, which otherwise would exist only by the conditional subventions of governments, parties, and pressure groups. It is also the provider of free radio and television entertainment for millions daily. Here, the prime object may be not to entertain, but to sell goods; yet millions are reasonably satisfied with, and grateful for, the fare they receive.

Why, then, do advertising men suffer from periodic qualms about their calling? Why do they not shrug off the criticisms of intellectuals, of those who demand a tax on advertising or who wish to see the 'fortunes' spent on it diverted to pay for public works? Sometimes the advertising men do shrug off these charges; sometimes they try to rebut them. If the society we serve is materialistic (they say) would it not be more fair to concentrate criticism on that society? If nations insist on over-producing, is it reasonable to blame the salesmen who try to keep themselves and those who hire them in a state of solvency – even if it means that the less enterprising or astute go to the wall? If society cannot thrive without waste or discontent, why brand the advertising man as an apostle of waste and a merchant of discontent? In any event (the apologists now argue) the advertising man cannot *create* new wants; he can only stimulate latent ones. Which is open to argument.

Perhaps the qualms of the advertising men spring from the knowledge – as Professor J. K. Galbraith has hinted[1] – that the keenest brains are employed to sell fringe commodites which fulfil no urgent public need, but which do something to lighten the rat race for which advertising is in some measure responsible – goods like tobacco, liquor, drugs, sweets, and gum. In a prosperous society there comes a point, as the professor indicates, when advertising no longer rewards the community with lower prices and greater efficiency. The manufacturer in a competitive market cannot conquer by price-cutting, for that way lies suicide; all he can do is to battle expensively, ingeniously, and perhaps unscrupulously for a bigger share of the existing market. This is unlikely to be achieved by a calm presentation of facts about his product, or by a plea for loyalty, but it can be done by a variety of tricks, among which is to invest the product with subjective qualities – offering romance with chocolates, poise with perfume, popularity with dance lessons, social prestige with motor-cars. In Shepherd Mead's *The Admen* (1958) a character says that toothpaste presents the real challenge to the advertiser, since there is not enough difference between one brand and another 'to put in your eye'. The same could be said of many cigarettes, most whiskies, nearly all petrols. Somehow the advertising man

1. *American Capitalism.*

must persuade the public that his brand is different, or more desirable; and if he does not do so, factories are going to close down and agencies disappear. He must find what arguments he can to solace his conscience. If, for example, it is ethical for doctors to prescribe useless medicines with a purely psychological value (placebos), why is it unethical to sell a sound product by investing it with a fanciful appeal?

Ought the Admass (Mr J. B. Priestley's word) to be protected from the wiles of the advertiser? The code which governs television advertising in Britain insists that no advantage shall be taken of the 'natural credulity' of children. Is it fair to take advantage of the natural credulity of adults? Should all advertising be so patently honest that 'wayfaring men, though fools, shall not err therein' (the phrase is Isaiah's, and the contention is that of America's Federal Trade Commission). The advertising man's reply is likely to be that if the public are to be protected against advertisements, they ought also to be protected against the editorial columns, which often contain an abundance of half truths, deceptions, and slanted misinformation. The public, he contends, brings a robust common sense to the assessment of advertisements; it can distinguish a flourish from a fact, a whimsy from a promise.

Yet the bulwark of common sense cannot always be depended upon to withstand the pounding and insinuating sea of suggestion. 'Nobody believes the nonsense in any one advertisement,' wrote Mr Herbert Agar in *A Time for Greatness*. 'Everyone is affected by the mist of deception which we continually breathe. The trouble is that we prefer to breathe that mist.'

Francis Bacon would have agreed. In his essay on truth, he wrote:

A mixture of a lie doth ever add pleasure. Doth any man doubt, that if there were taken out of men's minds vain opinions, flattering hopes, false valuations, imaginations . . . and the like, but it would leave the minds of a number of men poor shrunken things, full of melancholy and indisposition, and unpleasing to themselves?

Several writers, including Bertrand Russell and Aldous Huxley, have deemed it necessary to advocate teaching children distrust of advertising. Mr Huxley in his *Ends and Means* (1937) said that children ought to be shown that there was no logical connexion between the pretty girl in her expensive dressing-gown and the merits of the toothpaste she was intended to advertise. 'This lesson might be brought home by practical demonstrations,' said Mr Huxley. 'Chocolates could be wrapped in a paper adorned with realistic pictures of scorpions, and castor oil and quinine distributed from containers in the form of Sealyham terriers or Shirley Temple.' Then, having mastered the 'art of dissociation' in the field of commercial advertising, the young generation would be on their guard against political and religious propaganda.

Mr F. P. Bishop, author of that thoughtful book *The Ethics of Advertising*, argued that suggestions like those of Huxley and Russell amounted to 'cynical manipulation of the infant mind'. If that is so, what is the appropriate description of the tactics revealed in this extract from an American magazine, *The Sound Track*, in 1951:

Speaking of surveys, we tried an experiment the other evening. . . . To a curly-headed four-year-old being tucked under the covers we posed this question: 'Susie, which product brushes teeth whiter?' 'Colgate's of course, Gramp.' We couldn't resist another. 'Which product washes clothes cleaner?' Without a moment's hesitation: 'Tide.' We tried once more. 'Which coffee gives the best value?' When she replied, 'A and P, and now good-night, Gramp,' we hurried out of the child's room with other questions beating at our brain.

Where else on earth is brand consciousness firmly fixed in the minds of four-year-old tots? How many pre-school age Americans are pre-sold on how many different products? How can we get reliable data? What is it worth to a manufacturer who can close in on this juvenile audience and continue to sell it under controlled conditions, year after year, right up to its attainment of adulthood and full-fledged buyer status? It *can* be done. Interested?

From this it can only be concluded that the advertising man – or this kind of advertising man – is the new Jesuit: 'Give me your children before they are five and they are mine for ever.' To him all values are different. Fog is not something which delays trains; it is something which prevents people seeing posters. A well-framed solus picture of a sauce bottle on the end of a house is something which improves local amenities. For him words have different meanings: loyalty means always buying the same hair oil. A bride is not a young woman on the edge of a great adventure; she is a conditioned consumer who by buying the right cosmetics and right brassière has captured her man, and who, when she returns from her honeymoon, will go into the grocer's and automatically recite those branded names which have been most loudly dinned into her ears for the last twenty-one years. To him all problems can be solved in terms of advertising. The remedy for absenteeism in the mines is to make miners *want* more luxuries; the remedy for strikes is to saddle the workers with hire-purchase commitments. He has made women adopt men's habits (smoking, wearing trousers) and now he wants to make men adopt women's habits (using perfume). If he opens a Bible it is only because he has read that such an exercise is valuable as a reminder of 'the value of iteration', or, as in the parables, of the need to tell the story in the first sentence.

Perhaps that is an overdrawn picture of an advertising man (compare Mr Cyrus Ducker's more flattering picture in Chapter 9). It is fair and necessary to say that the industry has gone to exceptional pains within the last two decades to purify itself. The briefest glance at the newspaper files of the 1930s will show what a tightening up has taken place. The less fastidious newspapers of those days were sustained, on occasions, by advertisements which today would be illegal and by others which wore so shifty a face that the advertising and publishing industries agreed to renounce them. Not all the cleaning up has been voluntary; many controls have been imposed by Parliament in the last ten years.

Although the list of restrictions and self-restrictions is long, there are still fields in which advertising is wide open to criticism on social grounds. An obvious example is that of tobacco advertising. The motor-car and petrol industries continue to lay emphasis on speed and 'punch'. In 1962 an Italian car was advertised in a London evening newspaper thus:

A FANTASY IN SPEED: There's a rare quality about the — saloon that gives a new concept of carefree motoring. Streaking away at an un-hurried hundred . . . accelerating from traffic lights to 50 m.p.h. in 7·8 seconds . . . braking relentlessly with power-operated disc brakes on four wheels . . . the — carries you everywhere in relaxed comfort.

An advertisement of another car said: 'See how silently and safely you take the — up to speeds that leave 100 m.p.h. far behind.' Many more examples could be quoted. American car manufacturers at one time agreed to refrain from stressing speed, but the pact broke down. With traffic casualties scandalously high, the policy of inciting drivers to exceed 100 miles an hour in safety and relaxed comfort seems irresponsible to the point of imbecility. The imposition of a 70 m.p.h. limit throughout Britain by no means ended the emphasis on 100 m.p.h. performance. If the advertising man is content to blame the manufacturer for demanding this kind of copy, neither can complain if the Government intervenes.

On a different level, one of the least happy features of advertising remains the publication of testimonials by the famous and the titled. According to an American authority on etiquette, it is 'socially permissible' for anyone, if properly approached, to endorse foods, liqueurs, cosmetics, and cars, but not depilatories, toothpaste, or underwear. Nevertheless, society women have told the public how they rid themselves of blackheads, and actresses have boasted of their 'all-over loveliness'. This sort of thing raises the credit of advertising as little as it raises the dignity of the human race. Whether these testimonials are disinterested, whether they are venal, is beside the point; the point is that not two persons in a hundred *believe* them to be voluntary and disinterested. The public is resigned to the fact that anyone entering certain spheres of public life will feel impelled, sooner or later, to lend his or her name to some everyday product. George Bernard Shaw told in *Everybody's Political What's What* how a lady of his acquaintance had been paid £800 for a letter 'ascribing the beauty of her complexion, which was entirely and thickly artificial, to a well-advertised face cream'. He himself had been offered a big sum to attribute his mental powers to an equally well-advertised correspondence course.

Inevitably it will be retorted that an author has no cause to complain about the use of testimonials, since it is with the aid of them that his works are usually commended. The difference seems to be that reviewers, whatever their faults, are under no suspicion of venality. What is more, they write their own copy.

Is it not time that advertising, if it wants to be considered honest, should try to look honest – in this important respect? Would the loss of these 'vain opinions ... false valuations ... imaginations ...' really leave the minds of many people 'poor shrunken things, full of melancholy and indisposition, and unpleasing to themselves'?

1   The Mercuries

Sooner or later, the explorer seeking to track down the first advertisement in an English publication finds the trail petering out in a world of mermaids and two-headed children: the world of the Elizabethan broadsides and news-books which, at irregular intervals, purveyed 'miraculous newes' to the credulous.

Some of these publications were little more than elaborated versions of the handbills which were distributed at Bartholomew's Fair, calling attention to such attractions as 'a woman with three breasts, an admirable work of nature', or 'a male child born with a bear growing on his back alive'. The Elizabethans had a relish for abominations, which they liked to believe were the result of whoredom and worse.

Since these accounts contained the addresses of the objects they described, and such phrases as 'to be seen without a moment's delay' or 'unlikely to live long', they were in essence just as much advertisements as the handbills at the Fair.

Some of the earlier news-books had set out to give a sober and reliable service of news, both from home and overseas; but dispatches were slow, authority was obstructive, and men of culture were often contemptuous. It was not surprising that the writers lost heart and filled out their sheets with improbabilities. However, the outbreak of the Thirty Years War in 1618 quickened the literate public's appetite for news. The first regular English periodical appeared in 1622; it was the *Weekly Newes* of Nicholas Bourne and Thomas Archer. Closely following came Nathaniel Butter's *Newes from Most Parts of Christendom*. It was a later publication by Archer – the *Mercurius Britannicus* – which carried on 1 February 1625 one of the earliest known advertisements in a periodical:

An excellent discourse concerning the match between our most

Gracious and Mightie Prince Charles, Prince of Wales, and the Lady Henrietta Maria, daughter of Henry the Fourth, late King of France . . . with a lively picture of the Prince and Lady cut in bronze.

The Star Chamber harassed the publishers of these early sheets. When it was abolished in 1641, English journalism faced the future with more confidence. With the outbreak of the Civil War in 1642, 'mercuries' under all manner of extravagant titles began to appear, on both sides. In these, book advertisements were frequent. The *Mercurius Politicus* carried announcements of Izaak Walton's *Compleat Angler* and works by John Milton.

By mid century, most of the mercuries were printing advertisements, not only of books and freaks but of lost horses and the earliest patent medicines. In 1652 Samuel Sheppard, one-time assistant to Ben Jonson, noted that the writers of news-books had adopted 'another quaint device in their trading', explaining:

There is never a mountebank who, either by professing of chymistry or any other art, drains money from the people of the nation, but these arch-cheats have a share in the booty – because the fellow cannot lye sufficiently himself he gets one of these to do't for him.

Sheppard was sceptical, too, about those 'lost' horse advertisements. So was a writer in the *Man in the Moon*, who imputed deceit to Henry Walker, publisher of 'that Westminster catterwaule called *Perfect Occurrences*'. 'The sheet,' he said, 'was bumbasted out with a sixpenny story of a man that lost a walleyed mare at Islington', when the truth was that Walker himself stole the animal 'to carry his fardle of nonsense, heresy, and blasphemy to Uxbridge to infect his parish in the national sin of Atheisme'. Whatever the truth about the wall-eyed mare of Islington, it has to be recorded that the 'lost and found' advertisements soon began to cover a good deal of criminality.

The range of advertisements continued to widen in the decade which preceded the Plague. One historic announcement was this in the *Mercurius Politicus* of 30 September 1658:

THAT Excellent, and by all Physicians, approved *China* drink, called by the Chineans *Tcha*, by other nations *Tay* alias *Tee*, is sold at the Sultaness Head Cophee-House, in Sweeting's Rents, by the *Royal* Exchange, London.

Tea was to be the subject of rather less restrained advertising

That Prodigy in Nature,

By His Majesty's Authority,

At the Sign of *Charing-Cross*, at *Charing-Cross*.

THere is to be seen a strange and monstrous Child, with one Body, and one Belly, and yet otherwise it hath all the Proporsions of two Children, that is two Heads, two Noses, two Mouths, four Eyes, four Ears, four Arms, and four Leggs, four Hands, and four Feet, the monster is of the femal kind, it was born at Fillips Town on the Twenty Ninth of April, 1699 The Father of this monster is present where it is to be seen.

[*British Museum*

Among the earliest printed advertisements in England were handbills calling attention to monsters.

ere long. Coffee, first drunk in the Jamaica Coffee House in 1652, had already been hailed by Pasqua Rosée, its importer, as an excellent remedy and cure for consumption, dropsy, gout, scurvy, the King's Evil, and hypochondriac winds. 'It so incloseth the orifice of the stomach, and fortifies the heat within, that it is very good to help digestion . . . it much quickens the spirits and makes the heart lightsome.'

A year later came one of the earliest advertisements in a new class. It is from *Occurrences from Foreign Parts*:

At the *Rose* Tavern in Covent Garden, there is to be sold these Silks and Stuffs following at very reasonable rates: Silver Stuffs, Plushes, Sattains, Colour'd Tabbies, Colour'd Silk Mohairs, Silk Prunelloes, Podeswaies, Flower'd Tabbies, Taffaties, Silk Druggets, Tammies, Woosted Druggets, Serges, and all sorts of Bombassenes.

Other advertisements of this type offered Confaloes, Dorees, Elatches, Gelongs, Lungees, Mulmuls, Pelongs, Romals, Tanjeebs, Shahagerries, Farendines, Hair Shags, and Shaloons.

An early entrant in the field of hygiene was this, from the *Mercurius Politicus* of 20 December 1660:

Most Excellent and Approved DENTIFRICE to scour and cleanse the Teeth, making them white as Ivory, preserves from the Tooth-ach; so that, being constantly used, the Parties using it are never troubled with the Tooth-ach; It fastens the Teeth, sweetens the Breath, and preserves the Gums and Mouth from Cankers and Imposthumes. Made by Robert Turner, Gentleman; and the right are onely to be had at Thomas Rookes, Stationer, at the Holy Lamb at the east end of St Paul's Church, near the School, in sealed papers at 12d the paper.

The Merrie Monarch was not long on the throne before he himself sought the aid of the advertising columns. The most renowned of these advertisements, in the *Mercurius Publicus* in 1660, ran:

☞ We must call upon you again for a Black Dog, between a Greyhound and a Spaniel, no white about him, onely a streak, on his Brest, and Tayl a little bobbed. It is His Majesties own Dog, and doubtless was stoln, for the Dog was not born nor bred in *England*, and would never forsake his Master. Whosoever findes him may acquaint any at Whitehal, for the Dog was better known at Court than those who stole him. Will they never leave robbing His Majesty? Must he not keep a Dog? This Dogs place (though better than some imagine) is the only place which nobody offers to beg.

It must not be supposed that Charles II used the advertisement columns solely for the recovery of dogs. A king had his responsibilities to his people. In the *Public Intelligencer* of 1664 appeared the following:

Whitehall, 14 May 1664. His Sacred Majesty, having declared it his Royal will and purpose to continue the healing of his people for the Evil during the month of May and then to give over till Michaelmas next, I am commanded to give notice thereof, that the people may not come up to Town in the Interim and lose their labour.

By now the Press was again under restraint. Charles rewarded the loyal Roger l'Estrange, who had narrowly escaped execution by the Commonwealth, with the congenial task of supervision and suppression of newspapers. L'Estrange's personal conviction was that a newspaper 'makes the multitude too familiar with the actions and counsels of their superiors'. As justification for publishing two newspapers of his own – the *Intelligencer* and *The News*, both of which carried advertisements – he cited the need for prudent guidance of the public. He conducted night raids on printing shops, looking for treasonable works in the Press; nor was he disappointed.

The year of the Plague – 1665 – affords a notable example of a mass assault on the public by advertisers, using not only the public prints but the public streets. Daniel Defoe has told the story admirably in his *Journal of the Plague Year*. When the threat of the pestilence became real, he says, the public ran to 'conjurors and witches', eagerly 'storeing themselves with such Multitudes of Pills, Potions and Preservatives' that they 'prepared their bodies for the Plague instead of preserving them against it'.

It is incredible and scarce to be imagined how the Posts of Houses and Corners of Streets were plastered over with Doctors' Bills, and Papers of Ignorant Fellows; quacking and tampering with Physick, and inviting the People to come to them for Remedies; which was generally set off with such flourishes as these, (viz.) INFALLIBLE preventive Pills against the Plague. NEVER-FAILING Preservatives against the Infection. SOVEREIGN Cordials against the Corruption of the Air. EXACT Regulations for the Conduct of the Body, in case of an Infection. Antipestilential Pills. INCOMPARABLE Drink against the Plague, never found out before. An UNIVERSAL Remedy for the Plague. The ONLY TRUE Plague-Water. The ROYAL ANTIDOTE against all Kinds of Infection; and such a number more that I cannot reckon up; and if I could would fill a Book of themselves.

The claims were no more sweeping than some of those advanced in our own century on behalf of 'cures' for cancer and tuberculosis.

Here are some more advertisements quoted by Defoe:

An Italian Gentlewoman, just arrived from NAPLES, having a choice Secret to prevent Infection, which she found out by her great Experience, and did wonderful Cures with it in the late Plague there; wherein there died 20,000 in one day.

An eminent HIGH-DUTCH Physician, newly come over from HOLLAND, where he resided during all the Time of the great Plague, last year in AMSTERDAM; and cured Multitudes of People that actually had the Plague upon them.

An antient Gentlewoman having practised with great Success, in the late plague in this city, ANNO 1636, gives her advice only to the Female Sex. . . .

Defoe noted that one advertiser offered 'advice to the poor for nothing'. This advice, it turned out, was to buy the advertiser's physic. The Lord Mayor of London instructed the Royal College of Physicians to publish a list of cheap remedies, but nothing could prevent the public from throwing their money away on physic, charms, philtres, exorcisms, incantations, and amulets.

Many of the quacks who stayed on to snatch the last profits were themselves felled by the Plague. Others dosed themselves liberally with their own specifics, and died just the same. It is possible that many of the vendors honestly believed in the virtues of their potions, or at least were convinced that their remedies were no less efficacious than those compounded by the doctors. The state of medical knowledge at the time was illustrated by a belief that if a sufferer from the Plague breathed upon glass, an observer with a microscope would see 'strange, monstrous, and frightful shapes, such as Dragons, Snakes, Serpents, and Devils, horrible to behold'. But, said Defoe, 'this I very much question the truth of'.

For two years after the Plague no quacks were to be seen in the city. Some of the public thought they had been all swept away by the infection, as 'a particular mark of God's Vengeance upon them, for leading the poor People into the Pit of Destruction, merely for the Lucre of a little Money. . . .' Defoe preferred to believe that many of them had fled into the country, unloading the remainder of their wares on scared villagers, who were hourly awaiting the visitation from the cities.

During the Plague the journals of L'Estrange had advertised nostrums, official instructions, and closing-down notices by inn-keepers and others. When the Great Fire succeeded the Plague, merchants whose businesses were burned out were invited to advertise their new addresses in the public sheets (a facility denied, for security reasons, to burned-out traders in the 'blitz' of the Second World War).

London could take it, then as now. The business world struggled back to its feet. New and better coffee-houses sprang up, fre-quented by merchants, masters of vessels, lawyers, authors, gamblers, clergymen, promotors of the new joint-stock com-panies. England was on her rapid climb to commercial greatness. The fear of another Great Fire was partly allayed by a new facility now advertised: fire insurance.

In the annals of advertising, the outstanding name in the latter part of the seventeenth century is that of John Houghton, a one-time apothecary and general dealer. He was not the first to con-ceive a paper published primarily to carry advertisements, but he was the first to propagate the idea with vigour and imagination. In 1682 he launched a modest sheet entitled *A Collection for the Improvement of Husbandry and Trade*. It had indifferent success, but Houghton kept on. The world must be informed of the possibilities of advertising. For instance, there were great and unrealized opportunities in the fields of 'situations vacant' and 'situations wanted':

If I can meet with a sober man that has a counter-tenor voice I can help him to a place worth £30 the year or more.

I want a complete young man that will wear a livery, to wait on a very valuable gentleman; but he must know how to play on a violin or flute.

I want a pritty boy to wait on a gentleman who will take care of him and put him out an apprentice.

I know of several curious women that would wait on ladies to be housekeepers.[1]

1. 'Curious' was used in the sense of 'careful' or 'bestowing care'.

Houghton was concerned also with the exchange of commodities and services:

> If any want all kinds of necessaries for corps or funerals, I can help to one who does assure me that he will use them kindly; and whoever can keep their corps till I get to London and have a coffin set down may have them afterwards kept any reasonable time.
>
> At one Mr Packer's in Crooked Lane, next the Dolphin are very good lodgings to be let, where there is freedom from noise, and a pretty garden.

Houghton stimulated a peculiar traffic which persists down to the present day – in second-hand sermons. He advertised books, reading and recommending them gratuitously. At one point he had to chide booksellers for putting new titles on old books. He published quack advertisements, but told his readers that they were under no obligation to read them.

'Anything to oblige' might have been Houghton's motto. He even entered the matrimonial field:

> I know of several men and women whose friends would gladly have them match'd, which I'll endeavour to do, as from time to time I shall hear of such whose circumstances are likely to agree; and I'll assure such as will come to me it shall be done with all the honour and secrecy imaginable. Their own parents shall not manage it more to their satisfaction and the more comes to me the better I shall be able to serve 'em.

Houghton seems to have been one of those men whose passion it is to 'do business', no matter of what type. He has been called the 'father of advertising', and his naïve-sounding offers and protestations have been quoted widely at advertising conventions in the last hundred years.

He had sounder ideas about the stimulation of business than the publisher of the *Country Gentleman's Courant*, who wrote in 1685:

> Seeing promotion of trade is a matter which ought to be encouraged, the price of advertisements is advanced to twopence a line.

2   'Near to Perfection'

During the early years of the eighteenth century, the years of Steele and Addison, publications of all kinds sprang into life, flourished for a day, and subsided into oblivion. In 1702 appeared the first daily newspaper in Britain – the single-sheet *Daily Courant*.[1] Two years later Defoe started his *Review*, and poured his prodigious energies into it for the next nine years. Next came 'social' journalism, with a deliberate appeal to women, as exemplified by the *Tatler* (1709) and the *Spectator* (1711). Even the liveliest of these publications were usually in financial straits. When, in 1712, on Crown instigation, the Government set out to curb the activities of the Press, it did so by imposing a punitive stamp duty and an advertisement tax. Each paid announcement, whether it occupied a line or a column, was charged at the rate of one shilling; if this was not paid within thirty days the tax was trebled, one third being paid to the informer. With many others, the *Spectator* went to the wall, while the more disreputable sheets continued to flourish.

For a century to come, the advertisements in all these publications were directed mainly at a limited circle: the frequenters of coffee-houses, where the newspapers were read. There was little or no advertising of household goods. The advertiser was content to offer the wealthy their coffee, their tea, their turtles, their books and wines and wigs, their purges and 'cosmaticks'; to notify them of new plays and concerts; to offer them lottery tickets; to engage them servants and slaves. He was also prepared, as will be seen, to offer even more intimate help.

For a progress report on the art of advertising at the end of the first decade, it is necessary to turn to Addison's essay in the *Tatler* of 14 September 1710.

1. The first daily newspaper in America appeared in 1704: the *Boston News Letter*. It carried advertisements.

'It is my custom in a dearth of news to entertain myself with those Collections of Advertisements that appear at the end of all our Publick Prints,' wrote Addison. He saw advertisements as 'instruments of Ambition' – 'A man that is by no means big enough for the *Gazette* may easily creep into the Advertisements; by which means we often see an Apothecary in the same paper of news with a Plenipotentiary, or a running Footman with an Ambassador.'

Addison noted how advertisements during late years had been used for the furthering of controversy: 'The Inventors of "Strops for Razors" have written against one another this way for several Years, and that with great Bitterness.' He went on:

The third and last use of these writings [advertisements] is to inform the world where they may be furnished with almost every thing that is necessary for life. If a man has Pains in his Head, Cholic in his Bowels or Spots on his Cloathes he may here meet with proper Cures and Remedies. If a man would recover a Wife or a Horse that is stolen or stray'd, if he wants new Sermons, Electuaries, Asses' Milk or any-thing else, either for his Body or his Mind, this is the Place to look for them in. . . .

Addison told how a puff for Spirit of Lavender had been sent to him, with five shillings, for insertion among his advertisements; it was written in such a Ciceronian manner that he felt he ought to include it in the body of his paper. It ran:

The highest compounded Spirit of Lavender, the most glorious, if the expression may be used, enlivening scent and flavour that can possibly be, which so enraptures the spirits, delights the gusts, and gives such airs to the countenance as are not to be imagined but by those that have tried it. The meanest sort of the thing is admired by most gentlemen and ladies; but this far more, as by far it exceeds it, to the gaining among all a more than common esteem. It is sold in neat flint bottles, fit for the pocket, only at the Golden Key in Wharton's Court, near Holborn Bars, for three shillings and sixpence, with Directions.

'At the same time that I recommend the several Flowers in which this Spirit of Lavender is wrapped up, if the expression may be used,' went on Addison, 'I cannot excuse my fellow-labourers for admitting into their papers several uncleanly advertisements, not at all proper to appear in the works of polite writers.'

Among them I must reckon the 'Carminative Wind-Expelling Pills'. If the Doctor had called them 'Carminative Pills' he had been as cleanly as anyone could have wished; but the second word entirely destroys the decency of the first. There are other absurdities of this nature so very gross, that I dare not mention them; and shall therefore dismiss this subject with an admonition to Michael Parrot, that he do not presume any more to mention a certain worm he knows of, which, by the way, has grown seven foot in my memory; for if I am not much mistaken, it is the same that was but nine feet long about six months ago.[1]

Addison commented on some of the more elementary devices employed by advertisers to attract attention:

Asterisks and Hands were formerly of great Use for this Purpose. Of late Years the N.B. has been much in Fashion; as also were Cuts and Figures, the invention of which we must ascribe to the Author of Spring Trusses. I must not here omit the blind *Italian* character, which being scarce legible always fixes and detains the eye and gives the curious reader something like the satisfaction of prying in a secret.

He noted, too, the fomenting of controversy between rival merchants, who indignantly accused each other of 'base impositions', 'fallacious subterfuges', and so on. Also he remarked how the advertiser was expected 'to mention the universal Esteem or general Reputation of Things that were never heard of'.

The 'cuts and figures' mentioned by Addison were of varying standards, according to the skill of the blockmaker. Announcements of ship sailings were often introduced by small pictures of barques or brigantines in full sail. The column listing runaway apprentices was sometimes headed by a picture of a fugitive with his head turned back over his shoulder. Advertisements for horse thieves and men suspected of the more serious offences would be decorated by a neat little picture of a gallows, laden or otherwise. In due course embellishments came to be stipulated by almost every advertiser, so that the effect of them was lost and valuable space was wasted (shipping pages were strewn with more ships than ever sailed in the Armada). Many newspapers then imposed a ban on illustrations which lasted until almost the end of the nineteenth century.

Advertising occasionally masked the activities of out-and-out

1. The worm was sixteen feet long in the *Post Boy* of 27 April 1710.

rogues. In the *Daily Post*, which enjoyed the distinction of serializing *Robinson Crusoe*, appeared this innocent-looking announcement on 31 July 1724:

> LOST, the 28th inst. at the Installment at Windsor, a Gold Watch. . . . Whoever will bring the aforesaid Watch to Mr Jonathan Wild in the Old Baily shall have eight Guineas Reward; or if anyone will discover the Person who took the gold Watch, he shall have ten guineas Reward for such discovery to be paid by the aforesaid Mr Wild.

There was another advertisement in the same issue, in respect of a lady's watch. At this time Wild, the self-styled thief-taker, was at the height of his nefarious career. Under him served a corporation of thieves and highwaymen, who stole from wealthy victims nominated by himself; the pillaged goods were then sold back to the victims after such eye-washing formalities as public advertisements. In January 1724 Wild petitioned to be granted the freedom of London in return for his thief-catching services, for he handed over to justice many free-lance thieves (notably Jack Sheppard) and any members of his organization who defected. But already, by the time the above advertisement appeared, Wild was under strong suspicion. Six months later he was clapped in Newgate, where he still carried on business as best he could. Soon, however, he fell foul of a newly passed law making it a capital offence to take a reward for restoring stolen goods unless the thief was apprehended by the person rewarded. Wild was hanged at Tyburn on 24 May 1725. One result of his activities was that advertisers offering rewards were no longer allowed to say 'No questions ask'd'; a rule which had to be reinforced a century later.

The year 1728 saw friction between the coffee-house keepers and the publishers of newspapers. Grievances of the former were set out in a truculent pamphlet entitled *The Case of the Coffee-Men of London and Westminster: or an Account of the Impositions and Abuses put upon them and the whole Town by the present Set of News Writers*. Not least of the complaints was that the coffee men were 'made tools and properties of in the business of advertising'.

> They [the coffee-house keepers] stipulate for news, not advertisements. Yet the papers are ordinarily half full of them. The *Daily Post*, for example, is often equipped with thirty, which yields £3 15s. that day to the proprietors for the least. And sometimes that paper has

more. Well may they divide TWELVE HUNDRED POUNDS A YEAR AND UPWARDS! They are paid on both hands – paid by advertisers for taking in Advertisements and paid by the coffee men for delivering them out; which (to make use of a homely comparison) is to have a good dinner every day and be paid for eating it. Here's luck, my lads! Never was there so fortunate a business.

If the coffee-houses were closed, said the writer of this pamphlet, the advertisers would be forced back on their 'old habitations', namely gates, corners of streets, tavern doors, and public conveniences. 'And what would they be worth in such situations?' The coffee-house keepers threatened to start their own publications, but the storm gradually subsided.

The next noteworthy report on the state of advertising comes from Dr Samuel Johnson, who wrote in the *Idler* in 1759:

Advertisements are now so numerous that they are very negligently perused, and it is therefore become necessary to gain attention by magnificence of promises, and by eloquence sometimes sublime and sometimes pathetic.[1] Promise, large Promise is the soul of an Advertisement. . . .

As instances, Dr Johnson cited 'a washball that has a quality truly wonderful – it gave an exquisite edge to the razor', and a blanket 'warmer than four or five blankets and lighter than one'. However, a vendor of a 'beautifying fluid' had been candid enough to admit that it would not restore 'the bloom of fifteen to a lady of fifty'.

The technique of 'scaring the mother' had already been discovered. The Doctor noted how the manufacturer of an anodyne necklace 'warned every mother that she would never forgive herself if her infant should perish without a necklace'.

Dr Johnson was unhappy about the way in which 'a famous Mohawk Indian warrior, who took Dieskaw, the French general, prisoner' was being advertised as on exhibition 'with his face and body painted, with his scalping knife, tom-axe, and all other implements of war'. This noble warrior, Dr Johnson thought, suffered by being juxtaposed in the advertising columns with an offer of a fresh parcel of Dublin butter.

The Doctor then made the observation which has not failed to amuse later generations: 'The trade of advertising is now so near

1. 'Pathetic' meant 'impassioned', 'moving'.

to perfection that it is not easy to propose any improvement.' But he thought it time to administer a caution:

... as every art ought to be exercised in due subordination to the public good, I cannot but propose it as a moral question to these masters of the public ear, Whether they do not sometimes play too wantonly with our passions? as when the Registrar of Lottery Tickets invites us to his shop by an account of the prizes which he sold last year? and whether the advertising Controversists do not indulge asperity of language without any adequate provocation? as in the dispute about Strops for Razors, now happily subsided, and in the altercation which at present subsists concerning Eau de Luce. In an advertisement it is allowed to every man to speak well of himself, but I know not why he should assume the privilege of censoring his neighbour. He may proclaim his own virtue or skill, but ought not to exclude others from the same pretensions. Every man that advertises his own excellence should write with some consciousness of a character which dares to call the attention of the Public. He should remember that his name is to stand in the same paper with those of the King of Prussia and the Emperor of Germany, and endeavour to make himself worthy of such association. Some regard is likewise to be paid to posterity. There are men of diligence and curiosity who treasure up the Papers of the Day merely because others neglect them, and in time they will be scarce. When these collections shall be read in another century, how will numberless contradictions be reconciled? and how shall Fame be possibly distributed among the Tailors and Bodice-makers of the present age?

Dr Johnson's appeal to the advertiser to refrain from 'censoring his neighbour' is possibly the first move (an unavailing one) against 'knocking copy'.

In the latter part of the eighteenth century daily journalism entered a more responsible period. It was still an age of licence and frivolity in high places. It was the age that lost the American colonies, but it was also the age that founded an empire in India. Already the Industrial Revolution was on its way; the Black Country was beginning to stretch its shadow; mill towns were springing up on the northern moors; canals were streaking the green fields.

In 1772 the *Morning Post* appeared. In its early years it was a disreputable sheet, one of its first editors being a reverend rake who allowed both contributors and advertisers extraordinary latitude. It was a long time before respectability overtook the future organ of the squirearchy, a respectability fortified by lucrative columns of horse-and-carriage advertisements.

Then, in 1785, John Walter issued his *Daily Universal Register*, which three years later changed its name to *The Times*. From the beginning it promised to carry nothing which could tend to 'wound the ear of delicacy or corrupt the heart'. Advertisements would be inserted without fail the day after receipt, no matter how inconvenient this might be. John Walter's view was that 'A News-Paper in this particular ought to resemble an Inn, where the proprietor is obliged to give the use of his house to all travellers who are ready to pay for it and against whose persons there is no legal or moral objection'.

The Times had been in existence only a few months under its new name when the Bastille fell. From this point onwards the British Press found itself under stricter government surveillance, and the advertisement tax and stamp duty were further increased, in an attempt to drive journals with radical tendencies out of business. The advertisement tax had been raised to 2s. in 1757 and now jumped to 2s. 6d. It was a blow to new and struggling journals; but if a newspaper found advertisements were scarce, it was better to lift some from its contemporaries than to go without (a practice not unknown in a later day). 'In an emergency', says *The History of The Times 1785–1841*, 'the official announcements of the Victualling Office could be inserted without authority and the Minister afterwards brought by political pressure to pay for their insertion.'

The radical sheets refused to die; they were powerfully spiced with news of vice and crime. *The Times* itself was regarded with deep suspicion by the Government, and in the first year John Walter found himself imprisoned for libels on the royal dukes.

In those days of dangerous ideas an editor could not keep too careful a watch on his advertisement columns. John Mennons, editor of the *Glasgow Advertiser*, forerunner of the *Glasgow Herald*, explained to his readers one day in 1793 that he would have to suspend publication in order to answer an indictment in Edinburgh. He had innocently published, at the instance of a Gorbals gunsmith, an inflammatory announcement telling how the Sons of Liberty in Partick, having attentively perused the whole works of the immortal author of *The Rights of Man*, Thomas Paine, declare it as their opinion that if the nations would adopt the practical use of these works tyrants and their satellites would vanish like the morning mist before the rising sun, that social comfort, plenty, good order, peace and joy would diffuse their benign influence over the human race. . . .

Mennons escaped punishment, and resumed publication after nothing more than a bad fright. He was luckier than some who followed.

Many of the advertisements of the eighteenth century add such piquant footnotes to social history that the temptation to over-quote is strong. Some of the more general types of announcement may be noted here, leaving over the more scandalous ones, and those of the quacks, for separate attention.

Steele has told how, on going to the Bear Garden at Hockley-in-the-Hole, he had a paper thrust in his hand which read:

I, James Miller, sergeant, lately come from the frontiers of Portugal, master of the noble science of defence, hearing in most places where I have been of the great fame of Timothy Buck, of London, master of science, do invite him to meet me and exercise at the several weapons following:

Backsword	Single falchion
Sword and dagger	Case of falchions
Sword and buckler	Quarter-staff

For those who liked their fun unrefined, there was another kind of match, like this one advertised to take place near Whitechapel Mount:

I, *Mary Brindle*, of *New England*, well-known through the Provinces in *North America*, particularly that of Massachusetts, for my extra-ordinary Skill, Judgment and peculiar Dexterity in the noble Science of handling the Members, having by a series of Good Fortune discom-fited all those who have hitherto encountered with me, as well on the public as private Stage, throughout the American Colonies; and being desirous of aggrandizing my Character in this Part of the World, do hereby invite the famous Miss *Elizabeth Sturdy* to meet and fight me . . . for the Sum ten pounds old Tenor, and hope to convince the mistaken World that though born in the new-discovered Country we are no wise inferior in Point of Courage to any Woman upon the Face of the Globe.

Mary Brindle

I, *Elizabeth Sturdy*, from the Kingdom of *Ireland*, do readily accept to the above Challenge; and notwithstanding my present Indisposition, occasioned by the Scars lately received at *Guy's* and *St Thomas's*, *will not fail* of meeting this celebrated Heroine, and doubt not that I shall soon convince her, as I have several others before, of her Folly and Vanity in attempting to contend with one who possesses so great a Share of innate Courage so peculiar to her famous Hibernian Ancestors.

Elizabeth Sturdy

For this encounter, which was to be preceded by numerous 'bye-battles' between cinder-wenches and oakum-pickers, it was announced that 'commodious Seats are provided for the Ladies to separate them from the Mob; and if the Weather proves cold, Mr Smarvey intends to accommodate the Ladies with Pans of Charcoal-Dust gratis'.

An advertisement of a similar combat at Hockley-in-the-Hole stipulated that each woman should hold half a crown in each hand 'and the first woman that drops the money to lose the battle'.

If women were pitted against each other in public, how much mercy could animals expect? Alan St H. Brock, in his *History of Fireworks*, quotes this advertisement of an entertainment at the Bear Gardens, Hockley-in-the-Hole:

Likewise a green Bull to be baited, which was never baited before, and a Bull to be turned loose, with Fireworks all over him; also a mad Ass to be baited. With a variety of Bull baiting and Bear baiting and a Dog to be drawn up with Fireworks. To begin exactly at three of the Clock.

A later announcement (1730) promised 'a Mad Bull dressed up with Fireworks is to be turned loose in the same place; likewise a Dog dressed up with Fireworks; also a Bear to be turned loose. N.B. a Cat to be tied to the Bull's Tail.'

Not always were fireworks put to such dubious uses. The advertisements of the London pleasure gardens throughout this century tell of many ingenious and spectacular novelties. Those who visited Cuper's Gardens on 4 September 1749 were promised 'a curious and magnificent firework which has given great satisfaction to the nobility, wherein Neptune will be drawn on the canal by sea horses and set fire to an Archimedean worm and return to the Grotto'. Great sieges, like those of Quebec and

Gibraltar, were elaborately reconstructed. Ranelagh, towards the end of the century, staged a volcanic eruption which was a favourite for many years. There was a scene representing Mount Etna and the Cave of Vulcan, with the Cyclops forging armour for Mars 'as described in the Aeneid of Virgil', all to the accompaniment of music 'compiled from Gluck, Haydn, Giardini, and Handel'.

'Black boy' advertisements were a constant feature in the newspapers of this century. Those who are under the impression that slavery never existed in these isles will here find a rude awakening. To show that the keeping of black boys was not just a Metropolitan fad, here is an announcement from the *Edinburgh Advertiser* of 20 January 1769:

To be Sold

A BLACK BOY, about 16 years of age, healthy, strong, and well made, has had the Measles and Smallpox, can shave and dress a little and has been for these several years accustomed to serve a single gentleman both abroad and at home.

For further particulars, inquire at Mr Gordon, Bookseller, Parliament Close, Edinburgh, who has full powers to conclude a bargain.

Some of these boys came from Spain and Portugal, others may have been brought to Britain by the masters of slavers. Not infrequently, a boy fled his master, and then his virtues were sung less praisefully. He was described as pock-marked, instead of 'has had the smallpox'. He became bandy legged and wall-eyed, instead of handsome. Almost all runaways, whether black boys, apprentices, serving maids, or absconding clerks, seem to have been ugly, misshapen creatures. In an appeal for information about thieves who had stolen fishing tackle, an advertisement of 1775 said: 'The above banditti may be discovered by the following marks: they all walk *on one side*, are *short-sighted* and most of them are marked with the King's Evil.'

After describing a missing youth, another advertisement continued: 'Whoever meets him at a Billiard Table, or at a Bawdy House. . . .' Occasionally, however, a missing person was given the benefit of the doubt, as in an announcement in the *Daily Advertiser* in 1772: 'It is feared he has been surprised and engaged by some of those Persons employed to pick up Men for the India Company and is confined and deprived of Pen, Ink, and Paper.'

From time to time the advertising columns carried contrite apologies from those who had temporarily forgotten their station in life. The *Public Advertiser* on 25 January 1785 contained the following:

I, Richard Thomas, Footman to the Right Hon. Lady Vernon, do publicly acknowledge myself greatly to Blame, for staying out without Leave until Three O'Clock in the Morning and then making a Disturbance to gain Admittance. I am extremely sorry that by a Blow I gave my Fellow Servant, Edward Brett, I broke his Jaw-bone, which he kindly forgives; And I must humbly thank Lady Vernon for her Ladyship's Goodness in pardoning my insolent and impertinent Behaviour to her.

Newick Park, Jan. 17, 1785

Richard Thomas

And on 8 December 1785 the same newspaper published this:

We do hereby ask Pardon of the Gentlemen we insulted on Sunday Night last, at the Turnpike on the New Road near Islington, and promise never to offend in a like Manner again. We sincerely acknowledge the Lenity of those Gentlemen in dropping the Prosecution against us and hope all Turnpike Collectors will take warning by our example.

John Bottomley
John Benwell

At this time, the charge for insertion of advertisements 'of moderate length' in the *Public Advertiser* was 3s. 6d.; not an inordinate sum to pay in tribute to the magnanimity of one's betters.

When a vacancy occurred in the public service, aspirants to the post frequently put forward their claims by advertisement. In 1785 a collector of land tax called Till died, and the front page of the *Public Advertiser* carried daily solicitations for his post to the Lord Mayor and Aldermen of London. Henry Cranke humbly hoped that the character he had maintained for forty years in the conduct of an extensive trade, 'in which I have suffered losses to the amount of SEVENTY THOUSAND POUNDS', would be his most powerful recommendation. Another aspirant, Stanley Crowder, also presented his ill-success in business as a recommendation; he had suffered a series of difficulties 'which the utmost assiduity could not surmount'. If the selectors appointed him they would have 'the heartfelt satisfaction of reviving the drooping spirits of a family unaccustomed to distress'. In a later letter Crowder appended a postscript: 'Give me leave to add that I have an aged mother, whom I have maintained for many years, who is now entirely dependent upon me for support, and that I am totally out of business.' The successful candidate was the dead collector's son, Richard Till, who had never doubted, in his daily solicitations, that the post would go to him as a token of respect to his father's memory.

A learned monograph might well be written, with the aid of advertisements from this century and the next, on the bear's grease trade. There is room to quote only the following from the *Daily Universal Register*:

H. LITTLE, Perfumer, No. 1 Portugal Street, Lincoln's Inn Fields, acquaints the Public, that he has killed a remarkable fine RUSSIAN BEAR, the fat of which is matured by time to a proper state. He begs leave to solicit their attention to this Animal, which, for its fatness and size, is a real curiosity. He is now selling the fat, cut from the Animal, in boxes at 2s. 6d. and 5s. each, or rendered down in pots, from One Shilling to One Guinea Each.

A generation like our own, accustomed to smearing its hair with the 'scientifically prepared' contents (animal, vegetable or mineral – who knows?) of some highly advertised jar, recoils fastidiously when assured that its great-grandfathers used raw unprocessed bear's fat to nourish their scalps. The enterprising Mr Little was only one of a big band of bear's grease men. Unlike a certain rival, he did not caution his buyers to keep the grease off their hands lest they grow hairy paws. To the modern reader it is all very mysterious. Where did Mr Little obtain his bears? Where and how did he keep them? How did he fatten and exercise them? How did he mollify those neighbours who were downwind of the bears?

If bears were a nuisance, so were bugs – in spite of the heroic efforts of men like Andrew Cooke, of Holborn Hill, who boasted in the *Public Advertiser* of 1775 how, over twenty years, he had 'cured 16,000 beds with great applause'. He professed to be the oldest bug-destroyer in England, and was angry with a rival who styled himself 'Bug-Destroyer to His Majesty'. If anyone had a right to this title, said Cooke, it was himself, for he had worked at sundry apartments in the King's Palace.

Almost every social foible was reflected sooner or later in the advertising columns. At the end of the century a country gentleman in Lancashire was advertising for a recluse to sit permanently underground in his hermitage, for £50 a year. The successful candidate had to be willing to let his hair and nails grow as long as possible.

PUBLIC AND PERSONAL

The advertisements of the latter part of the eighteenth century project a startling light on urban morals. In the daily newspapers are to be found impassioned paragraphs in which some 'beauteous fair one' who smiled in the direction of a gentleman at such-and-such a place and time is implored to keep a rendezvous with him. Clearly it was not shyness which prevented these amorous gentlemen from making the lady's acquaintance in the first place, but the fact that she was under escort. Occasionally the advertiser received an encouraging reply; sometimes a stinging rebuff, possibly from the lady's escort.

An enterprising publisher issued, in 1750, a symposium of contemporary advertisements under the title *Love at First Sight*, or *The Gay in a Flutter*. One announcement reads:

Being at Covent Garden Play-house the fifth instant, saw a gentleman there that belonged to the Army, and afterwards went to a House in the Strand; if the Gentleman is of the same Mind, as he was then, and will leave a line at the said House for *M.B.*, where I can see him, I will certainly meet him.

Note.—If the Gentleman has forgot, the last Words were, *To Trust to Chance*.

One of M.B.'s sisters in the profession also sought to re-establish contact with a military friend:

Whereas on *Tuesday* night last between the Hours Nine and Ten a certain well and strong Backed Officer did go into a Lady's Bed-Chamber in a house in Dean Street and take from the Head of the Bed while she was in it a gold Watch with a Steel polished Woman's Chain with several seals, etc. hanging to it; this is therefore to give notice that unless he delivers the Watch etc. to the Owner within four days from the Publication hereof, or comes in Person to perform what was that Night expected, his Name will be published at Length and his Person described. . . .

Threats to publish the names of offenders were quite common. 'An old Fornicator whose sins have rendered his Limbs incapable to support him' was informed that he would be exposed if he did not stop annoying persons at a certain address; a warning which must have worried quite a number of aged gallants. Another threat of exposure was addressed to a lady who 'persuaded a gentleman to meet her on the other side of the water a month ago', and who had given him 'a most severe C—p'; but if the lady was prepared to render, in writing, a good explanation for her incivil action, the advertiser was prepared to hold his tongue.

Sometimes the motive of the advertiser is obscure. Was it merely a disinterested moralist who inserted the following announcement, or a woman jealous of her more adventurous neighbours?

This is to advise certain ladies to pay no more Visits to a certain House near Covent Garden; for it is a Place where Reputation may be lost but I have never heard of any got there.

Matrimonial offers are ten a penny. It was usual for a gentleman to stipulate that the lady must be in possession of a private income, and vice versa; and at the same time the partner had to be capable of returning 'a most sincere and ardent love'. Sometimes a gentleman politely deprecated his personal appearance, which probably meant he was little removed from Caliban; but usually he would make the most of any modest asset, as 'a gentleman of Hampshire, wearing his own Hair. . . .' There were plenty of brash announcements like this, from *Love at First Sight*:

If any Lady not yet past her Grand Climacterick, of a Comfortable Fortune in her own Disposal, is desirous of spending the Remainder of her Life with a tolerably handsome young Fellow of *great* Parts, about five feet six inches, she may hear of such a one to her mind by inquiring at the *Theatre* Coffee-House for Mr F., a Sophister of — College, Cambridge.

In May 1750 the *Daily Advertiser* carried the following:

WANTED: Tall and graceful in her Person, more of the fine Woman than the pretty one . . . good Teeth, soft Lips, sweet Breath, with Eye no matter what Colour so they are but expressive . . . her bosom full, plump, firm and white . . . a good understanding without being a wit, but cheerful and lively in Conversation, polite and delicate of Speech, her Temper humane and tender and to look as if she could feel Delight where she wishes to give it. If such a one there be! there is a Gentleman of £2,000 a year, 52 years next July, but of a vigorous Strength and amorous Constitution that will marry her, be her Fortune ever so small, and settle on her a clear Jointure of £600 a year . . . she must consent to live entirely in the Country . . . she must not be more than 14 years, nor less than seven years younger, than the Gentleman.

There were many dubious requests by impoverished single ladies for loans of money. One lady wishing to borrow £100 announced that 'the Security, though personal, may probably be very agreeable to a single Gentleman of Spirit'. She is more likely to have obtained her loan than the lady who inserted the following in the *Daily Advertiser* of 27 October 1752:

GENTLEMEN. It's well-known that many of you spare neither Pain nor Cost, when in pursuit of a Woman you have a Mind to ruin; or when attached to one you have already undone; But I don't remember to have heard of any considerable Benevolence conferred by any of you on a virtuous Woman: I therefore take this Method to let you know, that if there should be any among you, who have a desire to assist (with a considerable Present) an agreeable Woman, for no other Reason, than because she wants it; such a Person or Persons (if such there be) may, by giving their address in this Paper, be informed of an Occasion to exercise their disinterested Generosity.

As the century progressed the 'personal' advertisements became more and more bare-faced. In January 1775 the *Public Advertiser* carried several insertions of the following (one of them under an announcement of a new edition of the Holy Bible):

This Day is Published
Price 2s. 6d. with the original Introduction HARRIS'S LIST OF COVENT GARDEN LADIES; or, Man of Pleasure's Kalendar for the Year 1775. Containing an exact Description of the most celebrated Ladies of Pleasure who frequent Covent Garden and other parts of the Metropolis.
Printed for H. Ranger, Temple Exchange Passage, Fleet Street. Where may be had Harris's List for 1771, 1772, 1773, and 1774.

Who was Harris? And how did he compile his popular year-book? Was it a one-man task? Who (if anyone) reviewed it?

Even though it did not sell out every year, the guide must have been profitable enough to repeat. There was also a companion guide to the ladies of Piccadilly.

In the *Morning Post* in 1775 a young gentleman offered to devote his services to 'a lady of real fashion and fortune, who may wish to have some particular deficiencies thoroughly supplied, without subjecting herself to any disagreeable restraints'. Quoting this proposition, Henry Sampson suggested that young gentlemen like this, who 'knew what was marketable', may have done much 'to prevent the titles and fortunes of noblemen and gentlemen who married late in life from passing to remote branches'.[1] There was another way of preserving an inheritance. The *Public Advertiser* of 16 April 1776 contained the following under the heading 'Matrimony':

> A Gentleman who hath filled two succeeding seats in Parliament, is near sixty years of age, lives in great Splendour and Hospitality, and from whom a considerable estate must pass if he dies without Issue – hath no objection to marry any widow or single lady, provided the party be of genteel birth, polished manners and five, six, seven or eight months gone in her pregnancy. Letters to — Brecknock at Will's Coffeehouse.

According to the *Sporting Magazine* (November 1793 and June 1794) the advertiser was Edward Wortley Montagu, who wished to stop his estate passing to a branch of the Bute family. Several women answered his advertisement, of whom one was selected; but Montagu died on his way to meet her.

Occasionally there were advertisements by gentlemen anxious to pass on their unwanted mistresses into good hands. There were also numerous offers by benevolent ladies to help outcast girls, or to remedy any inconveniences suffered by young women of spirit and fashion. Here is one of many in the *Morning Post* of 1772:

> LADIES may be accommodated to lie-in, where care, tenderness, humanity, honour and secrecy may be depended on. Inquire of Mr Jenkins, grocer, Rathbone Place.

In what other age could ladies have hired humanity, honour, and secrecy at their grocer's?

1. *A History of Advertising.*

Running through all these personal columns was the oft-repeated advertisement of the 'respectable young woman with a good breast of milk'. There is something rather endearing about these announcements. It is pleasant to think that the young woman really was respectable; that she had not forfeited, and never would, her 'undeniable character'. Sometimes there was a sad, circumstantial tale explaining how the breast of milk came to be available. In one instance a couple who had lost their infant said that they were anxious to assuage their grief by helping some mother in distress.

In American newspapers of the eighteenth century also appeared intimate personal advertisements, reflecting the stresses of less sophisticated communities. In England, a husband might cynically wink at his wife's adultery; in New England a cuckolded husband reacted in more forthright fashion. Here is a top-of-the-column advertisement by a citizen of Boston in Benjamin Franklin's *New England Courant* one summer day in 1724:

Know all Men by these Presents that on the twenty-fourth of this Instant, at or between the Hours of Eleven and Twelve at Night, the Wife of me, the Subscriber, was caught in Bed with Samuel Butler, they being both undress'd, and in a very indecent Posture, contrary to the Peace of our Sovereign Lord the King. In Testimony whereof I have hereunto set my Hand this twenty-sixth Day of June Annoq. Dom. 1724.

The Mark *AH* of Arthur Hall.

Settlers' wives did not always stay silent in the face of published accusations by their husbands. In 1734 James Moore, of Woodbridge in New Jersey, inserted an advertisement in the *New York Gazette* saying that his wife Deliverance had eloped from his bed and board, and urging that credit be denied her. A few days later the *Gazette* published a spirited reply from Deliverance Moore, describing her husband's charges as absolutely false:

She has lived with him for eight Years under his Tyranny and incredible Abuse; for he has several times attempted to Murder her and also turned her out of Doors, shamefully Abusing her, which is well known to the neighbours and the neighbourhood in Woodbridge.

This was by no means an unusual exchange. Sometimes the parties to a domestic brawl would set out at great length the injustices they claimed to have suffered, blackening the characters of mother-in-law, parents, children, and neighbours in the process.

A successful advertiser in the *New England Courant* in the 1720s was John Phillips, who claimed to have sold 15,000 copies of his *Onania*, dealing with 'the hideous Crime of Self-Pollution and all its frightful Consequences in both Sexes'. Less in demand was a *Sermon on the Horrid Crime of Self-Murder*.

DISORDERS – SECRET AND OTHERWISE

The eighteenth century was an age of magnificent quacks, or 'empirics', if a kinder word must be used. Some, but not all, were blatant humbugs. A few were men of powerful personality and a high level of culture, personal friends of the literary men whose works they subsidized by their advertisements, and whose lives (in regrettable instances) they cut short by their pills and elixirs. In the empirics' favour it can be said that they often believed passionately in their nostrums, that they did not descend to inventing new illnesses, and that on the whole they did not market their goods by 'scare' tactics, being content to sing their virtues in extravagant language. Although they made the crudest claims for their purges, and went into revolting details about the length, hairiness, and voracity of the worms they conjured from the human gut, they did not proclaim that nine out of ten suffered from gravel. Their promises to cure stuttering by the application of ointment were no more absurd than some latter-day offers to stimulate the growth of hair by 'magic combs'. When they told a lie they told a resounding one to attract attention, leaving it to a later age to sell rubbish by false suggestion, by half-truth, and by words carefully chosen to mean nothing when challenged in a court of law. The modern medicine vendor is entitled to retort that even if his specifics do no good they rarely do harm, whereas the eighteenth-century quacks killed right and left.

Readers of the *Spectator* were offered cures for all kinds of bodily and mental ravages. A useful all-round restorative was a 'chymical Liquor' which, in a moment, would make 'the most nauseous Breath smell delicately Fine and Charming', as well as fastening any loose teeth and making the gums grow again 'when almost eaten away'. To lose one's sense of smell, in those days, was not perhaps an unmitigated disaster, but anyone who wished to recover this lost faculty could summon it back at once with the aid of an 'incomparable pleasant Tincture'. There were few faded powers which could not be restored:

Loss of Memory, or Forgetfulness, certainly cured by a grateful Electuary peculiarly adapted for that end; it strikes at the primary source, which few apprehend, of Forgetfulness, makes the Head clear and easy, the Spirits free, active and undisturbed, corroborates and revives all the noble Faculties of the Soul, such as Thought, Judgment, Apprehension, Reason and Memory, which last in particular it so strengthens as to render that Faculty exceeding quick and good beyond Imagination; thereby enabling those whose Memory was before almost totally lost to remember the minutest circumstances of their Affairs etc. to a wonder. Price 2s. 6d. a pot. Sold only at Mr Payne's at the Angel and Crown in St Paul's Churchyard, with directions.

Here is another from the *Spectator*:

Famous Drops for Hypocondriack Melancholy: Which effectually cure on the Spot, by rectifying the Stomach and Blood, cleansing them from all Impurities, and giving a new Turn to their Ferment, attenuating all viscous and tenacious Humours (which make the Head Heavy, clog the Spirits, confuse the Mind, and cause the deepest Melancholy, with direful Views and black Reflections), comforting the Brain and Nerves, composing the hurried Thoughts, and introducing bright lively Ideas and pleasant Briskness, instead of dismal Apprehension and dark Incumbrance of the Soul, setting the Intellectuals at Liberty to act with Courage, Serenity and steady Cheerfulness, and causing a visible, diffusive Joy to reign in the Room of uneasy Doubts, Fears, etc., for which it may be truly esteem'd infallible. Price 3s. 6d. a Bottle, with Instructions. Sold only at Mr Bell's, book-seller at the Cross Keys and Bible in Cornhill, near the Royal Exchange.

In other words, 'Wake up your Liver Bile'.

When the *Spectator* died, the fleas left the body and were made welcome elsewhere. In almost every paper were earnest offers to alleviate rheum, hypochondria, sinkings, the dry belly-ache, the irregular or flying gout, hectic disorders, scorbutic humours, griping of the guts, and even writer's cramp. A Dr Lowther offered a nerve powder to counter 'frightful dreams, confused ideas, failure of memory and horrors'. Freeman's Grand Restorer of Human Nature was directed against 'horrid Thoughts, Startings in the Sleep, and Decay of Nature'. There was the 'true

Royal Chymical Washball' mentioned by Dr Johnson, which besides ridding the skin of all Deformities, Tetters, Ringworm, Morphew, Sunburn, Scurf, Pimples, and pits or redness of the Small pox', was warranted to 'give an exquisite edge to the razor, and so comfort the brain and nerves as to prevent catching cold'.

Advertisers freely sneered at each other's products, often opening their announcements with such phrases as 'Whereas an ignorant pretender . . .' or asserting that their notices were 'not the hasty composition of an illiterate schemer or self-created Doctor'. Dr Radcliffe, creator of a savoury elixir which cured the effects of hard drinking along with the King's Evil, warned readers of the *Edinburgh Advertiser* in 1767 against 'sweet slops' and 'nauseous pills' which make 'thousands puke at the sight of the phial or pill box. . . .' Perhaps it was this queasiness of the public stomach that inspired Molyneux's Smelling Medicine (*Edinburgh Advertiser*, 1770), for curing 'scurvy, pimpled faces, bald heads, and all cutaneous eruptions by smelling only'; no bleeding, no physic, no anointing the body, and – a noteworthy advantage – no need to 'change either bed clothes or wearing apparel'. Not that cleanliness was entirely at a discount. An advertisement in the same newspaper announced the opening of 'A Neat Bath' for Gentlemen and Ladies near Edinburgh, and added: 'Every person is served with fresh water.'

Apart from pills and elixirs, some of the most extravagant claims were made on behalf of tobaccos and snuffs, medicated or otherwise. As far back as 1604 James I had noted some of the contradictory claims made by quacks on behalf of tobacco:

. . . it cures the Gowt in the feet, and (which is miraculous) in the very instant when the smoke thereof, as light, flies up into the head, the vertue thereof, as heavie, runs downe to the little toe. . . . It helpes all sorts of Agues. It makes a man sober that was drunke. It refreshes a weary man and yet makes a man hungry. Being taken when they goe to bed, it makes one sleeps soundly, and yet being taken when a man is sleepie and drowsie, it will, as they say, awake his brain and quicken his industrie. . . .

'Cephalick'[1] tobaccos were widely advertised in the eighteenth century; one of them, announced in the *General Advertiser* of 1749, professed to cure insanity.

1. 'Cephalic': relating to the head.

It hath set a great many to rights that was never expected, but there is but few, or none, that careth to have it published they were a little out of their Senses, although it be really an Ailment. ...

Some of the tallest claims on behalf of tobacco – 'The Famous Cephalick and Opthalmick Tobacco' – were advanced in early numbers of *The Times*. It was a miraculous weed:

Which by Smoaking a Pipe of it, is good for the *Head, Eyes, Stomach, Lungs, Rheumatism*, and GOUT, Thickness of Hearing, Head-Ach, Tooth-Ach or Vapours.

And to Restore Ancient Sight and preserve Young Eyes.

So that by using this *Tobacco* Persons may never come to wear *Spectacles*; And if they have already used them may leave them off, by its so *Strengthening*, and *Clearing* the SIGHT.

Likewise to bring away *Phlegm, Rheum* and *Foul Humours* from the Breast, Stomach and Lungs, and such terrible Wheezings that Persons can hardly fetch their Breath.

This Fine Tobacco is Prepared *Only* Up One Flight of Stairs, at the Sign of the *Anodyne Necklace*, against *Devereux Court*; at Mr Bradshaw's, at the Golden Key behind the Royal Exchange and at Messrs Peter and Abraham Brown's, in Bristol. Price 4s. a pound, or Any LESS Quantity proportionately down to Three Pence.

Another engaging field was that of aphrodisiacs, notably:

... viper wines, to make old age presume
To feele new Lust and youthful Flames again.

Baldwin's London Weekly Journal of 1772 contained numerous repetitions of the following:

The true Cordial Quintessence of Vipers.

The most noble and grand Preparation in the whole Materia Medica, for the real substantial Cure of Impotency in Men and Barrenness in Women, and is vastly preferable to Viper Wine or any other preparation of Viper whatsoever as being replete with the full and whole Virtues of them.

A few Days of it only give such a general Warmth, and so exceedingly delight the Vital and Animal Spirits, Senses and Nerves, as soon to show what it will do upon a little Continuance of it; for it not only promotes and prompts Desire, but also furnishes proper Matter for the Support and Establishment of a true and lasting Power and Inclination. Price 10s. 6d. a bottle.

In the *Morning Post* of 1776 was offered a 'Bath Restorative' of which the vendor wrote:

In the late decays of life it will supply the vital lamp with some recruits; it is admirable for those who have been almost worn out by women and wine ... where persons are not early happy in their conjugal embraces it will render their intercourse prolific and be of service to our rising generation; and those who have impaired their Constitution by the Act of Self-Pollution will find themselves a certain Remedy, as well as in all nervous Cases.

Another restorative balsam was 'for emaciated YOUTH and debilitated OLD AGE, particularly those who have impaired their constitutions by Excess of Women, secret Venery, etc. etc.' It was warranted to 'revive any Constitution that is not absolutely mouldered away'.

Those who offered to cure venereal disease sometimes referred to it as 'a Certain Disorder', 'the Secret Disease', or 'the French Distemper', but often it was bluntly named. A major handicap from the promotional point of view was that satisfied customers were so ungrateful as to refuse to sign testimonials; but the vendors of Leake's Patent Pills, which in 1785 were said to be curing sufferers at the rate of 5,000 a year, eventually found a volunteer. *The Star* of 31 December 1793 contained a long advertisement consisting mainly of a letter from the Clerk of St Michael's Church in Bristol, to Thomas Taylor, a surgeon of Blackfriars, London, describing how a distressed mariner named John Morris had been cured by Leake's Pills of 'a virulent Venereal Disorder' contracted at Bordeaux. The gruesome condition of the patient was set forth; he was already blind, deaf, and immobile, and had been given up by the faculty of a public institution. As a last resort, Leake's Pills were tried, and they restored his senses and ('we doubt not') his earning capacity. The grateful mariner not only authorized, but begged, the Clerk of the parish to make his case public, 'for the good of mankind'. The Clerk added his cordial congratulations to Thomas Taylor 'on possessing the most unparalleled, cheap, and safe Medicine in the Universe', which he promised to recommend on all occasions, both public and private. Thomas Taylor then explained where the pills could be obtained and – in case any customer was apprehensive that his cure might be hailed in the public prints –

offered 'in all cases the most inviolable secrecy'. The phrase 'N.B. A back door, and Lights in the Passage at Night' suggested a judicious blend of privacy and solicitude.[1]

Other practitioners in this field offered cures 'without Confinement, Hindrance of Business or the Knowledge of a Bed-Fellow', or 'without the Knowledge of the most intimate Relation'. Richard Rock, operating in Goose Lane, pulled teeth as a sideline, which made it less embarrassing to be seen entering his premises.

The advertisers who toiled in the service of Aphrodite were joined about 1779 by the ineffable Dr Graham with his Celestial Bed, designed 'for the propagation of Beings, rational and far stronger and more beautiful in mental as well as in bodily Endowments than the present puny, feeble and nonsensical race of Christians'. The 'Temples of Health' run by this handsome Edinburgh quack have often been described; it was in the Adelphi establishment that the future Lady Hamilton made her thinly-draped debut as 'Vestina, the Rosy Goddess of Health'. Graham, during a two-year stay in America, had watched Benjamin Franklin's experiments and had seen possibilities in electrical mumbo-jumbo. On his return to London he installed ornate and preposterous electrical machines in his Temples, the interiors of which were as lush as his prose style – 'oriental odours and aetherial essences will perfume the air while the hymeneal sopha blazes forth in the plentitude of the soft lambent celestial fire'. The great bed, made for £12,000 by a coiner who was hanged at Tyburn, was an extravaganza of crimson silks and glass pillars, perfumed with essences from 'the Grand Turk's seraglio'. It could be rented at £100 a night by childless couples, the fee including the Doctor's 'magnetico-electric' treatment. 'In a neighbouring closet,' he explained, 'is placed a cylinder by which I communicate the celestial fire to the bed-chamber, the fluid which animates and vivifies all, and those cherishing vapours and Oriental perfumes, which I convey hither by means of tubes of glass.' For good measure, there were 1,500 pounds of compound magnets which were 'continually pouring forth in an ever-flowing circle'. The mattresses were filled with 'the strongest and

1. Quoted by A. Fessler M.D. in 'Advertisements on the Treatment of Venereal Disease', *British Journal of Venereal Diseases*, vol. xxv. 1949.

most springy hair, produced at vast expense from the tails of English stallions'.

The Doctor took leave to doubt whether there existed anyone 'frigid enough to resist the influence of the pleasure of those transports which this enchanting place inspires. It furnishes the grossest imaginations with the means of refining its enjoyments, of multiplying its pleasures and of carrying them to their highest degree'. But he warned potential customers that 'such refinements of the pleasures of the senses abridge the period of life and relax the springs both of body and mind'.

The Celestial Bed made its appeal to a few jaded voluptuaries, but soon the fee dropped to £50 a night and even less. There is no evidence to show that any richly-endowed Christians were sired in it. In 1782 creditors began to close in, and Graham returned by devious ways to his native heath. He had sparked the trail for the electrical quack, a familiar figure in our own times.

The century, and this chapter, may fitly be rounded off with an epitaph which was inscribed in a churchyard at Godalming, Surrey:

Sacred
To the Memory of
Nathaniel Godbold Esq
Inventor and Proprietor
of that Excellent Medicine
The Vegetable Balsam
For the Cure of Consumption and Asthmas
He departed this Life
The 17th day of Decr 1799
Aged 69 Years
Hic Cineres, Ubique Fama

3   The 'Blast of Puffery'

The most rousing advertisement with which to start the nineteenth
century is a non-commercial one: Sergeant Hammond's famous
recruiting poster. When this call to arms was reproduced in a
London exhibition in 1949 it inspired a fourth leader in *The
Times*, which praised the writer for the 'rich perfection' of his
simultaneous appeal to the nobler sentiments and the human love
of comfort.

A HORSE! A HORSE!

MY KINGDOM FOR A HORSE!

Now, my lads, for the

14th LIGHT DRAGOONS

or the

DUCHESS OF YORK'S OWN

All you who are kicking your heels behind a solitary desk with too little
wages, and a pinch-gut Master, all you with too much wife, or are
perplexed with obstinate and unfeeling parents

may apply to

SERGEANT HAMMOND, ROSE & CROWN, WHITECHAPEL

You are quartered in the fertile County of Kent, where you have pro-
vision remarkably cheap. Luxurious living to the brave and ambitious
mind, is but a secondary object, else thousands would repair to the
Standard of the gallant 14th, could they obtain the honour of being
received.

Those of address and education are sure of preferment, your com-
forts in this Service surpass all clerks or mechanics, an hospitable table
and capacious bowl of punch that will float or sink the little Corsican
Chief.

N.B. Four Farriers are wanted, and a Master

for the Band.

'GOD SAVE THE KING'

As an example of the 'psychological attack' more than a
century before that tainted technique began to be developed,

Sergeant Hammond's poster is indeed notable. It leaves a better taste in the mouth than some of the recruiting posters ('Is Anyone Proud of *You*?') issued during the First World War.

There were vacancies, not only for private soldiers, but for commanding officers, in the enlisting of whom a less heroic note was sounded. Here is a bargain offer from the *Morning Post* of 21 April 1803:

ARMY. A LIEUT-COLONELCY in an Old Regiment at home to be DISPOSED OF. There are advantages attending this Commission, which render it peculiarly profitable. Letters, post-paid, addressed to Y.Z., Cannon Coffee-house, Charing Cross will be immediately attended to.

In those fateful days nepotism and place-hunting were carried to startling lengths. Here is an appeal from *The Times* of 16 April 1801:

FIVE HUNDRED GUINEAS will be given to any lady or gentleman who can procure the Advertiser a Permanent Situation of proportionate value in the Exchequer or any other office under Government where not more than three hours daily attendance is required. Strict secrecy may be relied on if requisite. Address to Mr Mason at 4 Salisbury Street, Strand. None but principals will be treated with.

Two years later the market appeared to have stiffened. An advertiser in the *Morning Post* of 26 May 1803 dangled a bigger sum and even offered to do an honest day's work:

A PREMIUM of One Thousand Pounds will be presented to any Person who can procure to the Advertiser a SITUATION in any of the PUBLIC OFFICES under Government. The Advertiser's object is to be employed six, eight, or ten hours of the day. Letters addressed to G.H.G., Orange Coffee-House, Haymarket will reach the Advertiser.

Sometimes an applicant specified the exact post he required – in one instance, that of Commissary of the Forces – and invited the existing incumbent to resign (for a consideration) in his favour.

The eighteenth century was still dying, lustily and lustfully. The 'naked fashion' caused some scandal; a woman's dress weighed as little as seven ounces. Belles of society had false faces, false hair, false breasts, and false bellies (for the fashion of the anterior bustle, giving an illusion of pregnancy, died hard). Mantraps and the pillory had still to be abolished. But reform was unmistakably in the air. Sir Samuel Romilly was seeking to whittle down the monstrous list of felonies for which a noose was the penalty – there were two hundred of them at the start of the century. In 1801 the *Aberdeen Journal* carried this announcement:

WANTED, AN EXECUTIONER

For the City of Aberdeen. Such persons as may wish to be appointed to the office are desired immediately to apply to George Turiff, Dean of Guild's Officer, who will give information respecting the salary and emoluments, which are considerable, besides a free house.

The Scots prided themselves that their law was less barbarous than the English, yet evidently there was sufficient work to justify the supposedly frugal city of Aberdeen in maintaining its own hangman.

It was a grim age, and not even the grave could always be relied upon for shelter. One advertiser boasted, however, that his patent coffins were 'on such a principle as to prevent their being opened'.

During the Hundred Days, the advertising columns of the newspapers gave little hint of tremendous events on the Continent. The respectable young woman with a good breast of milk, the pedlar of lottery tickets, the young orphan lady seeking the protection of a single gentleman, the pox-doctor, the Society for Suppression of Mendicity, the vendor of cauls (for those in peril on the sea), the promoter of panoramas, the auctioneer, the ventriloquist, the rakes of Ranelagh – all these were conducting business as normal. A Mr Gray, of the Royal College of Surgeons, announced an 'unprecedented' development in dentistry: artificial teeth could now be provided without springs, wires, or other anchoring devices – 'the teeth may be taken out with the greatest facility, cleansed, and replaced by the wearers themselves'. The cry of 'no springs, no wires' was soon to be taken up by dozens of competitors. There was internecine strife among the trussmakers; the firm of Salmon, Ody, and Company tried to work up public indignation against one of their rivals who had canvassed Army and Navy contracts by offering self-adjusting trusses, whereas the ones he was in a position to offer were not self-adjusting and did not even have universal joints. There was a whiff of a pre-Revolutionary world in the announcement of a powder which would give any woman 'the incomparable bloom of Ninon de L'Enclos'. On the day that the *Morning Post* carried the heading 'Glorious Intelligence – Defeat of Bonaparte by Duke of Wellington' it is unlikely that many readers had time to read the persuasive announcement on the front page of Slater's Patent Steam Kitchen and Range – 'Its various operations of steaming, boiling, roasting, baking, stewing and broiling, and supplying constantly from one to fourteen gallons of boiling water . . . are all performed by the use of one small fire.' The advertiser went on to make a claim familiar to modern ears – that his range used only half the fuel of any other.

During these years the Press was straining for its liberty. William Cobbett, back from exile in America, had launched his journal *The Porcupine* in 1800. This short-lived sheet contained the following pledge:

Not a single *quack* advertisement will on any account be admitted into the *Porcupine*. Our newspapers have been too long disgraced by this species of falsehood, filth and obscenity. I am told that, by adhering to this resolution, I shall lose five hundred a year, and excite the resentment of the numerous body of empirics; but their money I hope I shall never be so graceless as to covet, and as to resentment, I have nothing to fear from that, so long as I abstain from their death-dealing nostrums.

Cobbett ascribed the *Porcupine*'s ill-success, not to lack of advertising, but to his inability to stoop to the prevailing fashion of smirching reputations in the expectation of being paid to keep silence. It is worth noting that Leigh Hunt's brother John, on starting the *Examiner* (1808), declined even trade advertisements lest they impair the dignity of the paper.

The 'taxes on knowledge' were so severe at this period that only the best and the worst publications prospered. In 1803, as a war measure, the advertisement tax was raised to the crippling figure of 3s. 6d. Yet even under this handicap *The Times* and the *Morning Post* continued to make headway. Government advertising – an important source of revenue – was withheld from those papers which had the temerity to criticize the way the country's affairs were conducted. In 1803 Cobbett was deprived of Post Office advertisements; next year *The Times*, after a strong and well-warranted attack on the First Lord of the Admiralty, also lost its Government announcements. Ingeniously, John Walter the

Second surmounted the many obstacles the Government put in his path, and the mounting circulation of *The Times* was reflected in the increased number of advertisements (about 100 a day in 1800, 150 a day in 1810). Lesser publications suffered, flouted, or evaded the 'taxes on knowledge' as best they could.

Cobbett's England gave way to Dickens's England. The rotten boroughs were banished; a police force sprang into being; the railway boom began; illiteracy began to recede. Yet, because of the 'taxes on knowledge' there were fewer newspapers in the 1840s than there had been in the 1740s, even though the advertisement tax was lowered – in 1833 – to 1s. 6d. Often enough the new literacy was nourished on the 'last confessions' of criminals, the early 'penny dreadfuls', and the tasty *réchauffages* of police news served up by Edward Lloyd, founder of *Lloyd's Weekly Newspaper* (1842).

A powerful whiff of radicalism rose from this obstreperous organ, which vigorously defended the underdog. At first it was only lightly supported by advertisers, who favoured those papers circulating among 'carriage trade'. Both Lloyd's paper and *Bell's Life in London* carried announcements which would scarcely have been welcomed by the *Morning Post*; for example, the following from *Bell's Life* on 7 June 1835:

> Read the Pocket BLACK BOOK, containing Authentic details of the Revenue, Expenditure, and Taxation of the United Kingdom. The Income and Patronage of the Church, amounting annually to nearly Ten Millions! The Enormous Income and Patronage of the Bishops! A complete list of 1500 Ladies and Gentlemen, pensioners, place-men, sinecurists etc. who receive annually upwards of one million of the public money!

There was still much to outrage a good radical. In 1844 an advertisement in the *Cheltenham Free Press* by the Earl of Ducie's agent offered 'the ENTIRE VILLAGE of Nympfield, wherein are SIXTY-SIX HOUSES and the DUCIE ARMS, WITH POLITICAL INFLUENCE extending over 1200 HONEST YEOMEN'.

Punch commented: 'Has the Earl no *droits de seigneur*? ... Can he not lump in with the yeomen their wives and daughters?'

A new type of advertisement which began to appear in *Lloyd's Weekly Newspaper* was the undertaker's announcement. The Metropolitan Cemetery and Funeral Company offered a first-class funeral at £14 14s., with carriages built in the new Gothic style, use of cloaks, hatbands, hoods and scarfs for eight mourners, and – a considerable inducement – superintendent on horseback. Two mutes on horseback, with appendages, cost £2 2s. extra. The superintendent on horseback was still included in the fee for a second-class funeral, but in a third-class funeral he was present only on foot. The fourth, fifth, and sixth class funerals he left to his assistants. Incidentally, the sixth class funeral, at £2 2s., appeared to offer very sound value.

Gradually the nature of the advertisement columns was changing. The reproach that the advertiser was the rich man's pander could no longer fairly be made. Manufacturers of hair dressings and tooth powder were beginning to woo a wider market. Even household goods – blacking, polish, soap – were being lauded in print. They were also being lauded, with increasing blatancy, in the streets, where the 'fly posters' were beginning to scramble for every vacant patch of brickwork. Prince Pückler-Muskau, visiting Britain late in George IV's reign, commented on the 'ambulant' advertisers he saw in the City of London; for example, men with tall 'hats' proclaiming 'BOOTS at 12s. a pair – warranted'. There were also 'chests, like Noah's Ark, entirely pasted over with bills, and of the dimensions of a small house, drawn by men and horses slowly through the streets, and carrying more lies upon them than Münchausen ever invented'.

This increasing trend towards 'puffery' aroused much disdain in the scholarly reviews. The *London Magazine* offered some 'hints' to advertisers of the day in its issue of February 1825:

> The style should be firm and forcible, calculated to command respect and attention, and not going tenderly and gingerly to work merely to solicit observation. Judgment must be passed, not prayed for. The public must be cautioned against every thing on earth but the identical article advertised. The world must be challenged for a certain amount (a hundred guineas is an approved sum). The trade must be defied. The inventor must be 'ever anxious' or 'always emulous' to check imposition.

The *London Magazine* went on to tell how a 'certain prose writer of the present day' had been commissioned to write lottery puffs, but had had his efforts returned as being too modest. 'He thought that he could write,' commented the magazine, 'and the florid Mr Atkinson with a pen dipped in his own curling fluid[1] wrote a flourishing paragraph that put him quite beside himself.' There is good reason to suppose that the writer whose copy was spurned was Charles Lamb.

In the literary world the advertising methods of Henry Colburn (who published among others Disraeli, Mrs Shelley, Hood, and Fenimore Cooper) were the scandal of the day. Colburn was the proprietor of several papers which he used to push his own publications. He also had a share in the *Literary Gazette* which on one occasion, as the *Athenaeum* pointed out, carried twenty-one columns of extravagant commendations of his own works and one eighth of a column on a publication by John Murray. *Frazer's* and the *Athenaeum* belaboured Colburn regularly. They were incensed that he should seek to advertise literature on the same lines as blacking and tooth powder. In April 1830 *Frazer's* noted how Colburn kept clerks and writers solely to look after his papers and advertisements and said: 'And does not the little man boast of being able to stuff his uncomfortable trash down the reluctant maws of the public in spite of mazagines and newspapers and critics?' His puffs appeared in all newspapers, said *Frazer's*, except *The Times* and the *Morning Herald*.

On 17 July 1830, the *Athenaeum* returned to the attack:

There can be little doubt that the stupidest cluster of trashy papers, the most insignificant articles, may by dint of eternal paragraph be forced into sale. It could not otherwise happen that Day and Martin, Rowland, Colburn and Bentley, Eady, Warren and those after their kind could lavish so much money in the praises of their oils, their books, their pills and their polish if there did not exist a class of human being who are greedy of belief. It is the duty of an independent journal to protect as far as possible the credulous, confiding, and unwary from the wily arts of the insidious advertiser.

Flagrant though Colburn's methods might be, there was no doubt that many authors sighed to be published by him. His annual expenditure on advertising reached £9,000.

At this period publishers and booksellers accounted for much

1. Probably a reference to Curll, the notorious eighteenth-century book puffer.

advertising space. The first full-page advertisement in *The Times*, in 1829, was of a book: Edmund Lodge's *Portraits and Memories of the Most Illustrious Personages of British History*, published by the firm of Harding and Lepard, of Pall Mall East. Wordsworth is probably the only author to have complained that his publisher over-advertised his works. As he received only £9 8s. 2d. for the first edition of one of his books, and a bill from Longman's for advertising amounting to £27 2s. 3d,[1] his protest is understandable.

In 1843 the *Edinburgh Review* devoted a long article to the history of advertising. 'There is no disguising it,' said the writer, 'the grand principle of modern existence is notoriety. Hardly a second-rate Dandy can start for the moors or a retired Slopseller leave London for Margate without announcing the "fashionable movement" in the morning papers.'

The writer mourned the passing of that cautious attitude once expressed in the 'well-known aphorism':

> Be not the first to lay the old aside,
> Be not the first by whom the new are tried . . .

a piece of advice which if practised today would bring civilization down in ruin.[2]

The *Edinburgh Review*'s approach to advertising was one of wry but on the whole good-humoured resignation. By contrast, Thomas Carlyle was sourly unamused by what he called the 'all-deafening blast of puffery'. In his *Past and Present* (1843) he wrote:

> We take it for granted, the most rigorous of us, that all men who have made anything are expected and entitled to make the loudest possible proclamation of it, and call upon a discerning public to reward them for it. . . . Nature requires no man to make proclamation of his doings and hat-makings; Nature forbids all men to make such. There is not a man or hat-maker born into the world but feels, or has felt, that he is degrading himself if he speak of his excellences and prowesses, and

1. Quoted in *The Athenaeum*, by Leslie A. Marchand.
2. The Duke of Wellington did not believe in this aphorism. According to Richard Aldington's biography, he was an eager reader of newspaper advertisements and 'could never be prevented from buying any new invention which happened to catch his eye'. He was one of the first to purchase a new safety razor, but he declined to endorse the product.

supremacy in his craft; his inmost heart says to him, 'Leave thy friends to speak of these; if possible thy enemies to speak of these; but at all events, thy friends!' He feels that he is already a poor braggart; fast hastening to be a falsity and speaker of the Untruth.

Some of the advertisements which drew such heavy disapproval must now be reviewed. Robert Warren – one of those named by the *Athenaeum* – is generally supposed to have marketed the first nationally advertised household article, Warren's Shoe Blacking, which was launched on a sea of poetry. Little is known about him. The advertising appears to have been taken over after some years by Mrs Warren, presumably his widow. Said the *Edinburgh Review*: 'The praises of blacking were sung in strains which would have done no discredit to Childe Harold himself, even in his own opinion – for when accused of receiving £600 a year for his services to Mrs Warren – of being, in short, the actual personage alluded to in her famous boast "We keeps a poet" – he showed no anxiety to repudiate the charge.'

The reader may or may not be able to detect the influence of Byron in this specimen verse, which appeared in *Bell's Life* in January 1835:

> 'Friend,' said Aminadab to Obadiah,
> 'Why such amazement do thy features show?'
> 'To see, Aminadab, thy Boots on fire,
> And thou stand harmless in the burning glow!'
> 'Ah! Friend, dost thou so of discernment lack –
> Art thou so far to common knowledge barren,
> Not to perceive 'tis but the radiant black
> That's manufactur'd by Friend Robert Warren?'

Mrs Warren could also have boasted 'We keeps an artist' – and a distinguished one at that. Her much-admired picture of a cat spitting at its reflection in a Hessian boot was drawn by George Cruikshank, who was not the man to turn up his nose at Mrs Warren's profession. On occasions, Mrs Warren could be very much on her dignity, as the following extract from one of her announcements will show:

Imposture Unmasked

The progress of MERIT, although frequently assailed, is not impeded by Envy and Detraction. The aggression of ambuscade terminates in defeat; and conscious rectitude ultimately triumphs in the attainment of the grand object – public approbation. The test of experience is the guarantee of favour and has established Warren's Blacking in general estimation; of which there exists not a stronger proof than the tacit acknowledgment of a host of servile imitators who surreptitiously obtrude on the unwary a spurious preparation of the genuine article. . . .

'Rowland' – Alexander Rowland – was the originator of a commodity (still on the market) which became so popular that society was forced to defend itself – and it did so with the anti-macassar. Rowland's Macassar Oil first appeared about 1793. Twenty-one years later it was widely enough known for the Emperor of all the Russias to ask that ten guineas' worth should be sent to him without delay, through Foreign Office channels. In due course the firm was able to boast the patronage of 'Her Majesty, His Royal Highness Prince Albert, the Royal Family and nobility, and the several sovereigns and courts of Europe'.

Rowland's announcements were remarkable, in the opinion of the *Edinburgh Review*, for their 'confident tone of conscious superiority'. The 'elegant, fragrant and pellucid' oil was 'of vegetable ingredients', possibly a slap at the bear's grease trade, which still flourished in Dickens's day.[1] Its fame inspired Grimaldi to one of his stage illusions – turning a deal box into a hair trunk.

Rowland had other commodities to offer: Odonto, a dentifrice; Cerelaum, for headaches; Kalydor, 'an Oriental botanical pre-paration', for redness and pimples. One advertisement told of 'a whimsical occurrence' which had befallen a customer who had used Rowland's Essence of Tyre. A writ had been made out against him for some dereliction. As he walked past the bailiffs in the street he heard one say to the other: 'That's the man'. The other said: 'Why you fool, that gemman has black hair, and you know Mr — has grey.' Said the advertisement: 'This is one among the thousand instances of the beneficial effects of Rowland's Essence of Tyre in changing the colours of the hair.'

1. In *Master Humphrey's Clock* Dickens introduces an ill-starred barber who over-spends on bears. When taken ill, he loses all interest in life until the bears are 'stirred up a bit' and made to growl. In the year of the Great Exhibition *The Times* had an advertisement of a bear's grease 'depot' off Belgrave Square, containing an invitation to 'any gentleman desirous of shooting the bear' to communicate with the proprietor.

For those beset by bailiffs, there was also Spencer's Chinese Liquid Hair Dye, which 'changes in a few minutes without trouble red or grey hair, whiskers, eyebrows, moustaches, etc. to dark brown or black by simply using a comb wetted with this liquid . . . a pleasing and permanent change'.

The admiration of many was aroused by a Mrs Harden, with a place of business off Oxford Street, who announced herself ready to display to all comers her own hair dyed in stripes to demonstrate the full range of colours available. Anyone who was unable to stimulate the growth of his hair by the foregoing preparations could have recourse to Cantharides Oil ('Spanish Fly is the acting ingredient'). And if that failed there was always the assiduously advertised 'Gentleman's Real Head of Hair, or Invisible Ventilating Peruke'.

Another original advertiser at this period was Richard Tanner, who was trying to revolutionize the art of writing. Apparently the public clung to the quill, distrustful of Tanner's claim that his steel pens were 'the noblest invention of which mankind can boast'. So Tanner tried the emotional appeal. He assured his readers that the stripping of geese, as practised in Lincolnshire and Cambridgeshire, was a reproach to civilization. He dwelled on 'the streams of empurpled dye, and the half-expiring contortions of these birds', and asked: 'Cannot the science of writing be improved and increased without inflicting such violence?'

Tanner, like so many of his contemporaries, had a fatal affection for polysyllables. In one advertisement he told of his 'Tobago Permanent Anti-Corrosive Limpid Ink, and Immarcessible Atramental Fluid – That facilitates writing, by flowing from the pen in a certain gradual stream to the paper, obviating the unpleasant obstruents which are so justly complained of in other inks'.

No one can read the advertisements of this period without marvelling at the cumbrous Latin compounds, the grotesqueries of 'Greek' with which the advertiser sought to impress his public. Teeth were stopped with 'mineral marmoratum' or 'mineral succedaneum'; raincoats were 'siphonias'; hair cream was an 'aromatic regenerator'; hair dye was an 'atrapilatory'. There were 'pulmonic wafers' for the chest; there were Aethereal Oleine, Elmes's Arcanum, Winn's Anticardium, Olden's Eukeirogenion, and Rypophagon Soap. Some critics feared, as many have feared since, that the English language would never recover from the abuses of the advertiser.

The 'hungry forties' offered wide, if not perhaps lucrative, employment for those poets who were prepared to twang the lyre on behalf of commerce; Mrs Warren's example was widely imitated, not only in Britain but overseas. The *Illustrated London News* drew attention to itself in a saga 128 lines long. Goodman, a saucemaker of Berkshire, kept a poet who could praise his product in many languages. A stanza from the English advertisement went as follows:

> The goose that on our Ock's green shore
>   Thrives to the size of Albatross,
> Is twice the goose it was before,
>   When washed with Neighbour Goodman's sauce.
> And ye, fat eels and trout, may feed
>   Where Kennet's silver waters toss,
> Proud are your Berkshire hearts to bleed
>   When drest with Goodman's prime Vale Sauce.

In America, unhappy couples derived what cheer they could from stanzas like this:

> Lucina Cordial! – Barren wives
>   It turns to mothers fair,
> And the fond name of father gives
>   To husbands in despair.

Then, as now, advertising had its MacGonagalls; and the worse the style, the longer the poem. In a Sydney newspaper land speculators were urged to make up their minds to buy plots in a certain favoured area, or

> At last there'll be no 'lotments to be had,
> And many a one will say, 'My slowness was too bad.'

In Britain, another patron of poets was the firm of Moses and Company, sellers of cheap clothes. What the firm paid per stanza is not known, but its women shirt-makers received two-and-sixpence for every dozen shirts.

An advertising fashion much exploited in the forties was that of printing in bold type an arresting phrase like:

A Beautiful Young Girl Strangled

to be followed, in small type, by something like 'a cry of admiration when she saw our new blouses'.

Or perhaps

The Duke of Wellington Shot

followed by 'a glance of admiration at our hats'.

Punch's celebrated 'Advice to Those About to Marry – Don't' stemmed from one of these advertisements. In the original the word 'Don't' had been followed by a phrase on the lines of 'fail to visit our store'.

The inventiveness of the age was constantly finding its reflection in the advertising columns. In *The Times* were not only appeals 'To Capitalists' but appeals *from* capitalists, like the following dated 1 May 1845:

To Inventors and Patentees: From £1000 to £2000 will be given for any chymical or mechanical invention not expensive to manufacture and for producing economically some article of general consumption. – Apply, to Mr Dircks, King William Street, City.

Some article of general consumption ... something which a growing population could be persuaded to swallow, to smear on its hair, or to ride on or in. ... It was a confident, forward-looking age, and no better evidence is to be found than in the railway advertisements of the forties. In these columns of small-type advertisements can be read the story of a brave new world in the making – a new world which was no less brave because many fortunes were lost in the building of it. It is easy to see, even at this remove, how the minds of the Victorians must have been fired by the contents of these arid-looking columns.

By the early forties, gangs of Irish navvies were laying the glittering metals throughout the length of Britain. But that was only a fraction of the picture. The same issue of *The Times* that contained the announcement of the Coventry and Leicester Junction Railway would carry solicitations on behalf of the Great Mediterranean and Adriatic Junction Railway ('connecting the cities of Genoa, Turin, Milan and Venice'); the Enniskillen and Sligo Railway; the Namur and Luxembourg Railway ('shortest route to Baden'); the Northern Trunk Railway of France; the Jamaica South Midland Branch Railway; the Austrian and Sardinian Railway Company; the Central of Spain Railway; the

Great India Peninsula Railway; the Alto Douro Railway ('will connect the harbour of Oporto with the entire wine district'); the South London Suburban Railway; and a score of others.

Distended to many times their normal size by these advertisements, the popular newspapers of 1845 reaped an immense revenue. Special newspapers were started with no other idea than that of tapping the flow of gold. *The Times*, which carried as many as forty-four columns of railway advertisements in one issue, attacked the craze for speculation and turned away a great many advertisements which appeared over-reckless; these easily found harbour elsewhere. Very few editorial voices were raised in warning. Right until the end, some newspapers egged on their readers to invest, but were quick enough to abuse the public for its folly when the crash came.

It was a poor prospectus which offered less than a fifteen per cent return. The more ambitious companies hinted at profits which would be so great that the directors were hesitant to name them. Sometimes the reasons offered for constructing a line were peculiar, as in this plea by the promoters of the Somersetshire and North Devon Junction Railway:

The advantages which this Railway presents, in a national point of view, are of great importance and cannot fail to ensure the consent of Parliament to the line in question. It is evidently a Coast line, and is connected with the remarkable historical fact, that in the reign of Alfred the Great the vicinity of this line of coast was the seat of an actual invasion by the Danes, under HUBBA, their leader; but to the honour of the brave men of Devon, that hostile armament was wholly destroyed, their Chief HUBBA slain with all his followers and their supposed invincible standard, Reafan, taken. Supposing, therefore, that a modern or future HUBBA should attempt a renewal of invasion on this line of coast, what other fate could he expect in the face of a whole nation eager and hastening to receive him? Such are the advantages of defence which Railways afford to distant and apparently unprotected coasts.

Among the projected enterprises were atmospheric traction railways. The principle was that the driver's car was connected to a piston in a continuous tube laid along the track, and the piston thrust forward into a vacuum created by relays of pumping stations. In practice much trouble was caused by leaks, but the advertisement in 1845 by Pilbrow's Automatic Railway and Canal Propulsion Company (director, the Earl of Essex) was full of confidence:

The prominent advantages of this system of atmospheric traction are that the continuous valve is dispensed with, roads are crossed upon a level without interruption of main, one atmospheric railway can be intersected by another, thus saving bridges, approaches, and leakage, and it is confidently expected that a stationary engine every ten miles will be sufficient.

Increased safety is insured, also obstruction and destruction by weather and other sources are placed beyond probability by the mains being buried.

The bursting of the bubble ruined many besides George Hudson, the 'railway king'; but the railways went on. In 1848 a special train, chartered by W. H. Smith and Son, was run from Euston to Glasgow, *via* York and Newcastle, in ten hours and twenty minutes, a distance of 472 miles.

In 1849 an advertiser calling himself Y.Z. offered to readers of *The Times* the recipe for a 'superior' patent medicine. He ended his eulogy: 'It is a *gentlemanly employment*, requiring but little attention and from which a fortune may speedily be made.' The last claim was perhaps nearer the truth than the first one. It has been said that in the second half of the nineteenth century anyone with £10,000 to spend on pushing a patent medicine could not fail to make a large fortune. Whether or not the medicine had any virtue was of small consequence.

Out of the legion of medicine men in Victorian times (no one called them empirics any more) it will suffice to single out three leading pill-makers. The most provocative of the three, in an advertising sense, was probably James Morison, self-styled 'the Hygeist', creator of the Universal Pill. So assiduously and ingeniously did he advertise this concoction (chiefly gamboge) that Thomas Carlyle felt impelled to draw morals from it in two of his essays in *Past and Present*. Men and women, complained Carlyle, 'fancy that their religion, too, shall be a kind of Morison's Pill which they have only to swallow once and all will be well. . . . I advise thee to renounce Morison; once for all, quit hope of the Universal Pill.'

Morison was another of those enterprising Scots – this time from Bognie, Aberdeenshire – who exploited the credulous southerners to great purpose. According to his autobiography, of which excerpts were freely given in his advertisements, he himself endured 'thirty-five years inexpressible suffering' (spent mostly between Hanau, Riga, and Bordeaux) before discovering, about 1822, his simple secret – the swallowing of a few vegetable pills at bedtime, followed by a glass of lemonade in the morning. Morison's headquarters were in Hamilton Place, New Road, London, and were dignified by the name of 'The British College of Health'. His advertisements often included a picture of the building, which was imposing, detached, and surmounted by a couchant lion.

Morison claimed to have been the first to attack the medical practice of bleeding. He missed no chance to mock the doctors, and when well-known personages died he did not hesitate to criticize their medical treatment and imply that his Universal Pill would have saved them. If confronted with instances in which the pills had failed to fulfil expectations, he would simply assert that the sufferer had not taken enough of them. No one could say that he had not the courage of his convictions, for when he died in 1840 he was (so the story goes) in the act of reaching for another box of his own medicine.

Morison's vigorous tradition of advertising was maintained by his heirs and assigns. A specimen in the best popular style is the following, from *Lloyd's Weekly Newspaper* of 11 December 1842:

DIFFERENCE BETWEEN A DOCTOR'S BILL AND A
HYGEIAN'S BILL

A Doctor's Bill

Mr John Bull,
  To Bleed 'em and Kill 'em

	£	s.	d.
To Pills, Draughts, Bleeding, Leeching, Blistering, Cupping etc. for yourself and family during the last six months	£10	10	
To 182 visits at 5s. per visit . . .	£45	10	
	£56	0	

A Hygeist's Bill

Mr John Bull (now in his senses)
　　To Purge 'em and Cure 'em

	£	s.	d.
To 12 boxes at 1s. 1½d. (No 1 and 2) of Morison's Vegetable Universal Medicines for yourself and family during the last six months . . .	£0	13	6
To 12 boxes of vegetable cleansing powders . .		13	6
According to the Hygeian System *no* visits are necessary since you have only to take the pills whenever you feel pain or are unwell . .	0	0	0
	£1	7	0
Difference between the doctor and the hygeist .	£54	13	0

Note—All the Patients are radically cured and
　　some of the Pills still left in the house.

The scope of Morison's operations may be gauged from the fact that he paid the Government £60,000 in stamp duties between 1830 and 1840, and also from the reports he used to print in his advertisements from such far-flung representatives as 'John Mackinnon, Esq., of Her Majesty's 104th Regiment, now on half-pay, Hygeian agent for the islands in the Gulph of St Lawrence'.

The Hygeist's successors seem to have had a go-ahead agent in the region of Exeter, for in 1851 seventy-year-old Samuel Crabb, of Pinhoe, a man of infirm mind, was reported in the local Press to have been 'thoroughly restored to reason' by taking the Universal Pill. There was another instance in the same neighbourhood 'where a young man was effectively cured in a single night of insanity by swallowing the whole contents of a thirteen penny-halfpenny box of No. 2 Pills which had been inadvertently left in the bedroom'. And it was almost certainly a Morison pill which, at Winchcomb, 'fetched a man out of the Union Workhouse and sent him to provide for himself with his own hands'.

'Parr's Life Pills' were less sensationally, but no less widely advertised. They were said to be concocted from a secret recipe handed down by Old Parr, a venerable Salopian whose span of life is entered in the *Dictionary of National Biography* as '1483 ?–

1635'. Reputedly, Parr threshed corn when he was 130 years of age, and then was taken to London to be exhibited at the Queen's Head in the Strand. After his death William Harvey carried out an autopsy and asserted that the air of London had killed him.

The recipe of Old Parr was acquired by Herbert Ingram, co-founder of the *Illustrated London News*, who employed a schoolmaster to write the Pill's history. The advertisements were often introduced by pseudo-scientific rigmaroles like the following, from *Lloyd's Weekly Newspaper* in 1843:

The spring and fall of the leaf has been always remarked as the periods when disease, if it be lurking in the system, is sure to show itself. The coldness of winter renders torpid the acrimonious fluids of the body and in this state of inactivity their evil to the system is not perceived; but at the spring these are roused, and if not checked mix up and circulate in the blood, and thus the whole system is contaminated. . . .

Parr's Life Pills were said to increase the beauty of women, lending 'brightness to the eyes, cheerful animation to the features and agreeable vigour to the whole frame'. Dickens, no doubt, had Parr's Life Pills in mind when he published a skit on the 'Methuselah Pill' in *Household Words* on 5 October 1850.

The third of the pill-making trio, 'Professor' Thomas Holloway, was a man with strong claims to be classed as the first worldwide advertiser. Probably no single name was more widely blazoned over the earth in Victorian times than that of Holloway. It assaulted the eye on every wall in London; it was to be found in the ill-printed newspapers of China, India, and Peru; once it screamed from no less a hoarding than the Great Pyramid. But it failed to find its way into the pages of Dickens, who refused an offer of £1,000 for a 'puff'.[1]

Holloway was a soldier's son from Devonport, a fastidious town which later declined to accept largesse from him. His early rise is shrouded in apocrypha. One version has it that, as a merchant in London, he helped to obtain a hospital testimonial for one Albinolo, a leech-seller from Turin, who was seeking to popularize an ointment with the resounding name of 'Albinolo's

1. 'Authoritatively' reported in Sell's *Dictionary of the World's Press*, 1886.

or the St Come and St Damien Ointment'. Soon, to the leech-seller's chagrin, Holloway put an ointment of his own on the market, also fortified by a testimonial from a hospital, and followed it with a brand of pills. The leech-seller went to a debtor's prison, and in due course so did Holloway. He owed large sums to newspaper proprietors, most of whom he eventually persuaded to accept a settlement. Later he paid them all in full, with a ten per cent bonus for those who had trusted him. The pill had been slow to take on; in one week Holloway spent £100 and disposed of two boxes. For years the self-styled professor worked an eighteen-hour day seeking to expand sales. He would visit the docks almost daily, introducing his commodities to captains of vessels and their passengers, in the hope that goodwill for Holloway would thus be built up along the trade routes.

In 1842, four years after starting his business, Holloway was spending £5,000 a year on advertising. He had richly decorated offices in the Strand, on the site of the present Law Courts. By 1850 his advertising expenditure had risen to almost £20,000, which was twice the budget of either Rowland or Moses. In this year he was faced with a family embarrassment and found it necessary to obtain an injunction against his brother, who was also selling 'Holloway's Pills and Ointment' from an address in the Strand.

For his more cultured readers Holloway liked to quote the 'celebrated lines of Dante' – 'And Time shall see thee cured of every ill'. How gratifying, said Holloway, that this prophecy was now 'literally fulfilled' in nineteenth-century England! *Punch* twitted Holloway on numerous occasions; in 1843 it recorded how 'Mr Holloway with the modesty which is the invariable attendant on real merit declares that his "Universal Ointment" will mend the legs of men and tables equally well and will be found an excellent article for frying fish in'. In 1855 the *Quarterly Review* wrote: 'It does seem incredible that one house should expend upon the mere advertising of . . . pills and ointment a sum equal to the entire revenue of many a German principality. Can it possibly pay? asks the astonished reader. Let the increasing avenue of assistants to be seen "from morn to dewy eve" wrapping up pills in the "Professor's" establishment within the shadow of Temple Bar supply the answer.' A later historian was to marvel

c

that Holloway should employ 'two intelligent females whose sole duty it is to see that all the advertisements, whether at home or abroad, for the publication of which he has paid, are duly inserted'.

Holloway's career may as well be followed through, though it means running ahead of the period under review. He opened an agency in America in the fifties, and soon established an acknowledged supremacy. In 1870 the American advertising agent George P. Rowell wrote: 'Millions who have never heard of Napoleon, his victories and defeats, the sad story of his invasion of the frozen North [*sic*] and his woeful return, have heard of Holloway, the most general advertiser of today.'

Holloway's Press advertisements lacked the piquancy of Morison's. It was the scale, not the impudence, of his announcements which impressed the world. Like his rivals, however, he could produce some notable tributes when required. In 1850 the Earl of Aldborough professed to have been cured by Holloway's Pills after all the doctors on the Continent, and even the waters of Carlsbad and Marienbad, had failed. A lady living in Sydney, 'after having for twenty years been unable to make the slightest exertion', found it possible, since taking the pills, to run up mountains.

By the seventies Holloway, who now had offices in New Oxford Street, was spending between £40,000 and £50,000 a year on advertising, and taking a similar sum in profit. He had quietly dropped the title of 'Professor'. Friends now began to suggest ways in which he could atone for his wealth. Lord Shaftesbury recommended him to build a shelter for the mentally afflicted of the lower middle classes, and Holloway duly set up a sanatorium for this purpose at Virginia Water. In memory of his wife, he also created and endowed the Holloway College at Egham (now the Royal Holloway College, London University), which was opened by Queen Victoria. On the two buildings he spent more than a million pounds.

In his later years, Holloway watched without undue alarm the rise of a rival pill, one which, in the succeeding century, was to support an immense financial empire. Thomas Beecham laid the modest foundations of his business in St Helen's in the fifties, and it was there that he adopted the slogan 'Worth a guinea a box'.

Real expansion began when his thrustful son, Joseph, joined the business in 1866.

When Holloway died at Sunninghill in 1883, *The Times* referred to his 'enormous property, valued perhaps with exaggeration at more than five million sterling'. The London Stock Exchange, it added, was already in a flutter at the news. In a long leading article, the newspaper said this of the soldier's son from Devonport: 'He was one of that remarkable class who seem destined to become rich, who roll wealth together in a way which ordinary men fail either to follow or understand.' Making money had been his 'steady, unvarying purpose'. Of the pills which brought his fame, *The Times* leader-writer contented himself with saying: 'If they possessed one-tenth part of the wonderful virtues which have been assigned to them, their discovery may safely be set down as marking an era of no small importance in the progress of the curative art.'

Throughout the Victorian age, the crowned heads of Europe, and many of the lesser lights of the *Almanach de Gotha*, freely gave testimonials to patent medicines, though freely is perhaps not the right word. In 1848, the year of revolutions, *Punch* said: 'We perceive that the Emperor of Russia has been swallowing a lot of Revalenta Arabica for the sake of testifying to the merits of the article, when so many of the Continental kings are so badly off that it would be a charity to let them have the job of puffing the Revalenta if there is anything to be got by it.' The Tsars, the Grand Dukes, and the Grand Duchesses nevertheless continued to praise a variety of commodities. Not far behind them were the members of the royal house of Greece; but the easiest testimonials to obtain were those of the German princelings.

Punch, while poking fun at the claims made for Revalenta Arabica, often carried full-page advertisements for this product, which helped to combat, among other things, atrophy. In its issue of 25 March 1871 the list of testimonials contained the following:

The health of the Holy Father is excellent since, abandoning all other remedies, he has confined himself entirely to Du Barry's Revalenta Arabica Food, of which he consumes a plateful at every meal. It has produced a surprisingly beneficial effect on his health and His Holiness cannot praise this excellent food too highly.

This tribute was copied, allegedly, from the *Gazette du Midi*. The advertisement also mentioned that thanks to the Revalenta the Marchioness of Brehan had once again been rendered fit for social intercourse.

Numerous articles were advertised as in use in Queen Victoria's household, often no doubt without authority. One of these was the Balm of Syriacum, 'a sovereign remedy for both bodily and mental decay'. In the later Victorian years the Queen was portrayed, in a memorable advertisement, sitting in the royal train with a cup of Cadbury's Cocoa before her. In another advertisement, the Prince of Wales and Princess Alexandra were shown enjoying a *tête-à-tête* over the same privileged beverage.

The *Edinburgh Review* discovered that Mr Cockle's Antibilious Pills were recommended by, among others, ten dukes, five marquises, seventeen earls, eight viscounts, sixteen lords, one archbishop, fifteen bishops, the adjutant-general, and the advocate-general. 'This list,' commented the *Review*, 'may give rise to curious speculations about the comparative biliousness of the higher classes.'

The classified advertisements of Dickens's day offer endless treasure trove. Here is the employer seeking a well-educated governess willing to work for nothing – and the governess offering to work for nothing; the gentleman inviting a housekeeper to pay him £10 a year for the privilege of sharing his home and looking after him; the Christian lady in search of a helpmeet, who must not be a Tractarian; the High Church annuitant anxious to augment his income by copying for an attorney, but not one of High Calvinist, Socinian, or Unitarian views; the householder stipulating 'no followers', 'no encumbrances', and 'no Irish'; the managing clerk who promises to establish in all those about him 'habits of perseverance, self-denial, and fagging industry'.

There was a falling off in the vogue for matrimonial advertisements, traceable perhaps to the extravagant publicity which had attended the trial of William Corder, the Red Barn murderer (executed on 11 August 1828). It emerged that Corder, after stealthily disposing of Maria Marten, had inserted the following advertisement in the *Morning Herald* of 13 November 1827:

MATRIMONY—A Private Gentleman, aged 24, entirely independent, whose disposition is not to be exceeded, has lately lost the chief of his family by the hand of Providence, which has occasioned discord among the remainder, under circumstances most disagreeable to relate. To any female of respectability, who would study for domestic comfort, and willing to confide her future happiness in one every way qualified to render the marriage state desirable, as the advertiser is in affluence. The lady must have the power of some property, which may remain in her own possession. Many very happy marriages have taken place through means similar to this now resorted to, and it is hoped that no one will answer this through impertinent curiosity; but should this meet the eye of any agreeable lady, who feels desirous of meeting with a sociable, tender, kind, and sympathizing companion, they will find this advertisement worthy of notice. Honour and secrecy may be relied on. As some little security against idle applications, it is requested that letters may be addressed (post-paid) to A.Z. care of Mr Foster, stationer, No. 68 Leadenhall Street, which will meet with the most respectful attention.

According to J. Curtis's account of the Red Barn case, the stationer Foster delivered forty-five letters to William Corder, one of them from Mary Moore, whom Corder married. Corder also advertised in the *Sunday Times* of 23 November, but did not bother to go through the fifty-three letters sent in. Curtis quotes from several of the letters. Some sound genuine enough, and more than one applicant admits to being not very handsome.

Curtis may safely be left to point the moral:

We heartily hope that the sad experience of the unfortunate Mrs Corder will deter our female readers from embarking in a speculation where the chances are five hundred to one against them. An upright, prudent and moral man would hardly, we conceive, make his desires in matrimony known through the medium of a newspaper. There may be here and there a platonic lover, a quixotic sentimentalist or a *timid being*, who might resort to such a measure; but what female would like to link her destiny through life with either of those characters, however unobjectionable he might be from a moral point of view?

Our experience is, and it is founded upon considerable experience arising from a long acquaintance with the public press, that those advertisements generally emanate from speculative, sensual, and sordid men, whose aim is to obtain a *mistress*, or a *fortune*, rather than a wife. How many there have been who will ever curse the day when they were induced to form an alliance with such adventurers!

The 'agony' column of *The Times* in the middle of the nine-teenth century is worth special study. It contained a great deal of what Sherlock Holmes, at a later date, was to describe as 'Bleat, Watson, unmitigated bleat'. That is, cries of 'Come home, all is forgiven', 'Would Philip like to hear of his Mother's Death?' and professions of undying passion. Some were in the most melo-dramatic language, composed regardless of cost; for instance, this of 29 May 1850:

To A xxxxxx If humanity has not entirely fled from your breast, re-turn, oh! return ere it is too late, to your heart-broken, distracted wife you have forsaken – ere the expression of those soft eyes that won you be lost in the bewildered stare of insanity – ere they may gaze on you and know you not; write, tell her, oh! tell her where you are, that she may follow you – her own, her all – and die. See her once more.

Sometimes the agony was disguised in code. The breaking down of such messages seems to have provided the more leisured readers of *The Times* with mental recreation akin to that to be obtained nowadays by solving the newspaper's cross-word puzzle. A large number of these cryptic advertisements were assembled in book form a generation later by a Miss Alice Clay, who seems to have been a code-breaker of more than ordinary talent.

Some of the codes were dismayingly naïve. It is doubtful whether the master of 35, Upper Seymour Street, Portman Square, would have been baffled for very long if, suspecting a domestic intrigue, he had turned to the agony column of *The Times* on the morning of 27 June 1861:

ABZ si yltsenrae detseuqer ot etacinummoc tuohtiw yaled. ma ni yrev taerg elbuort. Dna eriuqer etaidemmi ecivda. 53 Reppu Ruomyes-teerts, Namtrop erauqs.

It was an equally naïve advertiser who inserted the following on 12 July:

Smude. Eht tsop eciffo ta Hgiel si dehctaw, Lotsirb lliw od. Ekat erac.—July 11.

A trifle more ambitious was the coding of this one on 11 October 1869:

SKZPCJJY. BCYP Dyllw, kccr wmsp bgqrpyarcb dpgclb zclcyrf rfc ugjjmu zw rfc jyic.

Solving of this involves moving each letter forward two positions in the alphabet; the message is then seen to be an assignation with Dear Fanny. Other codes were of considerable complexity, as even the *Quarterly Review* admitted. Occasionally a solver was caddish enough to play the marplot, inserting his own message, to the confusion and alarm of the parties concerned. Sometimes a marplot intervened even when the messages were in clear. For instance, Miss Clay quotes:

Eighth May. You are not despised – quite contrary. (13 May 1852)
Eighth May. I feel delighted and shall get mad with joy. Pray do answer. (14 May 1852)
Eighth May. Heed not yesterday's advice. (15 May)
Eighth May. The advertisement under this head on the 15th is not inserted by the same party as that of the 14th. (17 May)

Certain personal columns were used for negotiations with 'finders' of 'lost' property. The Larceny Act of 1861 banned anew the use of the phrase 'no questions asked'. Common informers have since collected money when publications have erred in this respect.

The agony column of *The Times* was as well conducted as such a column can be, which is more than can be said for that of the *New York Herald*. On occasions *The Times* would go to pains to help readers in unusual difficulties, as when, in 1845, it broke its rule not to allow illustrations and reproduced a specimen of the handwriting from a threatening letter addressed to one of its readers.

Probably the 'finest hour' of *The Times* agony column was at the time of the siege of Paris in 1870. French residents and refugees in England greatly distended the column in their anxious efforts to communicate with relatives and friends in the French capital. The newspaper hit on a way to help them. The front page was photographed on thin transparent paper one and a half inches long and one inch wide, nothing being legible save under a microscope. These photographs were sent to Bordeaux, and later flown by pigeon into Paris. There they were enlarged by magic lantern and projected on to a screen. Clerks transcribed the messages and sent them off to the addresses indicated by the advertisers. It was all part of *The Times* service.[1]

'EXTERNAL PAPER HANGERS'

Many ambitious merchants of Dickens's England were far from convinced that the Press was the best advertising medium. There were hundreds of thousands of people who did not read newspapers, and who were yet, in a sense, literate. Their attention was best secured by enlisting the aid of the 'external paper hanger', as the bill-poster of the day liked to be described. Moreover, bills pasted on walls were not subject to the advertisement tax.

In the thirties and forties London was papered over, nightly and often twice-nightly, until it vanished from view. Everywhere prowled fustian-jacketed guerrillas with their big pockets bulging with posters, their paste boxes suspended from their shoulders, their long rods at the ready. A householder leaving his home in the morning might find a poster stuck on his own front door and an undertaker's announcement chalked on the pavement just outside. Every vacant wall was pasted and overpasted with shrieking announcements barbarously printed. The Metropolitan Police Act of 1839 made it an offence to post up bills without the consent of the owner of the property, but it seemed impossible to enforce the law. Even the Fleet Prison was treated as a hoarding. Charles Knight says that some of the bill-posters had 'consuetudinary bye-laws of their own'; that is, they made it a point of honour not to paste over another man's poster until it was dry. The real problem for the 'external paper hanger' was to operate early enough in the day to escape interference, yet late enough to be able to cover a rival's posters. Contractors banded together some of these guerrillas, with the result that pitched battles occurred from time to time between rival gangs. Since the fly-poster's stock-in-trade consisted not only of paste but of blacking to deface the enemy's handiwork, these encounters were as spirited as anything in a Keystone comedy.

1. In February 1950 Mr G. R. Pope, assistant manager of *The Times*, told members of London Publicity Club that frequent attempts were made to abuse the advertisement columns of that newspaper. The classified advertisements manager had a close link with Scotland Yard, and there was a 'black list' of 5,000 names.

Engaging details about the days of unregulated bill sticking are to be found in an article by Charles Dickens in *Household Words* of 22 March 1851. If the 'King of the Bill Stickers' who is interviewed in this article is to be believed, bill-posting in its heyday was by no means an ill-paid profession. When lotteries were still legal (that is, up to 1826), the 'trampers' employed by the State Lottery Commissioners were paid 10s. a day and expenses. Sometimes they might be on the road for six or eight months at a time. As the day of the draw neared, London bill stickers in the service of the Commission would earn as much as £8 or £9 a week. They often dined ceremonially together. With the banning of lotteries, however, all the good fellowship vanished, and cut-throat rivalry took its place. The new élite were the auctioneers' men, 'mostly respectable and intelligent', who were paid 7s. for a day's work, a shilling for a night's lodging, and a shilling for paste.

A few bill-posters were illiterate. Their sheets were handed to them right side up, and in a fixed order, and the men took such good care not to confuse them that it was rare to find a bill posted upside down. But the 'King of the Bill Stickers' was contemptuous of the intelligence of some of his rivals. He himself took pride in having been the first to post bills under the arches of the Thames bridges. His imitators had posted their bills at low tide, and these had been washed away.

The 'King of the Bill Stickers' told his interrogator how, after the passing of the Metropolitan Police Act, one poster contractor had employed a gang of ruffians to beat up those free-lance bill stickers who refused to respect his territory. After spending £500 in a fruitless attempt to rout the guerrillas, the contractor capitulated, but not before he had shaken hands with the enemy and congratulated them on their tenacity.

By mid century, it appeared, the bill sticker had fallen on lean times. In order to prosper, a man had to erect and maintain his own hoarding, unless he was prepared to spend his time haggling with piermasters and builders' foremen for permission to post bills on premises under their control. If a building was found to be tenantless or derelict, fly-posters still descended on it in droves. Dickens cited 'an old warehouse which rotting paste and rotting paper had brought down to the condition of an old cheese . . . it was so thickly encrusted with fragments of bills that no ship's keel after a long voyage could be half so foul'. The doors and even the water spout had been billed over. Finally the whole place had become so rank and encrusted that even the fly-posters had abandoned it.

Not only towns were plastered with posters. Edward Lloyd carried his message far and wide into the countryside. According to Thomas Catling, who worked for him, 'the more remote the place for sticking a bill the more tempting it was to Mr Lloyd.' In the head office the cry was always for 'more slips for palings and gates', and 'six-sheet bills for the rocks in Wales'. Lloyd gave free copies of his newspapers to toll-keepers to induce them to post his bills at the roadside.

The trade of 'external paper hanger' was not one that could be learned in a day. Nor, it seems, was the art of handing out leaflets, as practised by those hypnotic, and often distinguished-looking, gentry who stood at every other street corner. 'Any man,' said Charles Knight, 'can stick up a bill upon a wall, but to insinuate one gracefully and irresistibly into the hands of a lady or gentleman is only for one who, to natural genius, adds long experience.' Reluctance on the part of ladies and gentlemen to accept these leaflets was heightened by the well-founded suspicion that many of them were concerned with 'cures' for disreputable diseases. Eventually the street leaflet scandal became such that Parliament passed the Indecent Advertisements Act (Chapter 4).

Numerous contractors found it more satisfactory to attach advertisements to human beings than to walls. Down-and-outs by the score were rounded up and sent out in droves carrying placards back and front (it was Dickens who invented the phrase 'sandwich-men'). Sometimes they were made to patrol carrying banners on long poles, like down-at-heel heralds. The sandwich-men were the infantry of advertising; but the more resourceful advertiser threw cavalry and mobile columns into the battle. A man on horseback could carry a more imposing placard than a man on foot, and a vehicle – as Prince Pückler-Muskau noted – could be adapted to carry all manner of ingenious devices.

Knight has mentioned one vehicle – 'an undescribable column mounted like the tower of Juggernaut upon the body of a car – a hybrid between an Egyptian obelisk and the ball-surmounted column of an English country gentleman's estate. It bore an inscription of "washable wigs". . . .' Another had a revolving device full of Gothic niches in which tailoring styles were displayed.

Dickens's interview with the 'King of the Bill Stickers' was conducted on board one of a procession of advertising carts touring the streets of London. There is no detailed description of the vehicles, but each one drew violent attention to the contents of a sensational Sunday newspaper (presumably Lloyd's). 'Robbery, fire, murder, and the ruin of the United Kingdom – each discharged in a line by itself, like a separate broadside of red-hot shot – were among the least of the warnings to an unthinking people.' Yet, says Dickens, 'the Ministers of Fate who drove the awful cars leaned forward with their arms upon their knees in a state of extreme lassitude, for want of any subject of interest'. During the frequent traffic hold-ups, angry carters struck blows with their whips on the sides of the advertising carts.

Carlyle found time to complain of one vehicular monstrosity in *Past and Present*. He wrote:

The Hatter in the Strand of London, instead of making better felt hats than another, mounts a huge lath and plaster Hat, seven-feet high, upon wheels; sends a man to drive it through the streets; hoping to be saved *thereby*. He has not attempted to *make* better hats, as he was appointed by the Universe to do, and as with this ingenuity of his he could very probably have done; but his whole industry is turned to *persuade* us that he has made such! He too, knows, that the Quack has become God.

There were advertisements on London passenger vehicles before Queen Victoria came to the throne. Madame Tussaud paid £90 a month to the Atlas Omnibus Company for the privilege of putting her bills on the outside of their vehicles. When the proposal was made that advertising should be allowed *inside* the vehicles (1848), *Punch* was scandalized:

How will you feel sitting for an hour opposite to a pleasant list of the wonderful cures of some professor's ointment? . . . The testimonials of these gifted gentlemen are as little noted for their delicacy as for their truth, and do not form the kind of reading we should exactly prescribe to the fairer portion of the public who patronize omnibuses. . . . Do in mercy allow us to ride for a day's pleasure to the Bank to receive our dividends without compelling us to sit vis-à-vis to Moses and Son, or having Rowland's Kalydor perpetually thrown in our faces. Let us be a nation of shopkeepers as much as we please but there is no necessity that we should become a nation of advertisers.

The city of Glasgow held out against allowing advertisements on its trams and buses for more than a hundred years after London succumbed.

Punch kept a critical eye on all extravagances of publicity; noting how advertising boats were making a nuisance of themselves in the middle of the Thames during regattas; recording with sharp disapproval how Barnum's visit with Tom Thumb had resulted in a rash of posters over the Egyptian Hall shouting the attractions of the *lusus naturae* within ('deformity seems to grow by what it feeds upon'). On another occasion *Punch* sarcastically observed that people would be advertising on umbrellas next; and the suggestion was gratefully put into practice.

Any award for audacity in advertising at this period must inevitably go to Edward Lloyd. He began to stamp the copper coin of the realm with the words 'Lloyd's Weekly Newspaper', paying half the wages of his men with this money in order that it should be well distributed. Belatedly the Government took action and frustrated this enterprise; quite a sizeable sum had to be voted to replace the mutilated coinage. The writer has searched *Hansard* in vain for any expression of indignation at a practice which now carries the penalty of a year's imprisonment. Oddly enough, this was not the end of advertising on coins. Thomas J. Barratt, of Pears' Soap, hit upon a scheme of much ingenuity; it belongs to a later chapter.

4   The Tax is Lifted

By the middle of the nineteenth century the agitation against the advertisement tax and the stamp duties could no longer be brushed aside. As operated, the tax was unjust. The catalogue of the Great Exhibition contained fifty-three pages of advertisements, all tax-free; the announcements in the railway carriages paid no tribute; nor did the posters of Thomas Holloway. Yet a clerk in search of a job had to pay a tax of 1s. 6d. if he advertised in a newspaper.

Tax officials showed great zeal in discovering what they called 'separate interests'. If a steamboat announcement mentioned a hotel and an omnibus service, the tax collectors demanded an additional 1s. 6d. for each reference. Even news items about the arrival of early fruit or vegetables were decreed to be advertisements. The *Publishers' Circular* avoided payment of advertisement tax only by omitting the publisher's name from the announcement of a new book. More ludicrous was the practice of taxing a favourable review as an advertisement; an author whose book was savaged by an impecunious periodical could be pardoned for harbouring base suspicions.

One simple argument in favour of abolishing the advertisement tax was that a single small advertisement could easily elicit as many as 200 letters, all of which bore postage stamps and thus contributed to the revenue; if the advertiser answered some proportion of those letters, that meant a further expenditure on postage stamps. Thus, if small advertisements were allowed to multiply, the Exchequer would soon recoup the modest £178,000 received from the tax. The Chancellor of the Exchequer remained unconvinced. As a gesture he suggested cutting the tax to sixpence, but the abolitionists carried the day. That was in 1853.

It was a momentous period for the Press. Two years later the stamp duty on newspapers was abolished, and in 1861 the last remaining 'tax upon knowledge' – a duty on paper – was lifted. 'Of all decades in our history, a wise man would choose the 1850s to be young in', a historian has said. Certainly of all decades it was the one in which to start a newspaper (the *Daily Telegraph*, for instance, made its appearance in 1855). There were some 640 newspapers in Britain in 1855; by the end of the century there were more than 3,000. It is perhaps ungenerous to speculate how many of these would have appeared if it had not been for the open-handed advertising of quacks. Truth, knowledge, culture, piety, and wit – these, whether the world likes it or not, were propagated by pills, salves, pick-me-ups, elixirs, and aphrodisiacs.

The golden age of the fifties and sixties was not yet the golden age of advertising. In spite of the manifest success of Thomas Holloway, all but a few manufacturers had yet to be convinced that advertising was necessary. They were quite certain that it was ungentlemanly. Some may even have agreed with Carlyle that it was against nature. The ideal, the traditional way to do business was to surround oneself with a circle of customers and to cultivate personal relations with them; excellence of goods and word-of-mouth recommendation would do the rest. If wider markets were necessary, the way to tap them was to send respectable travellers out on the road and pay them commission. The last thing to do was to chalk the firm's name on the sides of quarries or to insert vulgar little paragraphs in the newspapers, in the contaminating company of truss-mongers, snuff-sellers, pox-doctors, body-snatching undertakers, and cut-price abortionists.

That was the only attitude a gentleman could adopt towards advertising, which he preferred to call 'puffing'. Yet what if an honest capitalist, in this inventive age, planned to build and market a complex machine like a steam cultivator or a traction engine or a mechanical piano? Hundreds of separate processes were involved in the making of these things. If only half a dozen articles were to be turned out in a year, the selling price would be prohibitively high. Unless a ready market could be assured, how was such an enterprise to be sustained? Similarly, if a man invented a new processed food – and scores of these were now being created – how could he offset the cost of plant if there was no certainty of buyers? How could people buy a product when they had never heard of it? Distasteful though the idea might be, there seemed to be no other way of ensuring a market than by advertisement, or perhaps – was this a way out? – by *announcement*. Thomas Russell, a former advertisement manager of *The Times*, has argued that it was because advertising, at this period, was still held in such widespread contempt that manufacturers contented themselves with little more than a bald statement of the firm's name and product; the technique of proclamation rather than persuasion. Since all advertisers' announcements were assumed to be mendacious, it was better to make no claims at all, but to let the public investigate for themselves, and having assured themselves of the excellence of the product, tell their friends.[1]

Hence, contends Russell, the unsubtle and monotonously repetitive advertising of the latter part of the century – 'Pears' Soap', 'Reckitt's Blue', 'Hot Bovril', 'Mellin's Food', and so on, reminder phrases which were regarded as complete and sufficient advertisements in themselves. As yet there was no difficulty in selling novel and need-filling goods, once their existence was made known. There was no necessity to bludgeon or cajole people into buying. The population was fast expanding, and it was a population which was anxious enough to be wooed by the advertiser. An ambitious, lightly taxed middle-class demanded the outward trappings of prosperity and progress, and usually it was able to pay for these things out of income. Although the seeds of hire-purchase had been sown – a Singer sewing machine could be hire-purchased in 1856 for 35s. down and 35s. monthly – it was not until the twentieth century that the 'never, never' system reached its monstrous flowering.

The older generation's fierce distrust of advertising and the advertiser was rooted deep in newspaper editors. Abolition of the 'taxes on knowledge' had enabled the selling price of newspapers to be lowered, but the costs of running a newspaper, with all the services and features which the public had grown to expect, were becoming ever heavier. Editors were curiously reluctant to admit that it was the advertiser who enabled them still to publish at a penny. They looked on the man as a pariah to be frustrated and disciplined as much as possible. He must be made to pay in advance, and he must bring his copy, cap in hand, to be edited.

1. Thomas Russell: *Commercial Advertising* (1919).

Why, some of the more importunate quacks were even demanding display advertisements, as if the newspapers were a public
hoarding! They were asking to use big black type, and pictures of
voluptuous women with billowing manes of hair. They wanted to
abolish column rules in the interests of more vulgar presentation.
Apart from disfiguring the newspaper (ran the editorial argument)
such concessions would only play into the hands of the biggest
advertisers, at the expense of the little men. By common consent
the newspapers put a ban on the use of any type larger than
minion. So, from the sixties onwards, began that tiresome era
when the advertising columns were filled with endless, pattern-
making repetitions of a firm's name or product. The idea, possibly,
was to goad the newspaper proprietors into relaxing their rules
against display by making the columns look as foolish as possible.
(American advertisers revealed a special gift in this direction –
Chapter 5.) *The Times* enforced a rule against the endless repetition of the same phrase; each line had to be followed by explana-
tory matter. Thus:

ROSSETTER'S HAIR RESTORER
is not a dye
ROSSETTER'S HAIR RESTORER
contains no oil
ROSSETTER'S HAIR RESTORER
prevents hair falling
ROSSETTER'S HAIR RESTORER
promotes the growth of hair

And so on, for as long as the advertiser cared to spin it out.

Then, in an evil moment, the trick was discovered of building
up large capital letters by grouping together small letters, in
appropriate shapes, thus:

TTTTTTT	HH HH	EEEEEE
TTTTTTT	HH HH	EE
TT	HHHHHHH	EEEE
TT	HHHHHHH	EEEE
TT	HH HH	EE
TT	HH HH	EEEEEE

If the letters were built up sufficiently, capitals three or four
inches deep could be constructed. The name CUTICURA was

spelt out one letter to a column across the top of an eight-column paper, subsidiary headings being constructed on a lesser scale. Many papers refused to allow column rules to be removed, with the result that words were arbitrarily split. Other gruesome feats of typographical topiary were perpetrated. A hatter would stipulate that the type in his advertisement be set out in the shape of a top-hat; an oculist would mangle his message into the shape of a pair of spectacles. These advertisements, which must have caused unspeakable profanity among compositors, now appear to be eyesores of the most futile kind; but the editors thought that anything was better than to let advertisers loose among the big black type. It was perhaps not surprising that some of the more frustrated manufacturers began to concentrate on outdoor advertising. There was no ban on the size of letters which could be painted on the side of a cliff.

It is time to review some of the new commodities which were invented in this fast-expanding age – commodities which carried the names of their backers into every household and into every mouth, yet rarely into the reference books. From now on a man could make a million pounds yet never rate an obituary in *The Times* or *Daily Telegraph*.

It was the age of new foods. In 1850 it was discovered that the virtues of beef could be stored in a small bottle, but it was fifteen years before the Liebig Extract of Meat Company (LEMCO, parent company of Oxo) was founded and began to advertise aggressively. During those years, Baron Liebig had been content to keep 200 or 300 cattle, and to supply extract of beef for purely medicinal purposes. By 1867 the LEMCO Company had been awarded a gold medal in Paris for originating 'a new industry productive of an article eminently cheap and useful'. Not until 1884 did Johnson's Fluid Beef come on the market under the name of Bovril, and the frisky bull ('I hear they want more Bovril') become familiar to millions.

Almost simultaneously with the condensing of the cow came the condensing of its milk. This lucrative feat was achieved, not without numerous setbacks, by Gail Borden in Connecticut and by Henri Nestlé in Switzerland. In 1869 a restless young chemist from Heligoland, Gustav Mellin, invented an infant food in powder form. Soon Nestlé and Mellin were unable to move far without being confronted by their own names. In 1869 a French chemist, Mège Mouriés, was commissioned by Napoleon III to find a butter substitute; out of his test tubes he conjured margarine, on the popularizing of which many fortunes were to be spent.

If a common commodity like milk could be processed and patented, why not bread? Richard Smith, in the eighties, produced a loaf with the singularly unappetizing title of 'Smith's Patent Germ Bread'. Rechristened Hovis (from *Hominis Vis*) it was swiftly propelled to fame. Others took the view that bread had enjoyed too long an innings, and began to devise breakfast foods in flake form. These had the advantage that weight for weight they could be sold at many times the price of bread.

Then there were the mechanical inventions which changed the business and social habits of the age. In 1874, after scores of patents had been taken out, the American firm of Remington put the first effective typewriter on the market. It typed only in capitals; but four years later a shift key was triumphantly announced. At the Great Exhibition of 1851 a model of a sewing machine had aroused no especial interest (ten years previously the Paris mob had wrecked the establishment where Barthelemy Thimmonier was using sewing machines on Army contracts); but as the century wore on, and patent litigation abated, Singer sewing machines began to conquer the world. One firm abandoned the trade, however, in favour of making bicycles – the Coventry Sewing Machine Company (later the Swift Company). Hobby horses and velocipedes had long since been laughed off the streets; the cycles which the Coventry firm marketed were low-built machines and had originally been intended for France, but the outbreak of the Franco-Prussian War compelled the firm to seek a home market. Bicycle races helped to 'improve the breed', and winners were much publicized. Ball bearings came in the late seventies, and in 1889 arrived John Boyd Dunlop's pneumatic tyre, paving the way for the great cycling boom of the nineties.

George Eastman, in America, announced the first portable roll-film camera in the late eighties, and a new popular hobby was born. 'You press the button – we do the rest' was the slogan on which Kodak sales subsequently soared. The gramophone had a long way to go before its makers could boast 'purity of tone'; this was the cry of the makers of player-pianos.

Modernized baths, furnaces, stoves, and water-closets also began pressing on to the market. In the latter years of the century there was a campaign to install a Turkish bath in every middle-class home. Many of the pictures in these advertisements suggest scenes of penance, with naked men or women sitting over equally naked lamps. From one apparatus emerges the head of a woman bearing an expression such as might be found on an elderly governess who has had the misfortune to be buried up to her neck by Touaregs. As time went on the bathers' expressions became less strained and most of them were depicted reading books.

*The Lady with the Lamp
c. 1900*

All these were new commodities, new inventions, and the public had to be told about them. But there were also old commodities, about which the public had never been sufficiently informed. As long ago as 1789 Andrew Pears had devised his transparent soap, but until the middle of the nineteenth century it had been very modestly advertised. In 1865, when the firm's annual bill for advertising was £80, a young man of twenty-four, Thomas J. Barratt, became a partner in the firm, and ushered in a vigorous new régime. It was too vigorous for Francis Pears, grandson of the founder, who thought that Barratt's reckless expenditure on advertising could bring only ruin. He withdrew from the business in 1875, while (as it seemed to him) there was still a business left; luckily for himself, he left £4,000 in the firm.

One of the many 'fathers of modern advertising', Barratt is on record as saying: 'Any fool can make soap. It takes a clever man to sell it.' When he finally took over control of Pears he raised his expenditure on advertising to between £100,000 and £130,000. In justification he never tired of pointing out that he was enabled to sell soap thirty per cent more cheaply than if he had not advertised it.

Barratt's policy was summed up with perfect simplicity in one of his own advertisements: 'How do you spell soap?' – 'Why,

P-E-A-R-S, of course.' 'Pears' and 'soap' had to be linked so
deeply and ineluctably in the public mind that it would be
impossible to think of one without the other. Ultimately the
public would be so conditioned to the association that they would
go into a shop and instead of asking for soap would ask for
'Pears' Soap', or even for 'Pears'. That was, and is, the advertising man's dream. It accounts for the tens of thousands of tedious
and apparently futile signs bearing the names of household
products – notably the indestructible enamel signs which stud the
approaches to railway stations. It is wrong to say that no one
reads them; they are not there to be read, but to be absorbed,
just as a capsule is not meant to be tasted, but to be swallowed.

Barratt's policy has been called one of hypnosis. Certainly his
puzzle posters, in which crowds of perhaps fifty persons stood for
as long as twenty minutes staring at optical illusions, suggested
hypnotic trance. If the crowds did not quite fathom the illusion,
at least they went away, it is said, with 'Pears' Soap' tattooed on
their sub-conscious.

The visual attack did not satisfy Barratt, however. He decided
he must have a catch-phrase which would make the whole country
say 'Pears' Soap'. His staff were invited to nominate the com-
monest phrases in daily use. Inevitably, somebody suggested
'Good morning'. The result was the notorious 'Good morning!
Have you used Pears' Soap?' which scourged two continents.
There were many who never forgave Thomas Barratt for debasing
this traditional, friendly greeting. The sensitive shrank from
saying 'Good morning', knowing that it would only spark
off the exasperating counter-phrase in the mind of the person
addressed.

The opposition from rival soap firms was far from negligible.
Since the 1840s Hudson's had been boasting that their new soap
powder spelled 'washing without tears' – a cry which was still
being dinned in the ears of British housewives by a score of rival
manufacturers a century later. In the mid eighties a grocer's son
from Bolton, William Hesketh Lever (the first Lord Leverhulme),
who had been casting around for an atttactive name for his soap,
decided that he could do worse than use the word 'Sunlight'. In
1888, after studying publicity methods in America, he cut the

first sod of Port Sunlight. Lever's was to prove the most formidable competition of all. Many of his advertisements and catchphrases – like 'Why does a woman look old sooner than a man?' – were to enjoy as wide a currency as anything conjured up by Barratt. In 1890 he had an advertisement of an old woman washing clothes in a tub. It was headed 'A CHEERY OLD SOUL', and the copy ran: 'It is possible for a woman with increasing years to continue to do laundry work. Thousands who would have been laid aside under the old system of washing have proved what Sunlight Soap can do in reducing labour.' When the soap war became really sharp, some of the advertisements took on a certain sharpness, too. One firm ran a 'knocking' campaign directed specifically at Pears.

By the eighties, there were a number of advertising agencies which offered to prepare the manufacturer's copy for him. There had been earlier agents, but they had owed allegiance to the newspapers rather than to the advertisers; they had been debt-collectors at best and fee-snatchers at worst. Now agents began to identify themselves with the advertiser and to offer him advice on the most suitable publications for his purpose. The number of newspapers was so great that only a specialist could keep track of them all and form a view as to their usefulness.

From the handbooks issued by agents in the eighties some idea of the advertising methods and philosophy of the day can be gained. Two of the livelier (not the first) directories were Samuel Deacon's *Newspaper Handbook* and Henry Sell's *Dictionary of the World's Press and Philosophy of Advertising*. Both Deacon and Sell solemnly warned their readers against the folly of the argument: 'The father did not advertise, why should the son?' Henry Sell deplored that many old-established businesses of undisputed probity were crumbling away from dry rot. Fifty years previously, the public had been obliged to patronize these firms. The world had been smaller then and there had been little rivalry.

Straightforwardness and honesty are as necessary, and we believe as frequently met with, now as heretofore, but even these qualities in a business house, unassisted by publicity, will fail to keep it in the leading rank. The public like to be asked for their custom and they naturally go to the people who invite them.

Henry Sell understood perfectly the art of marketing an everyday commodity. 'By the exercise of a little ingenuity it is easy to make a speciality. . . . Give it a name, register it, and Advertise it, so that the public *must* come to *you* for it.' Then came a few elementary lessons in psychology. Many people, he said, would have seen this sign in the window of a house:

A
MANGLE
KEPT HERE

How much better to put up signs in the windows of near-by houses reading:

MANGLING WITH A
NEW PATENT MANGLE
IS CAREFULLY DONE
BY MRS JONES
NO. 20 IN THE NEXT COURT

Samuel Deacon told a curious story about M. Millaud, founder of the prosperous *Petit Journal*, who had assured a gathering of Paris editors that the most worthless article could be sold if advertised sufficiently. Émile de Girardin, of *La Presse*, had joined issue with him. 'What will you bet,' said Millaud, 'that I cannot sell in one week 100,000 francs' worth of the most common cabbage-seed, under the pretext that it produces mammoth cabbage heads? All I have to do is advertise it once in a whole-page insertion in the daily papers of this city.' Émile de Girardin said he would present a page of *La Presse* free if Millaud was successful; so did the other editors. At the end of a week Millaud had sold twice as much cabbage-seed as he had promised, and the orders were still flooding in. It was decided to fulfil no more orders, on the grounds that the joke (if joke it was) had gone far enough.

The authors of both handbooks quoted advertisements of the day which had caught their fancy. Deacon thought highly of the following:

MR BRADLAUGH. The Struggle in the Lobby of the House of Commons. B. S. WOOLF, the celebrated City and Anglo-American tailor of 9 and 10 Poultry EC and 292 and 294 Edgware Road W, having witnessed the struggle in which Mr Bradlaugh's coat was unfortunately torn, will be glad to replace the same if Mr Bradlaugh will honour him with a call at either of his establishments.

Deacon was impressed, too, by the vigorous advertising of the Royal Insurance Company, which had expanded its business greatly in consequence. He urged some of the older-established and ultra-conservative insurance firms to follow the Royal's example. When they did take space in the Press, he said, their manner was so apologetic as to recall the impoverished gentleman, reduced to crying fish in the streets, who exclaimed: 'I hope to goodness no one hears me.' This reproach could not be levelled against the Railway Passenger Assurance Company, which in the seventies had column-length advertisements in the *Daily News* inviting readers to insure against a variety of risks, few of them connected with railways.

Each handbook contained aphorisms on advertising from newspapers and magazines of the day. To American newspapers were attributed such sayings as: 'Advertising is a blister that draws trade'; 'Trying to do business without advertising is like winking in the dark. You know yourself that you are keeping up a powerful winking, but no one else is aware of your exertions'; 'The chap who could get all the business he wanted without advertising has been compelled to advertise at last. The advertisement is headed "Sheriff's sale"'; 'Don't fear to have a small advertisement by the side of a big one. The big one can't eat it up'. Horace Greeley of the *New York Tribune* had said that to do without advertising was 'to close one's eyes to the light and insist upon living in perpetual darkness'. In Greeley's view advertisements were now read by between five and ten times as many people as twenty years before. No less a figure than Lord Macaulay was quoted as saying: 'Advertising is to business what steam is to machinery – the great propelling power.'

One truth which had already been discovered in the eighties was contained in an unascribed quotation: 'Ceasing to advertise in dull times is like tearing out a dam because the water is low'. Henry Sell told a cautionary tale of the (unnamed) manufacturer who for twenty years had been spending £10,000 a year on advertising. Convinced that his product must at last be familiar enough to the public, he cut his appropriation to £5,000. In the following year he had to spend £20,000 to recover his position.

Between them, Deacon and Sell did their utmost to convince the advertiser that he could get nowhere without enlisting the aid of an agent. 'Would you leave or enter a port without a pilot?' asked Sell. 'Would you commence to prosecute a law case without a legal adviser?' Like Mrs Warren, of blacking fame, Henry Sell could boast 'We keeps a poet'. He offered copy in prose or verse, explaining: 'I am in constant communication with gentlemen of literary ability'. Deacon assured his clients that he was trying to break down the reluctance of many newspapers to declare their circulations – the beginnings of a campaign which was to go on for fifty years.

Although as late as 1887 Henry Sell was still boasting of his firm's virtuosity in typographical pattern-making, many newspapers – among them the *Daily News* – were beginning to allow display advertisements, in light-face type across two columns, even with an occasional thumb-nail illustration. In illustrated magazines like the *Graphic* bold pictorial advertisements were now appearing. Some of these were creditable efforts; the worst of them were appalling. Having commissioned and accepted a drawing, the advertiser, or his agent, would set about disfiguring it. If it showed a family at table, he would run his slogan for sauce along the bottom of the tablecloth. If it showed a beauty leaning forward in her box at the theatre, he would inscribe his message vertically up the pillars of the box. Some advertisers, less inhibited, stamped their name or slogan on a lady's bare back or chest. Others again went in for symbolism. A nude girl rising from the Borax lakes waved her wand at a flight of unclean shapes labelled 'Disease' and 'Decay'. She was an attractive nude, and to ward off possible criticism she was labelled 'Spirit of Purity'. Undraped females were more plentiful in the advertisements of this period than might have been expected. Nude children abounded, too; so did odiously winsome little girls, into whose mouths were put words like 'I'm helping dear Mother by taking Ridge's to my baby Brother'. By 1890 'pretty girl' advertising was firmly established. The cigarette firm of Player had a girl with a cigarette in one of their advertisements. She was holding it in her hand, upraised above her head, and the expression on her face was one of near-ecstasy. If challenged, she would probably have explained that she was holding it for her brother. At this period there was a noticeable tendency to associate girls with cigarettes, without going so far as to put the cigarettes between their lips. If people chose to assume that these girls were smokers, well and good.

Player's famous bearded sailor had a predecessor, also framed in a lifebuoy. He was a very young-looking sailor, and the new face, adopted in 1898, was undoubtedly an improvement. It came as a surprise to many, in the summer of 1951, to learn that this was the portrait of a real sailor, Thomas Huntley Wood, who died in that year. Wood's likeness first appeared in the *Army and Navy Illustrated* in 1898, whence it was borrowed for advertising purposes. A friend of Wood's wrote to the firm suggesting payment of a fee of £15; Wood reduced this to a sum of two guineas 'and a bit of baccy for myself and the boys on board'. The firm paid, in cash and kind. Some time later, tiring of people pulling out a packet of Player's and asking 'Is that really you?', Wood shaved off his beard. An O. Henry or a Damon Runyon could have built an enchanting whimsy round the story of Thomas Wood – the man who sold his face for a song, only to be haunted by it ever afterwards.

Not every Victorian advertiser, by a long way, was willing to yield the composition of his advertisements to an agent. The most eccentric, the most obstinately 'different' advertisements in late Victorian magazines, and for a long time afterwards, were those personally devised by the founder of Eno's Fruit Salts. Three quarters of his space would be taken up by high-flown quotations on the theme of man's unconquerable mind, from the ancient and modern philosophers. The underlying theme, as far as it was distinguishable, was the sin of allowing the human intellect to be harnessed to a sluggish gut; but often the quotations came so thickly and haphazardly that it was impossible to trace a continuity of thought behind them. Now and again the compiler would throw in an uplifting poem which had taken his fancy, or perhaps an original rhymed tribute from a retired major-general. He kept an artist busy drawing scenes in which lost wanderers stumbled into forest glades and found words like 'Integrity' mysteriously carved on the rocks, or in which seated greybeards solemnly drew the attention of milkmaids to moral phrases graven on the ground before them. Sometimes the descent from the cloudless peaks of the intellect to the mucous walls of the intestinal canal was achieved almost in one sentence. For a

☞ The Bottle Imp of Disease Germs, contamination and malodorous vapours, the remnant of a wreckage on the shores of health, speedily succumbs to the powerful antidote, CALVERT'S CARBOLIC, the Popular Disinfectant.

Advertising art of the eighties

generation the strong-minded founder of the firm fought off any suggestion that he should 'modernize' his announcements. Eventually his product was advertised, like all the others, with the aid of pretty girls.

No review of this period can omit the highly individual publicity methods – adapted, some said, from Barnum himself – which were employed in the city of Glasgow by one of her most resourceful sons, Thomas Lipton. The stunts began with the driving of fat pigs through the streets under a banner 'Lipton's Orphans'; they continued with parades of cadaverous males inscribed 'Going to Lipton's' and parades of fat men labelled 'Coming from Lipton's'. Then came the importing of gigantic cheeses, drawn by traction engine or elephant to Lipton's shops, there to be stuffed with sovereigns and sold to milling crowds. Alec Waugh tells of these exploits in *The Lipton Story*; not omitting Lipton's offer of a monster cheese to Queen Victoria to mark her Jubilee in 1885. 'The cheese which I purpose presenting to your Majesty . . . would weigh about 11,200 pounds or not less than five tons and be made from one day's milk of 8,500 cows,' he wrote. The Queen replied that she could not accept gifts from persons to whom she had not been introduced; however, in due course the Sovereign who refused this humble tribute conferred a knighthood on the man who had offered it.

As a national and international advertiser Lipton did not get into his stride until the late eighties, when he took Ceylon for his colony and began to plaster the world with 'Lipton's Teas'. About 1890 he boasted of paying £35,000 Customs tax on his teas; but ten years later it was Mazawattee who claimed to have written the world's largest duty cheque: £85,862 8s. 8d.

THE LAW STEPS IN

The year 1853 had seen the 'emancipation' of advertising. It also saw the passing of measures designed to frustrate two of the more importunate classes of advertiser. The London Hackney Carriage Act made it illegal to send placard-covered vehicles or poster-carrying cavalry or infantry through the streets of the capital to the obstruction of others. Henceforth, if a man was determined to operate a vehicle shaped like a top-hat or a bottle, it had to be capable of carrying goods. From time to time the courts were called upon to decide whether certain wheeled devices were primarily advertisements or vehicles.

The other advertiser to come under a ban was the betting shop proprietor. Unfortunately the 1853 Betting Bill, which had sought to shut down betting shops and make it illegal to advertise them, merely had the effect of driving the owners out of England and into Scotland or the Channel Isles. From these tolerant sanctuaries they were at liberty to advertise as seductively as they wished in English sporting papers, and to flood the whole kingdom with circulars.

When a new Betting Bill came up in 1874, the House of Commons was regaled with some of the unscrupulous 'discretionary' advertisements from current sporting papers. A typical one from a Guernsey address read: 'Three Splendid Speculations. Great Success. For the trifling stake of 15s. you can realize £3,000; for £1, £12,000; and for £8, £37,000.' A 'discretionary' bet was so called because the punter handed over a stake to be invested at the discretion of the advertiser, who afterwards rendered to his client an account of the transactions. Most often, the punter who had been assured that he could not fail to win a fortune received a letter saying that, inexplicably, and for the first time since the business was founded, the system had failed; but that, as it was clearly impossible that such a cruel stroke of luck could happen twice, a further investment should be sent without delay. Sometimes a promising client was allowed to make modest wins at the outset.

The House was told that 'discretionary' advertisements were refused by all reputable papers. Those publications which accepted them, knowing that they were mostly fraudulent, adopted the curious course of charging three times the usual rate. Occasionally the editors warned their readers not to be ensnared by the specious offers in their pages. What more could they do?

Not all Members of Parliament were convinced that it was necessary to prevent rogues from exploiting fools, but the Bill was passed and the loophole plugged.

Another stage in the clean-up of advertising came in 1889 with the passing of the Indecent Advertisements Act. The discussions in Parliament on this measure were conducted in such veiled language that it is not easy, at first glance, to ascertain what the offending advertisements were about; but the Earl of Meath permitted himself to say that the Bill was directed against vendors of cures for 'a certain class of disease of a nameless character'. He added: 'It is quite impossible that I can bring before your Lordships' house all the evidence I have to show the need of such legislation.'

No one, said the Earl, could pass down certain streets of London without having thrust into his hands 'indecent and filthy publications which ought not to come before the eyes of any decent man or woman', leaflets which were 'inducements to promiscuous sexual intercourse'. Within recent years, 'a person connected with one of the societies interested in this subject' had had 20,000 papers thrust into his hands. In less populated districts it was usual for these leaflets to be stuck on gates and posts.

The Archbishop of Canterbury told how pernicious leaflets were given away in school playgrounds. 'While some girls were taking their recreation in a meadow attached to their school,' he said, 'two men drove rapidly by in a gig and flung over the wall packages of literature of the most horrible description. Fortunately one of them happened to fall at the feet of one of the mistresses and the mischief intended was not done.'

It was characteristic of the age that these advertisements should be attacked on the grounds of indecency and not because the treatments they offered were useless. Possible contamination of the mind was regarded as a greater peril than corruption of the body.

One speaker on the Bill in the House of Lords thought it odd that newspapers were still to be allowed to advertise cures for venereal diseases. Others thought it no less odd that the Press should be allowed to publish advertisements of abortifacients.

That same year the country read about the exploits of the rascally Chrimes brothers, whose profanation of the medium of advertisement outclassed even the efforts of Jonathan Wild. Richard, Edward, and Leonard Chrimes were charged at the Central Criminal Court, London, with attempting to extort two guineas from a married woman, Kate Clifford. It appeared that, under various aliases, and by heavy advertising, they had worked up a brisk business in abortifacients, one of their lines being entitled 'Lady Montrose's Miracle Female Tabules'. The newspapers which accepted these advertisements charged five times the normal tariff – 'a somewhat significant increase' as the prosecution pointed out. In all, the Chrimes brothers spent more than £2,000 in advertising their products; then, dissatisfied with the rate of flow of wealth, they conceived a plot of classic effrontery. On the morning of 8 October 1898, between 8,000 and 10,000 women up and down the country received a disturbing letter in the post. It ran:

> Trafalgar Buildings,
> Northumberland Avenue.

> Madame, I am in possession of letters of yours by which I can positively prove that you did on or about — commit, or attempt to commit the fearful crime of abortion by preventing or attempting to prevent yourself giving birth to a child. Either of these constitutes a criminal act punishable by penal servitude and legal proceedings have already been commenced against you, and your immediate arrest will be effected unless you send me on or before Tuesday morning next the sum of £2 2s., being costs already incurred by me, and your solemn promise on oath before God that never again by whatsoever means will you prevent or attempt to prevent yourself giving birth to a child. No notice whatever will be taken of your letter unless postal orders (cheques, stamps etc. will not be accepted) for the above amount are enclosed and received by me on the aforesaid day. Failing to comply with these two requests, you will be immediately arrested without further warning. All legal proceedings will be stopped on receipt of the £2 2s. and the incriminating documents . . . will be returned to you and you will hear nothing further of the matter.

> I am, Madame etc
> (signed) Charles J. Mitchell, Public Official

The letter addressed to Mrs Kate Clifford was opened by her husband, who showed it to the police. Between 14 October and 17 October detectives intercepted 1,785 letters addressed to 'Mitchell', 413 of which contained money. Excerpts from one letter were read by the judge:

> . . . the child that you are alluding to is a big fine girl, as healthy as any child could be, and is eight months old. . . . But if I have done wrong

I ask you to forgive me as I did not know I was doing wrong. I will promise that I will never do wrong any more, for Christ's sake. Amen.

This letter was one of those which contained two guineas.

The jury which found the three men guilty added a rider saying that:

... such a vile plot, even with all the ingenuity displayed in it, could only have been possible by the acceptance of such immoral advertisements by a section of the Press – religious and secular – well knowing their nature.

The hint was not taken, not even by the religious Press. The Chrimes brothers were awarded a total of thirty-one years' penal servitude, and ten thousand wives breathed freely again.

Two years later another class of advertiser came under a legislative ban – the moneylender who made a speciality of sending circulars to boys at boarding school. The Earl of Aberdeen assured his fellow peers that no other body of individuals in the country suffered more from the importunities of moneylenders than did the members of that House, as sons or fathers.

I have a boy of twelve, and therefore not old enough yet to be in a public school, who has received a good many of these circulars at his private school, in which he is told that if he borrows any money his father need not know anything about it, but that if in due course it becomes necessary he should know it, he would no doubt be delighted to pay the money.

For a moneylender to be able to ensnare the scion of a noble house at an early age was excellent business. With luck the victim would be on the firm's books for a lifetime.

As was to be expected, the Betting and Loans (Infants) Bill suffered no obstruction in the Lords, and the measure reached the Statute Book. Moneylenders' methods of advertising continued on unseemly and often outrageous lines, but Parliament was slow to take further action.

The year 1892 brought a legal case which deeply disconcerted the more conscienceless class of advertiser – the Case of the Carbolic Smoke Ball. In this, Mr Justice Hawkins laid down the vexatious rule that words, in certain circumstances, mean what they say.

In the *Pall Mall Gazette* of 13 November 1891 had appeared this advertisement:

£100 REWARD

WILL BE PAID BY THE

CARBOLIC SMOKE BALL CO.

To any person who contracts the increasing Epidemic,

INFLUENZA,

Colds, or any diseases caused by taking cold, AFTER HAVING USED the BALL 3 times daily for two weeks according to the printed directions supplied with each Ball.

£1,000

Is deposited with the ALLIANCE BANK, REGENT-STREET, showing our sincerity in the matter. During the last epidemic of Influenza many thousand CARBOLIC SMOKE BALLS were sold as Preventives against this Disease, and in no ascertained case was the disease contracted by those using the CARBOLIC SMOKE BALL.

One **CARBOLIC SMOKE BALL** will last a family several months, making it the cheapest remedy in the world at the price—10s., post free.   The BALL can be RE-FILLED at a cost of 5s.   Address :—

CARBOLIC SMOKE BALL CO.,
27, Princes-street, Hanover-sq., London, W.

A Mrs Carlill, of whom no personal details seem to have been handed down, bought a Carbolic Smoke Ball, used it as directed for two weeks, and contracted influenza. On her recovery she requested £100 from the manufacturers. When they declined to pay, she took them to court.

The defendants offered a variety of pleas. There was no contract, they said; or if there was a contract, it was void on the ground that a wager was involved, or that it was contrary to public policy. They also argued that a contract could not be binding unless it was made with a specific person. Queen's Counsel for the company was the future Lord Oxford and Asquith. He pleaded: 'The advertisement was a mere representation of what the advertisers intended to do in a certain event. The defendants did not, by issuing it, mean to impose upon themselves any obligation enforceable by law.' To this remarkable defence, Mr Justice Hawkins said: '. . . It must be remembered that such advertisements do not appeal so much to the wise and thoughtful as to the credulous and weak portions of the community.' A vendor making a promise 'must not be surprised if occasionally he is held to his promise'. The Court of Appeal upheld this decision, saying that the promise by the Carbolic Smoke Ball Company had been 'as plain as words could make it'.

Mrs Carlill collected her £100, to the envy, no doubt, of many who wished they had thought of the idea first. Today the case of Carlill *v.* The Carbolic Smoke Ball Company is a red light over the desk of the advertising copywriter. It was the first case of its kind and it should have been the last; but it was not.

In less sophisticated lands, the advertiser who made specific promises and attempted to go back on them sometimes received shorter shrift. In 1900 a New Orleans dealer sent a consignment of toothache drops to an agent in Chile. The drops were 'warranted to cure the worst case of toothache in ten minutes'. The first customer who tried the remedy did so on the spot; he took out his watch, and after ten minutes, finding that he still had toothache, had the agent arrested. The penalty imposed was a fine of one thousand dollars with three months' imprisonment. Only with great difficulty did the American consul succeed in having the jail sentence cancelled.

THEN CAME 'BUBBLES'

In the latter part of the nineteenth century the fly-posters were gradually squeezed out by the big hoarding contractors. The excesses of the free-lance banditti had been such that no one was prepared to shed tears over the eclipsing of the 'little man'. Jokes about fly-posting were slow to die, however. The Victorians took an innocent delight in the production of satirical prints showing enormous hoardings on which posters had been pasted, one partly over the other, in such a way as to produce 'messages' like: 'Funerals Conducted with Dignity and Decorum by FUNNY FOLKS EVERY WEDNESDAY with a Band and Chorus of 700 Performers in A. LYNES AND SONS 13s. TROUSERS.' Or perhaps: 'Mr J. L. Toole will PUNCH EVERY WEDNESDAY the Rev. Dr Parker.' The joke was played for all it was worth; sometimes no doubt juxtapositions little less farcical did appear on unregulated poster stations.

It is on record that by 1860 there were 'orderly and attractive'

D

hoardings in many English cities. Much of the credit goes to Edward Sheldon, of Leeds, who rose above the scuffle and forced the public and his rivals to respect his orderly, rented bill stations (see Cyril Sheldon's *A History of Poster Advertising*). He was a founder of the United Kingdom Billposters Association, which took shape in Manchester in 1862. This assembly of hardy individualists was often at loggerheads with itself and the world, but it originated and enforced a rough code of ethics designed to crowd out parasites. To begin with, it compiled a directory of responsible bill-posters, all of whom could reasonably be relied upon to paste up the bills with which they were entrusted instead of burning them or tossing them over the nearest hedge. Unfortunately a rival bill-posting association was formed soon afterwards, and the two bodies jeered at each other unflaggingly until 1889, when they buried the hatchet and called themselves the United Bill Posters Association. The more far-sighted members could see trouble looming; public criticism was growing, and there were restrictive Bills to be filleted.

The new Association even began to consider voluntary censorship of lurid theatrical posters, which were earning the trade a bad name. For the members by now craved respectability. From 'external paper hangers' they had degenerated in mid century to bill-stickers; slowly, as Cyril Sheldon points out, they had struggled upwards to the status of bill-posters, and now they were beginning to call themselves outdoor advertisement contractors.

Though the poster industry in Britain got away to an early start, it was not until colour lithography began to be perfected in the eighties that the hoardings could be described, even playfully, as an art gallery. The first British poster of any artistic merit is generally agreed to have been Fred Walker's black-and-white woodcut advertising the stage version of Wilkie Collins's *Woman in White*, in 1871 – 'a first attempt at what I consider might develop into a most important branch of art', said Walker modestly. No such development was visible in Britain until twenty years later, however.

The civilizing influence came from France, where Jules Cheret, having extended his lithographic knowledge in London, took the boulevards for his studio and covered them with vivid, sparkling posters in praise of everything from aperitifs to oil lamps, from ice-rinks to music-halls. Karl Huysmans in 1880 said that there was a thousand times more talent in the smallest poster by Cheret than in most of the canvases in the Paris salons. The public agreed; and very little criticism was heard of the high-spirited, frothy posters by the *Maître de l'Affiche*, whose output ran into four figures. A writer in the magazine the *Poster* said (1899):

Cheret has revived the traditions of Watteau; like Verlaine in dreamland gardens he brings his masks and pierrots; but true son of his time, he spices the eighteenth century, its 'Fêtes Galantes' and all graces of a past epoch with a striking note of modernism.

Cheret can make fair claim to have fathered the 'poster girl', a creature always radiant, wholesome, and eupeptic; of indeterminate age and of no recognizable social background; starry-eyed in her loyalty to her sponsor's toffee, purgative, or – latterly – beer.

Less starry-eyed were the damosels portrayed by Toulouse-Lautrec, whose posters also lent colour and vigour to the boulevards. Lautrec's mordant compositions embarrassed the critic of the *Poster*, for was not this artist in the pay of the Moulin Rouge?

. . . just as the source of [Lautrec's] inspiration is unclean so is the outcome, not unclean of deliberate purpose but essentially and intrinsically unclean. It must not be supposed that Lautrec has sought to glorify the mean erotics of the home of the can-can; he depicts the frequenters of the place with terrible reality.

Yet, sighed this critic, how preferable, with all their occasional Gallic shortcomings, were the posters of Lautrec and Cheret, Steinlen and Manet, to the 'ferocious orgies of the colour-printers' hacks' in Britain!

Mr James Laver has asserted that in France by the middle of the nineties 'the art of the poster was at the highest point it has ever reached, before or since. Magnificent designs were produced, so it seemed, as a matter of course. . . . It is a curious thing that so many arts come to their full stature immediately, and this is true of the poster. . . . No one will ever design better posters than Toulouse-Lautrec. . . .'[1]

Certainly Toulouse-Lautrec showed an exemplary personal

1. In a foreword to *Art For All*: *London Transport Posters 1908–1949*.

interest in the technique of poster printing. With his pockets stuffed full of old toothbrushes (for imparting delicate *crachis* to the lithographic stone) he would linger for hours in the workshop, experimenting and adding loving touches. He accepted at least one commission from an English advertiser, a confetti-maker of Charing Cross Road, London. Another poster, advertising a British bicycle chain, was abandoned.

It was a long time before British painters of repute could be persuaded to paint for, or to allow their works to appear on, the hoardings. Finally, they had to be tricked into it. Loud was the indignation which greeted the appearance of the famous 'Bubbles' poster, in 1887. Sir William Ingram had bought this work by Sir John Millais for the *Illustrated London News*; afterwards he disposed of it to the firm of Pears for the sum of 2,000 guineas. When Thomas J. Barratt called at the artist's studio with colour reproductions there was a considerable scene, but after the first explosion Millais seems to have been mollified by the excellence of the engraving. Less ready to forgive was Marie Corelli, who made a character in *The Sorrows of Satan* say:

I am one of those who think the fame of Millais as an artist was marred when he degraded himself to the level of painting the little green boy blowing bubbles of Pears' soap. *That was an advertisement*, and that very incident in his career, trifling as it seems, will prevent his ever standing on the dignified height of distinction with such masters in Art as Romney, Sir Peter Lely, Gainsborough and Reynolds.

Millais prevailed on Miss Corelli to expunge this passage from subsequent editions, after convincing her that he had not painted the picture specifically for Pears.

Two years later, it was W. P. Frith's turn. In a moment of rashness, he had painted a picture of a little girl holding up a white pinafore, with the title 'The New Frock'. The future Lord Leverhulme, who was not above following in the footsteps of Barratt, bought the picture and turned it into a poster entitled 'So Clean'. Frith made a show of anger, and the still smouldering controversy flamed up anew. Millais by now had decided that he had no feelings one way or the other about advertising, though he said he would object if a reproduction were badly executed. According to Barratt, Millais shortly before his death was about to undertake commissions for Pears.

Lord Leverhulme is on record as saying that Sidney Gross, who commissioned leading artists for Sunlight, and Thomas J. Barratt did more than any other men in the world to infuse Art into advertising. Others have argued that Barratt did Sir John Millais a considerable disservice by causing him to be remembered, in the popular mind, by one of his worst pictures. The Art Critic of *The Times*[1] was one of the many to make the point that the 'Bubbles' poster 'hindered rather than helped the development of the poster, by leading advertisers to bank on circumstantial interest instead of on the direct appeal of form, colour and rhythm'.

To those artists who still regarded the hoardings with abhorrence the future was a dismaying one. How could they safeguard their works from profanation, apart from choosing subjects which could not conceivably be used to further the sales of soap? If there was a falling-off in the number of nudes at the Royal Academy of 1890, the reason must be that artists were apprehensive lest their visions of Aphrodite be pasted up piecemeal on gable-ends, before ribald mobs, with a legend 'So Clean'. Nor was the peril confined to pictures depicting or implying cleanliness. A study of fat kine might be snapped up by a meat extract firm. Any canvas expressing a mood of *joie de vivre* might appeal to a pill manufacturer. There was no end to it all. And one day the Old Guard saw, without surprise, that a picture by Sir Edward Landseer was being used to advertise dog biscuits. Happily they did not live to see the day in the 1920s when a titled artist – Sir Reginald Blomfield – designed, not a poster, but a hoarding to carry posters.

Not all Royal Academicians waited to be tricked into advertising soap. After some persuasion by Thomas J. Barratt, Stacey Marks drew his picture of the two monks at their ablutions – 'Cleanliness Is Next to Godliness'.[2] Barratt was equally prepared to pay

1. In 1928.
2. Barratt wrung the utmost capital out of this saying. He told in a posthumously printed article in the *Strand Magazine*, September 1914, how, when visiting America, he decided he must have an inspiring testimonial for Pears Soap from a man of the highest distinction. Ruling out President Grant, the Governor of New York, and various Civil War heroes, he marked down as quarry the eminent divine, Henry Ward Beecher. One evening he called unheralded at Beecher's home in Brooklyn, and found to his consternation

handsome fees to an 'unknown', as when he bought the 'Dirty Boy' statuette which figured in a variety of Pears' advertisements. The sculptor was Focardi, an indigent Italian whose genius had begun to wilt in the uncongenial atmosphere of a boarding-house in Preston, Lancashire. One day when he rang for breakfast he received no answer, so he set off downstairs to find the landlady. Through a neighbour's open door he saw a rugged beldam scrubbing a dirty, howling boy. She was exclaiming, 'Drat the boy! Will he never come clean?' Here was Focardi's inspiration. Not without difficulty, he persuaded the old woman and the boy to pose for him. A suitable expression was maintained on the boy's face by pouring soapy water over his head at frequent intervals. For the resulting marble, Barratt paid the sculptor £500. What the boy received is not on record.

After Fred Walker, the first British poster artist of repute was probably Walter Crane. If the mantle of Cheret fell on anybody, it fell on Dudley Hardy, whose designs had a certain colourful ebullience, and whose posters were to be seen on the hoardings for many years to come. At the opposite pole were the brooding designs of Aubrey Beardsley, who was widely but not wisely imitated in America. A poster of two enigmatic nymphs, hot from the Decameron, poised above their Barlock typewriters, may have done much to fill moralists with misgivings about the wisdom of employing women in offices. The Beggarstaff Brothers (James Pryde and William Nicholson) developed a new technique of starkness and flatness, oddly powerful. The style was too flat and economical for some sponsors, however; it seemed hardly worth paying good money for such large expanses of white. When the Beggarstaff Brothers' design for the 1895 pantomime at

---

a party in progress. He shook hands all round ('perhaps they took me for a visiting English preacher or writer') and parried questions until the guests had gone. When Beecher learned that his visitor was soliciting a testimonial for soap, his face 'underwent a sudden change'; but as Barratt expatiated on the merits of the soap, the preacher checked him with a laugh, wheeled round in his chair and wrote on half a sheet of paper the soon-to-be-famous testimonial beginning, 'If cleanliness is next to godliness. . . .'

Like many celebrities who have given testimonials, Beecher apparently had little or no acquaintance with the product; but unlike many, he seems to have accepted no reward other than the advertiser's understandably 'hearty' thanks.

Drury Lane was displayed on the stage of that theatre, Sir Augustus Harris disapproved heartily, and Dan Leno said the design looked as if someone had spilled a pot of paint down it. At that point Phil May entered the theatre. Quickly sizing up the situation, he congratulated Sir Augustus Harris on his taste in selecting such an admirable poster. After that there was nothing to do except to send the design to the printer.

Gradually poster artists learned the secrets of simplicity, the effectiveness of bold, simple humour. One of the most popular of Pears' posters was the reproduction of the Harry Furniss drawing from *Punch*, showing a tramp writing a testimonial – 'Two years ago I used your soap – since then I have used no other.' Long in favour, too, was the picture of the baby stretching out of his bath to pick up a cake of Pears' soap – 'He won't be happy till he gets it.' Cartoonists freely adapted this poster, converting the baby into the Tsar or the Kaiser and the cake of soap into the disputed territory of the day. Nestlé had their famous two cats on a wall, with Fat Cat saying to Thin Cat: 'Hullo! You *are* looking bad, old man – been feeding on skim milk, eh?' Bovril indulged in a good deal of simple humour, too. The advertiser's message, as a rule, was mercifully brief. Mere reiteration of name or slogan was usually enough.

Occasionally there were unhappy dabblings in impressionism and symbolism. One poster showed a ship on a grassy ocean, surrounded by savage rocks, heading to a horizon where rose the sun, burdened with a brand-new typewriter. 'Dawn of a New Era', said the title; 'past praying for', said the critic of the *Poster*.

The bicycle advertising of the period was gently guyed by Jerome K. Jerome in *Three Men on the Bummel*. Jerome's man George, pedalling painfully through the Rhineland, complains that his bicycle is not like those advertised on the posters. On only one poster has he seen the rider represented as doing any work, and on that occasion a bull was pursuing him. The general purpose of the artist was to convince the hesitant neophyte that bicycling consisted of being wafted along by unseen heavenly powers. Usually the rider was a lady, wearing the kind of costume which might cause an old-fashioned landlady to refuse her lunch; she would float effortlessly, with one foot on the saddle and the other on the lamp, lighting a cigarette or waving a Chinese lantern.

Less often it is a mere male thing that rides the machine. He is not so accomplished as is the lady; but simple tricks such as standing on the saddle and waving flags, drinking beer or beef tea while riding he can and does perform.

According to George, the only haggard-looking persons seen riding bicycles, on the posters, were those who bestrode machines of inferior make.

There was an attempt to represent cycling as the sport of princes. 'The best I have ever used,' said Prince Ranjitsinhji, of the Dursley Pedersen cycle. Prince Henri of Bourbon was allowed to praise the Bantam in his native language: '*Depuis plusieurs mois je me sers presque tous les jours du 24 in. Bantam. Jamais je n'ai eu de bicyclette plus agréable et j'ai complètement écarté pour mon usage les autres machines.*'

But the girl in the saddle was a more potent sales force than princes. The symbol of the age, she appeared in all kinds of advertisements – for hats, clothes, health foods, and toffees, much as the sports girl was to appear a generation later, and the bathing girl a generation after that.

As the century ended the cycling girl was temporarily eclipsed – by the British soldier. The South African War might have been won earlier, it would appear from the advertisements, if soldiers had spent less time standing on *kopjes* waving packets of cigarettes in the air, or marching up to exposed positions under enormous Union Jacks superimposed with the names of meat extracts. Advertisers quickly learned how to tie in patriotism with the product; for once, there was value in the testimonial of a humble warrior. One gallant soldier who suffered alike for King and Commerce was Baden-Powell, who was hailed as smoking somebody's cigarette. He was a non-smoker.

The poster of the cheaper theatrical show was as unregenerate then as the cinema poster is now. When the United Bill Posters Association began to pass judgement on some of the offending sheets, censoring daggers, pools of blood, beds, female breasts, and other inflammatory detail, loud protests were voiced by the theatrical companies. Nor were music-hall posters immune. In 1890 the National Vigilance Association opposed renewal of the

London Aquarium's licence because of a 'suggestive' poster showing a woman acrobat in flesh-coloured tights. By modern standards the poster does not seem to have been very reprehensible.

Some excessively prudish criticisms of posters were voiced during this period. Cyril Sheldon records that even the Bovril bull was condemned by the town of Cork, for the reason that it was too obviously a bull. This is no subject for superior mirth, for in our own times prize bulls have been emasculated by the photographic retouchers of Fleet Street.

NOTHING SACRED

> How, with this rage, shall Beauty hold a plea,
> Whose action is no stronger than a flower?
>
> *William Shakespeare.*

In the last years of the nineteenth century outdoor advertisers sowed their wildest oats. And appropriately it was an oats-selling firm which achieved one of the less forgivable enormities: the erection of a monstrous signboard half way up the white cliffs of Dover.

In November 1892 readers of *The Times* began to report advertising excesses which had been forced on their attention, not only in Britain but overseas. It was from the indignation aroused by this correspondence that the Society for the Checking of Abuses in Public Advertising (S.C.A.P.A.) was born in the succeeding year; its founder was Richardson Evans. Some of those who wrote to *The Times* were out to abolish advertising totally. One of them pointed out that 'the colossal and flourishing biscuit works at Reading have never advertised – a proof among many that "good wine needs no bush" '. (This red-rag proverb inspires in an advertising man the same reaction as 'The Lord will provide' in an insurance agent.) It was not long before Thomas J. Barratt joined in the correspondence to suggest that, instead of seeking to put down advertising, those whose feelings were harrowed would be better employed trying to improve its standards. That, in effect, became the policy of S.C.A.P.A. The Society did not urge its supporters to follow the example of Miss

Frances Power Cobbe, the feminist, who took a pot of paint and a long-handled brush on her rural drives in order to deface defacements; and, whatever its secret sympathies, it offered no encouragement to those other vigilantes who believed that the best criticism of an offensive hoarding was to haul it down, by night, with a rope.

At this period, all over the world, beauty-spots were exercising a suicidal fascination over the outdoor advertiser. There was a stark simplicity about the advertiser's logic: the best announcements were those which were seen by the most people; more people were likely to visit beauty-spots than any other spots; therefore a progressive advertiser must be first in the beauty-spots. Seaside resorts were, in many ways, ideal, because a holiday-maker had an unoccupied mind and was therefore more susceptible to persuasion than when going about his daily occasions.

Travellers returning to Britain told of outrages everywhere. A Gothenburg margarine factory had painted its slogans on the walls of the fiords, right up into the Arctic Circle. The rock faces of the Thousand Isles of the St Lawrence were hideously daubed with slogans for stove polish and tooth powder. Out of the Mississippi rose letters twenty feet high testifying to the virtues of a chewing tobacco. Voyagers on the River Hudson at night were regaled, whether they liked it or not, by endless hoardings on the banks, picked out for their benefit by the ship's roving searchlight. Every other rock in the canyons of Nevada was disfigured. In one of the loveliest bends of the River Reuss in Switzerland a giant boulder had been painted brown, with a chocolate firm's name on it. High on the Rigi were enormous gilt letters advertising a hotel. Even the remote hills of the Sudan carried slogans for soap. It was gratifying to find, however, that the Rock of Gibraltar – contrary to all expectations – was not disfigured by the name of the Prudential Insurance Company.

Those homing travellers who hoped to save Britain from similar insult found that they were too late. Pollution was everywhere. Indeed, there were many who held that Britain was far more widely and provocatively vulgarized than the continents of Europe or America. Rudyard Kipling was one of them; William Archer was another.

The newly formed Society was encouraged by the fact that, here and there, public opinion had achieved its victories over the advertiser. In the eighties Niagara Falls had been saved at the eleventh hour from being overrun by bill-posters and jerrybuilders; though, unfortunately, from a strip of unprotected territory an enormous hoarding still looked down on the Falls. The Cape Town authorities, despite tempting offers, refused to lease Table Mountain as a hoarding. Holloway's name was no longer to be read on the Pyramids. In 1890 a soap company had been compelled, by public outcry, to remove from Ludgate Hill the sky sign behind which it was seeking to conceal St Paul's; but, to offset this, at the rail approach to Durham an advertiser had succeeded in shutting off the famous view of the Cathedral and Castle.

The S.C.A.P.A. reformers went into battle with a sonnet by Alfred Austin, soon to be Poet Laureate:

> Is nothing sacred then? nor grove, nor mead,
> Nor silent pool, nor solitary lane,
> Where tender souls, world-weary, may obtain
> The peace they covet and the rest they need?
> Shall woodland aisle and flower-paved pasture plead
> For loving head and reverent touch in vain,
> But every unclean huckster may profane
> Heaven's sylvan shrines with sacrilegious greed?
> By lust of gain divorced from Nature's heart,
> And quitting primrose brake and babbling brook
> For sordid joys of meretricious mart,
> Now they return, invade each shady nook,
> Each fair seclusion, and with impious art
> Deface the innocent Beauty they forsook.

That summer, members of the Society heard themselves described by speakers of the United Bill Posters Association as 'sickly', 'maundering', 'querulous', and 'super-sensitive faddists'. Said the leading orator: 'They talk about "destroying the appearance of our towns, ruining street architecture". These are but empty phrases. Take London, for instance. How little there is of street architecture worth approval!' The 'Society of Busybodies', if allowed their way, would put men out of employment. It was a free world and there were endless opportunities in it. The speaker said he would prefer to echo the words of another bard:

> Behold to what a goodly world we come,
> For us the spacious bounty of the air,
> The impregnable pavilion of the heavens,
> And silent muster of the disciplined stars. . . .

It was a quotation of unrealized and sinister aptness, for a generation later advertisements were to be towed by day through the spacious bounty of the air and projected at night against the impregnable pavilion of the heavens.

That same year S.C.A.P.A. bloodied its nose in an unsuccessful attempt to promote a Bill which would have given local authorities power to ban any outdoor advertisements they disliked. A similar Bill brought forward by Mr W. S. Caine to limit advertisements in rural districts made no progress. The bastion was not to be destroyed by a single mine; much patient sapping was required.

Like all reforming bodies, S.C.A.P.A. suffered from the over-enthusiasm of extremists, some of whom refused to admit that even derelict building sites, strewn with garbage and dead cats, were better screened off in orderly fashion behind a hoarding of gay posters. Hoardings, they pointed out, too easily became a screen for immoral acts; and what about the innocent people who had been injured by falling hoardings in Hyde Park, in the great gale of 1891? Then, as now, there was much arguing at cross purposes. 'The posters are the nation's picture gallery, and there is no charge for admission,' proclaimed the bill-posters, pointing proudly to the Academy pictures of the soap kings. Or, on another level: 'Who but a curmudgeon would prefer to gaze at a blotched and dilapidated gable-end rather than at the head of a pretty girl?' The critics retorted that it was a strange sort of academy in which ninety per cent of the exhibits consisted of paintings of whisky bottles, jars of ointment, and cocoa tins. 'Come to my window,' someone would say, 'and I will show you a once-decent gable-end bearing nothing whatever but the letters "—'s Pills" in ten-foot letters.' So it went on, neither side listening to the other's arguments.

The year 1894 produced some ingenious examples of desecration.

After dark on Trafalgar Day in London, advertisements for pills, blacking, and watches were projected on to the side of Nelson's Column by a magic lantern device, and also, for the sake of variety, on to the pillars of the National Gallery. S.C.A.P.A. took counsel's advice and were informed that 'the owners of the buildings affected by the advertisement can proceed for trespass or nuisance'. But, asked the Society, 'Cannot the County Council or the First Commissioner of Works do something for us at once?' A resourceful reader of *The Times* suggested 'jamming' the advertisements by a more powerful beam. Eventually the offenders desisted, after being informed that if they did not the necessary legislation would be sought.

That same year a leading pill company announced its scheme for a brighter Britain. It offered a free mainsail to every boatman and fisherman in the country, the sail to bear a slogan praising the firm's pills. In the face of criticism, this offer was represented by the company as a generous gesture to indigent fishermen. Eastbourne Council viewed the offer in a harsher light and prosecuted a local fisherman who had equipped his craft with one of the sails; the charge was 'disfiguring the foreshore'. At the Royal Academy banquet Lord Rosebery invited his listeners to consider how the illustrious Turner, if he returned to life, would feel on seeing the luggers and the coasting ships which he had made so glorious in his paintings converted into media for the advertisement of pills.

On Lake Windermere the same pill company erected a large metal sign at Bowness. When local vigilantes threw it into the lake, the company retorted by advertising on the sails of a boat. Thereupon the vigilantes drilled a hole in the bottom of the boat and sank it, but by that time the company had fished out the sign and re-erected it. The battle might have gone on long enough, but surprisingly the pill company agreed to withdraw on being assured that a personal request for the removal of the sign had been received from John Ruskin. 'They are evidently very aesthetic people at Windermere,' a representative of the company told the Press.

While pill companies were seeking to raise the standard of living of fishermen, other advertisers were generously saving farmers from bankruptcy by hiring strips of their fields, alongside railways, on which to erect signboards. The practice inspired such comments as:

> Ill fares the land, to hastening ills a prey,
> Where posters flourish and where crops won't pay.

Carter's Pills offered, in 1894, to withdraw their railside advertising where satisfied that public taste was being offended. But advertisers dared not trust each other. Thomas Beecham said he would remove his advertisements from Scarborough bathing huts on condition that no other firm was allowed to advertise there. 'While they are open to be used in this way the decoration may as well be "Beecham's Pills" as any other,' he said.

The year 1894 also saw the consolidation of rules restricting sky signs in London. For some years advertisers had been setting up names and slogans above the roofs of buildings in such a way that the letters stood out tall and stark against the sky. The result was that the roofs of London presented a crazed alphabetic silhouette calculated to make any painter throw away his brushes. Even a single-storey building might boast a sky sign reared sixty feet above it, on a metal gantry stayed with cables, like a tremendous gibbet. Nor was this the only kind of roof advertisement which had been gaining ground; those who drafted the Act found it desirable to impose a ban on 'balloons, parachutes, or similar devices'. Soon afterwards by-laws were passed restricting the use of flashing electric signs, which had been blamed in coroners' courts for causing street accidents. In these forms of advertisement, Britain appears to have been ahead of America. William Archer, in his *America To-day* (1900), said that sky signs were unknown in New York, and so were 'the flashing out-and-in electric advertisements' which vulgarized 'the august spectacle of the Thames by night'. One Thames-side building much favoured by electric sign advertisers was the old Waterloo Shot Tower, now demolished.

In 1896 a Royal Academician, W. B. Richmond, told S.C.A.P.A. of a startling new form of advertising:

I was in my garden and I heard sudden reports of artillery. Presently from the sky fell masses of green and red paper advertising a tooth powder. These fell all over my garden and I am not exaggerating when I tell you that these were spread over two acres at least. It took my gardener a week to collect all these pieces of paper which were blown out of guns into my garden.

Other members had reported that handbills were being flung into the air in such quantities as to make horses bolt; but advertising artillery seems to have been a solitary phenomenon.

Next year a piece of opportunism by a pill-maker rebounded. Nelson's battleship *Foudroyant*, on exhibition at Blackpool, was driven by a storm from her anchorage and lay half-capsized. The local agent for Thomas Beecham sent a telegram to his employer: 'Warship *Foudroyant* wrecked on beach at North Pier. What am I to do?' The reply came: 'Do the best you can at a reasonable price – "England Expects Every Man to Do His Duty And Take Beechams' Pills" '. This message was painted in three-feet letters along the ship's starboard length, facing the town. At Liverpool the *Foudroyant*'s owner claimed damages for 'insulting trespass' and was awarded £50. (Sir Thomas Lipton once cashed in on a shipwreck, too. He was passenger on a ship which was stranded in the Red Sea, and to the master's annoyance he stencilled 'Drink Lipton's Tea' on bales of cargo as they were jettisoned.)

So it went on. In 1897 a meat extract firm proposed to erect a giant advertisement along the open side of Princes Street, Edinburgh, to the detriment of the view of the Castle. The city of Edinburgh protested sharply, and the project was abandoned, but not before the firm had pointed out that, on an earlier occasion when it had given up a proposed site, a rival had stepped in and seized it. Taking no chances, the city of Edinburgh secured the passage of a protective Bill through Parliament.

The worst was still to be. On 19 October 1900, this letter to *The Times* from Richardson Evans, secretary of S.C.A.P.A., inaugurated a new battle:

Sir: Few Englishmen can have eyes so blind and souls so dull as to contemplate without an emotion of pleasure and of pride the novel panorama of the bay of Dover.

Many a home-returning traveller has felt that on all his wanderings he has found no scene richer in historical interest or natural beauty. For some time past the delight has been qualified, if not destroyed, by the intrusion of a colossal disfigurement. One of the American food companies has got some one to erect high up on the cliffs two monster boards on which the name of their product is painted in letters that dominate and degrade the whole prospect.

We ought perhaps to regard with a resentful sense of gratitude the feat of this remote Chicago firm in demonstrating to what lengths in the absence of rational restraint the instinct of vulgar competition can go in affronting the public eye.

But those who love Dover cannot afford to take this grimly philosophical view of the wrong that is being done to them. A memorial has been prepared for presentation to the Mayor and Town Council, asking them to exercise such influence as a municipality possesses for procuring the removal of the eyesore. . . .

As soon as the people who resort to these barbarous modes of soliciting custom realize that the community is alive to its rights, they will desist. It is a mere question of establishing an authoritative standard of decency.

There appears to have been rivalry between the oats firms at this time to make their names the first words decipherable wherever ships made landfall. A sign similar to the Dover one was erected over Southampton Water, but was removed as a result of action by the landowners. Another, by a different firm, dominated New York harbour.

Representatives of S.C.A.P.A. wrote to the London agents of the Chicago firm but received no reply. The Society also sent many letters to newspapers and enlisted much editorial support. Worried by the extent of the agitation, a deputation representing the London advertising trades tried to persuade the firm to pull down the sign, in the wider interests of the advertising business. They were met with a harsh refusal. 'A man sitting in a counting house in Chicago has only to draw a cheque for so many thousands of dollars, and lo! the glory of an English harbour is destroyed!' exclaimed Richardson Evans.

But Dover had not been idle. An Improvement Bill on the Edinburgh model was passed through Parliament, giving the town control over unsightly advertisements; and a year after the sign was erected it was pulled down, all eight tons of it. Thereafter many towns which felt themselves threatened by the advertiser promoted Bills to give them the same powers as Edinburgh and Dover.

Since those days America has been schooled to a suitable reverence for the white cliffs of Dover, though an urge to erect extravagant edifices there still persists. Immediately after the Second World War an American business man expressed a keen desire to see built on 'Hell Fire Corner' a giant statue of Mr Winston Churchill, with an ever-glowing cigar to serve as a beacon to mariners.

Street advertisers also had their setbacks during the nineties. A firm which packed the tops of London omnibuses with garishly dressed figures, all engaged in extravagant pantomime in praise of a brand of tobacco, was successfully prosecuted. Seven men who were seen patrolling along Leadenhall Street to Aldgate pump and back, holding close to their noses copies of a certain newspaper, were each fined one shilling. This represented a major part of their day's income, for they were paid 1s. 6d. to patrol from ten in the morning until six in the evening.

The derelicts of the big cities were submitted to endless indignities in the name of advertising. In London a number of them were dressed in convict's garb and made to patrol the streets clanking their chains to advertise a serial story. Much preferred to the uniform of Her Majesty's Gaols, however, were those of Her Majesty's Forces. In the early nineties it was no rare sight to see processions of seedy old men, dressed in the Queen's scarlet, trudging along the gutters of London, advertising the inevitable soap or pills. This was not a sight calculated to encourage the young man who had just accepted the Queen's shilling.

The scandal became such that a Uniforms Bill, designed to prevent military and naval uniforms being worn by others than soldiers and sailors, was introduced into Parliament in 1894. On the second reading, Members told of abuses which had come to their personal notice. Colonel A. M. Brookfield had seen a procession of 'bluejackets' marshalled by an individual in the uniform of a naval officer, with cocked hat and sword. More recently he had emerged from Charing Cross Station to see a procession of men dressed as Royal Marine Light Infantry, with pith helmets. One contractor had dressed his men in the uniform of the Artists' Rifles; and when the adjutant of that regiment protested the agent 'heard him with the greatest good temper and urbanity and in answer to his representations clothed all his men in the uniform of another battalion'. The colonel reported that he had even seen a man dressed as a Staff officer standing on the kerb handing out leaflets; and he felt that even Staff officers deserved some protection.

Major F. C. Rasch assured the House that it was because of the way the Queen's uniform was degraded in the streets of London that officers were unwilling to wear uniform when off duty. Indeed, it was considered such a hardship among young officers to be seen in uniform that a refractory subaltern had recently been ordered by Field-Marshal the Duke of Cambridge to wear his uniform in public for a specified period as a punishment.

Another Member, Stuart Wortley, said that when he was at the Home Office news had been received that an advertising contractor was proposing to dress up his sandwich-men as Napoleon's Old Guard. This had been felt to be most undesirable, and on private representations the plan was dropped. Yet Whitehall had not been stirred to take action to protect the uniforms of British regiments.

The Bill went through without much difficulty, though one or two Members feared that innocent persons might be arrested for wearing uniforms at fancy dress balls or on the stage.

Some advertisers who found these frustrations too much for them began to turn their eyes to Paris, where nobody greatly worried even if bills were pasted on churches or public monuments (if the posters were by Cheret, so much the better). On payment of a few francs bills might even be stuck on pillar boxes, police kiosks and *urinoirs*. In 1889 the French capital had been the scene of perhaps the most frenzied poster battle ever staged. For once, it was an electoral, not a commercial, occasion. According to Mulhall's *Dictionary of Statistics*, General Boulanger hired 15,000 bill-posters, who put up 900,000 bills at a cost of £8,000. His rival Jacques fielded 10,000 men who put up 500,000 bills at a cost of £5,000. 'In some places,' says Mulhall, 'when they were torn down after the election, there were found sixty layers, alternating, of the rival placards.' Such was the spirit of enterprise in Paris that a machine had been invented capable of sticking posters on sites fifty feet high. Yet when the new century dawned, even the indulgent French were driven to found a *Société pour la Protection des Paysages*.

The biggest eyesores of the period did not necessarily generate the greatest heat. Much bitterness was voiced at minor advertising innovations which are now taken for granted. A reader of *The Times* protested in 1892 at the 'brutal vulgarity' of inserting advertisements through the text of magazines instead of segregating them at the end. A man who bought a volume of Pepys was incensed to find that it contained fifty-six pages of advertisements at the back, instead of an index. 'To tack advertisements of 1896 on to a diary of the seventeenth century is a gross impertinence,' he wrote. No sooner had the safety curtain been introduced into theatres in the nineties than angry theatregoers saw it degenerate into a bill-board which ruined the atmosphere and dignity of the auditorium. And Rudyard Kipling spoke for many, then and now, when he complained of the 'beplastering of railway platforms with every piece of information in the world except the name of the station'.

Thomas J. Barratt badgered the Government to allow him to advertise on postage stamps and succeeded in getting tributes to Pears' Soap on the back of the penny lilac of 1881 and halfpenny vermilion of 1887.[1] The Government rejected his offer to print all the census forms of 1891 for nothing, provided that the back of the form bore an incitement to use Pears' Soap. Barratt also clashed with the Government over a publicity scheme which involved importing a quarter of a million bronze ten centime coins from France and stamping 'Pears' on them. At this period French 'pennies' were accepted as tender in England. Barratt issued the stamped coins, at fourteen to the shilling, for distribution all over the country. However, the Government failed to appreciate the beauty of the scheme. It bought up the coins and melted them down and after that no more foreign money was suffered to circulate in Britain.

1. According to the *Unilever House Magazine*, March 1953, many British advertisers used the backs of the New Zealand stamps in 1893. The slogans were printed on top of the gum and came off on people's tongues.

America:
5   Barnum and the Bennetts

Unrestricted by 'taxes on knowledge', American newspapers in the eighteenth century had expanded rapidly. In the early years of the nineteenth century they were devoting between one half and three quarters of their space to advertisements. The price of a newspaper was only three halfpence, as against sevenpence in Britain.

In 1829, when British newspapers published a total of 630,000 copies weekly – one to thirty-six inhabitants – Pennsylvania, with a population of 1,200,000, published a weekly total of 300,000 copies, or one copy to four inhabitants. The editor of the *Scotsman* computed that in one year twelve daily papers in New York had published 1,456,416 advertisements, while in the same year 400 newspapers in Britain had published 1,020,000. The cost of a twenty-line announcement, repeated every day for a year in a New York newspaper, was £6 18s. 8d.; in a London newspaper, £202 16s.

In content, the American advertisements were not vastly different from those in English newspapers: announcements of sailings, stage plays, books, freaks, and patent medicines. But there was one conspicuous difference. Whereas the British upper classes had almost ceased to advertise their black boys for sale, American advertisers still trafficked in human flesh, often in outrageous terms.

Charles Dickens recorded a selection of advertisements for the recovery of runaway slaves in his *American Notes* (1842). The notices would appear under a bold black heading, 'CASH FOR NEGROES', sometimes illustrated with a line block showing a manacled runaway cowering before a top-booted planter. Dickens quoted, among others:

RAN AWAY, a negro boy aged about 12 years old. Had round his neck a chain dog-collar with 'de Lampert' engraved on it.

RANAWAY, a negro woman and two children; a few days before she went off I burnt her with a hot iron on the left side of her face. I tried to make the letter M.

RANAWAY, a Negro named Arthur. Has a considerable scar across his breast and each arm, made by a knife; loves to talk much of the goodness of God.

RANAWAY, the Negro Ham. Has a ring with iron on his left foot. Also Gresi, his wife, bearing a ring and chain on the left leg.

RANAWAY, Sam. He was shot a short time since through the hand and has several shots in his left arm and side.

RANAWAY, my man Fountain. Has holes in his ears, a scar on the right side of his forehead, has been shot in the hind parts of his legs and is marked on the back with a whip.

Whip marks in themselves hardly seem to have been a sufficient guide to identity, since many of the runaways were said to be 'much scarred' in this way. Others had 'a good many teeth missing' – the violent punching out of teeth was a popular way of marking a slave. Phrases like 'has lost all her toes except the large one', 'the rim of his right ear has been bit or cut off', and 'one of his ears cut off and his right hand cut with an axe' suggested the use of mutilation both as a punishment and as a means of identification.

As a rule, a negro lost his value when he ceased to be able-bodied; but there were exceptions, as for example the carefully preserved Joice Heth, whose frail body served as the first stepping-stone to fame of a young Connecticut Yankee, Phineas T. Barnum, that rogue elephant of advertising. In the *Philadelphia Inquirer* of 15 July 1835 appeared the following advertisement:

CURIOSITY: The citizens of Philadelphia and its vicinity have an opportunity of witnessing at the Masonic Hall one of the greatest natural curiosities ever witnessed: viz Joice Heth, a negress aged 161 years, who formerly belonged to the father of General Washington. She has been a member of the Baptist Church 116 years and can rehearse many hymns and sing them according to former custom. She was born near the Old Potomac River in Virginia and has for 90 or 100 years lived in Paris, Kentucky, with the Bowling family. All who have seen this extraordinary woman are satisfied of the truth of the account of her age. The evidence of the Bowling family, which is respectable, is strong, but the original bill of sale of Augustine Washington in his own handwriting, and other evidence which the proprietor has in his possession, will satisfy even the most incredulous.

At the suggestion of his friend Coley Bartram, Barnum bought the Negress Heth for 1,000 dollars. She played her part well, being 'pert and sociable', and suitably garrulous about 'dear little George'. Though she died the following year – not surprisingly, of old age – Barnum had seen that his future lay in showmanship. In 1841 he acquired the American Museum in New York, and ran a non-stop entertainment featuring educated dogs, industrious fleas, ventriloquists, living statues, albinos, giants, dwarfs, rope-dancers, glass-blowers, and Red Indians. It is not by his newspaper advertising that Barnum is remembered, though sometimes his small-type advertisements had the quality of an incantation:

> VISION OF THE HOURIS
> VISION OF THE HOURIS
> VISION OF THE HOURIS
> A Tableau of 850 Men
> Women and Children
> CLAD IN SUITS OF SILVER ARMOUR
> CLAD IN SUITS OF SILVER ARMOUR
> CLAD IN SUITS OF SILVER ARMOUR

Barnum put much of his effort into flaming posters and transparencies, handbills, flags, banners, and bands. Over his museum he erected a gaslit sign as effective as many an 'electric spectacular' of the following century. He was an adept at engineering free publicity, which brought him into clashes with James Gordon Bennett, proprietor of the *New York Herald*. One day when a down-and-out begged for 'any kind of job' at a dollar a day Barnum gave him a coin to buy breakfast and then presented him with five bricks. These he was instructed to lay one at a time on the sidewalk at busy points; then he was to march rapidly from one point to the other and change the bricks round; and at the end of every hour he was to pass through Barnum's Museum. The man said it was 'all one to him so long as he could earn a living'. Half an hour later 500 people were watching his movements. As instructed, he marched from point to point with military bearing, and refused to answer questions. Each time he entered the museum a dozen or more spectators would accompany him, out of curiosity. The game went on for days until the police complained. Such pranks as these, and the erection of the famous sign 'This Way to the Egress' (designed to speed the passage of laggard spectators through his zoo), earned Barnum more renown than columns of paid advertising could have done.

Barnum's triumphal tours with 'General' Tom Thumb (his London visit infuriated *The Times*) and his sponsoring of Jenny Lind made his name world-famous. Though there was much to criticize in many of his earlier exploits, he gave the public a run for its money.

Gradually Barnum formulated a philosophy of advertising, which he set out in his autobiography, published in mid-century. 'You may advertise a spurious article and induce many people to call and buy it once, but they will gradually denounce you as an impostor,' he said. (Nevertheless, for generations to come, impostors were to make quick and gratifying 'killings' out of useless articles, especially medicines designed to alleviate conditions capable of spontaneous improvement.) Barnum was one of the first to pronounce that 'advertising is like learning – a little is a dangerous thing'. He quoted a French writer as saying: 'The reader of a newspaper does not see the first insertion of an ordinary advertisement; the second insertion he sees, but does not read; the third insertion he reads; the fourth insertion he looks at the price; the fifth insertion, he speaks of it to his wife; the sixth insertion he is ready to purchase; and the seventh insertion he purchases.'

If a man has not the pluck to keep on advertising, said Barnum, all the money he has already spent is lost. As illustration, he told the story of the scrounger who asked a gentleman for ten cents, saying that he wanted to save himself a dollar. When the gentleman asked for an explanation, he said: 'I started out to get drunk, but I have not quite succeeded, although I have spent a dollar. Another ten cents would suffice to make me drunk and thus save the dollar I have already expended.'

Barnum's advice, perhaps for no other reason than that it was Barnum's advice, was warily received, and it still has to be reiterated today. Hamilton Basso, in *Mainstream*, says of him: 'Out of a wedding of the circus and the New England commercial instinct was born a new and generic art which forever after was to be the most beguiling maidservant of business, teaching a nation to want things it did not need and throw away other things it could still use.'

In the same year that Barnum acquired the moribund body of Joice Heth – 1835 – James Gordon Bennett, a Scots immigrant, put out from a basement the first issues of his *New York Herald*, of which he was editor, publisher, and advertisement manager. This was the start of a new journalism. Built up on sensational stories of clashes with his rivals – 'MR JAMES GORDON BENNETT PUBLICLY HORSEWHIPPED,' 'MR JAMES GORDON BENNETT HORSEWHIPPED A SECOND TIME!' – the *Herald* became in little more than ten years the leading advertising medium in America. At the height of his success Bennett was strong enough to be able to impose his own terms on advertisers. These were: cash down, all announcements in small type, no illustrations, and copy to be changed daily. The first of these restrictions was one which only the more prosperous publishers could impose; the less prosperous, as in Britain, were frequently forced to accept payment in kind, which meant anything from bottles of elixir to Vinegar Bitters.

Bennett at first allowed advertisers to use bigger type and double-column displays, but later he ruled out these experiments on the grounds that the smaller advertisers were overshadowed by the big ones. His *Herald* was to hold out stubbornly against display long after the battle was lost. The boast 'Advertisements Renewed Every Day' may have given a certain freshness to the paper, but from the advertiser's point of view the rule was less than reasonable. It is an axiom that a successful advertisement should never be changed for the sake of change.

Bennett's restrictions were cleverly challenged by Robert Bonner, publisher of the *New York Ledger*. He had been impressed by the policy of repetition adopted by English advertisers in *The Times*, and decided to carry the idea a great deal farther. He began to lease entire pages in the *Herald*, then as many as four pages at a time, filling the columns with endlessly repeated sentences like 'Fanny Fern writes for the *Ledger*' or 'Read Mrs Southwold's new story in the *Ledger*'. Tackled by Bennett, Bonner pointed out that there was no rule saying that advertisements must be changed *every line*. The public also began to show a certain exasperation, and Bonner's friends, learning that he was spending as much as 2,000 dollars in a single issue, began to fear for his financial stability. 'What is the use of your taking the whole side of the *Herald* and repeating that statement a thousand times?' a critic asked him. 'I put it in,' replied Bonner, 'to attract your attention and make you ask that question.'

Publishers who leased space to Bonner now began to show considerable apprehension as to how he might use it. Sometimes he varied the policy of repetition by taking a page and leaving it almost blank except for a few small notices. Angry editors complained that he was disfiguring their sheets and holding them up to ridicule; to which Bonner was able to reply that he had used the size of type stipulated, so where was the offence? At other times he filled pages of the *Herald* with the opening chapters of new serial stories which he was about to publish in the *Ledger*, cutting them off at an exciting point with some such notice as: 'No more of this story will be published in the *Herald*. It will be continued in the *Ledger*.' Yet he steadfastly refused to have advertisements in the *Ledger*, preferring to derive his revenue from a high circulation. He paid handsomely for literary contributions – $5,000 to Tennyson for a short poem, the same to Dickens for a short story.

Because his policy of repetition was mocked in fashionable quarters, Bonner hatched an ingenious plot. *Harper's Magazine* was then being started in a blaze of respectability. To various publications Bonner sent advertisements which consisted of 'Buy *Harper's Magazine*' monotonously repeated. When these appeared the scoffers had to admit that there must be something to be said for Bonner's style of advertising, since *Harper's* were not above using it. *Harper's* took the prank in good part.

Although James Gordon Bennett laid typographical restrictions on his advertisers, he allowed them to say anything they wished. To complaints that quacks abused his columns, he retorted: 'Business is business, money is money ... we permit no blockhead to interfere with our business.' In this attitude he did not greatly differ from his rivals, who held that so long as the language of the announcement was decent, the publisher had no further responsibility. Even Horace Greeley's temperate *New York Tribune*, which declined the more obnoxious quack advertisements, preached the doctrine of *caveat emptor*.

During the Civil War, American publishers had a brief taste of an inconvenience which Britain had at last shaken off: a tax of three per cent was imposed on advertisements. It does not seem to have caused much hardship. Editors were still strong enough to hold out advertisements on days when the war news was unusually exciting; and the war provided a useful excuse for putting news on the front page and relegating advertisements to the interior – a policy which was maintained in the years of peace.

One authority has attributed to the Civil War the proliferation of patent medicines in the next two decades, contending that it was among the ill and dispirited survivors that rough-and-ready nostrums found acceptance. According to one of the leading medicine men, Dr James C. Ayer, the demand chiefly arose from the pioneers pushing westwards. Earlier generations had lived in small settlements, with doctors in their midst; now adventurous men and women were becoming increasingly dispersed. Even on horseback, a doctor could not carry enough medicines to meet the demand. Nor, for that matter, could the itinerant quacks with their free shows and their bogus Red Indian chiefs selling coloured pump water.

The name of Holloway, the English pill-maker, was in the forefront in mid-century, but he had formidable rivals. One of them was Dr Benjamin Brandreth, born in Leeds, who had begun to sell his pills, a box at a time, in New York in 1835 – three years before Holloway began his struggles in London. When he had sold enough boxes Brandreth put an advertisement in the *Sun*, and kept on using his profits in this way. In due course he was surprised to find that the druggists were selling more of Brandreth's Pills than he was making, and he then issued strongly worded pleas to the public to avoid substitutes. At a critical time in the *Herald*'s early history, James Gordon Bennett made a lucrative advertising contract with Brandreth, whom he later denounced as a rogue. By 1870 Brandreth owned several blocks of real estate in New York, including 'a huge pile on Broadway worth its weight in gold', and a big laboratory at Sing Sing. It was estimated that he spent two and a half million dollars on advertising.

Dr Henry T. Hembold, 'Prince of Druggists', specialized in 'fluid extracts'. His leading nostrum was 'Buchu', a name which (as a writer admiringly testified in 1870) adorned 'every dead wall, fence, rock, and telegraph pole from the Atlantic to the Pacific'. Three million bottles of 'Buchu' were sold in 1868–9. Then there was Dr Joseph H. Schenck, who acquired a mansion and 300 acres on the Delaware, and a fine yacht, from the sale of his Seaweed Tonic (originally mixed in a barrel in a back yard), not to mention his Mandrake Pills and Pulmonic Syrup.

Dr Ayer, who has already been mentioned, ran his own paper mill to ensure that his wrappers and labels should be difficult to counterfeit. He died 'worth millions'. Others were Dr Jayne, whose business was so large that he had difficulty in spending the profits, and Dr Wolcott, creator of Pain Paint, whose offices were always crowded with the afflicted. For all their wealth, it seems that none of the great pill men could force an entry into fastidious society.

To the rising advertising man the patent medicine field offered a great professional opportunity. This is admitted by Claude C. Hopkins, in *My Life in Advertising* (1927). Indeed, this form of advertising 'offered the supreme test of a man's skill', since a medicine was worthless merchandise until a demand was created. 'The greatest advertising men of my day were schooled in the medicine field . . . it weeded out the incompetents and gave scope and prestige to those who survived.'

Hopkins, who wrote copy for Dr Shoop's Restorative, is one of the few who have given patent medicine manufacturers any credit for honesty. 'I have never known higher-minded men than those who engaged in these enterprises,' he says. 'They felt that they were serving humanity by offering good remedies for common conditions at very modest cost. They were aiding those who could not afford physicians. There was much reason in their arguments. Every medicine maker received thousands of testimonials. And I still believe that those medicine makers did far more good than harm.'

In the year that the Civil War ended, a young freebooter, George P. Rowell, conceived a happy idea for diverting some of the riches of advertising into his own pocket. He set about organizing 'space selling' on a more efficient basis. Many unscrupulous middlemen were already in business, their chief object being to extort the maximum commission from both sides, in return for the minimum of service. Secret fees were freely pocketed, secret rate adjustments were negotiated in taverns, and accounts shamelessly filched. Rowell's plan was to buy up advertising columns from country newspapers for a period of twelve months, and lease these to advertisers at one hundred dollars an inch, on the understanding that each advertisement would be inserted four times in 100 newspapers. Though this brought Rowell a spectacular profit, the country editors were well content; they were relieved of the worries of drumming up trade, and Rowell guaranteed prompt payment in cash instead of bitters. Two years later, in 1867, Rowell opened an agency in New York. He did not disguise that he was in business for himself alone, owing allegiance neither to publisher nor to advertiser. In his eagerness for quick riches, he decided to market his own patent medicine. But 'Ripans Tabules', made of nothing but rhubarb and soda, and sold at a tremendous profit, failed to take on, despite all the arts of promotion lavished upon them. Possibly as a result of this unfortunate venture, Rowell's views changed, and in later life the one-time freebooter did much to bring order, organization, and respectability to advertising.

Already, from 1869, the agency of N. W. Ayer and Son, of Pennsylvania, had shown that a policy of truth in advertising was not the reckless and disastrous course that it might appear to many. Though the Ayer agency handled patent medicine accounts (including Dr Williams's 'Pale Pills for Pink People'), it shed this line of business before its rivals did. But the man who has been widely hailed as 'the father of honest advertising' was John E. Powers. He came to prominence in the eighties, when advertising agencies were beginning to assume responsibility for preparing their clients' advertisements. Powers turned out some of the early announcements for John Wanamaker's store, and became a highly paid consultant to many firms, ranging from Castoria to Scott's Emulsion. He wrote in short, simple sentences, scorning the exaggeration which had hitherto been considered essential. Indeed, it is probable that Powers did as much to make advertising literate as to make it honest. He arrived during a period when many small-town advertisers chose their slogans from handbooks containing 'suitable' phrases for all occasions, like 'Enormous slaughter in every department' (just as football reporters were once able to turn up handbooks to find phrases like 'rattled the upright' and 'nettled by this reverse').

John E. Powers had a partiality, which became a fetish, for dressing up his advertisements in Caslon Old Style type. Rivals who imitated his make-up are said to have found great initial difficulty in telling a lie in Caslon Old Style.

Once, in Pittsburg, Powers was called in to advise a big store which was in financial straits. He told them (says Claude C. Hopkins) to publish a prominent advertisement saying something like this: 'We are bankrupt. We owe $125,000 more than we can pay, and this announcement will bring our creditors down on our necks. But if you come and buy tomorrow, we shall have the money to meet them. If not, we go the wall.' The hitherto unprecedented blend of truth and showmanship appealed to the public, who responded on such a scale that the store was saved.

The growth of big-store advertising was one of the most important features of the last thirty years of the century. To the agents it was a welcome development, respectable as well as profitable, enabling the more successful among them to unload their patent medicine accounts as gracefully as possible on to less prosperous firms. Among the pioneer big-store advertisers were Marshall Field, of Chicago, A. T. Stewart, Macy, and John Wanamaker of New York. Their early advertisements showed no especial originality. John Wanamaker's 'new kind of store', launched in 1877, got away to a shaky start. Mass production threatened to choke the many departments; a quick turnover of goods was imperative. John Wanamaker knew that there was no solution in the old-fashioned publicity methods, in the deferential listings of taffetas and tulles. He scorned handbills; the type of person who accepted them was too poor to be interested in the kind of bargain he offered. Newspaper advertising, as he admitted, was his salvation; and John E. Powers was the man who engineered it.

The rival stores took advantage of the quickening competition in popular journalism to wring concessions in the way of display types. Even the jealously hidden black types were reluctantly produced in the eighties. Double-column displays came slowly, and when they were sanctioned the advertisers demanded three- and four-column displays. At least one advertiser in the *New*

York Tribune in 1880 achieved the equivalent of a four-column display by tipping his proclamation on end, so that the paper had to be turned on one side to read it. The advertisement was still contained within the compass of a single column.

Soon Joseph Pulitzer's *New York World* was making heavy inroads into the circulation of the *Herald*, and it was Pulitzer who relaxed many of the hitherto sanctified restraints – at a price. In 1887, armed with a dollar club, William Randolph Hearst began to beat his way into the popular newspaper field. Not until 1895 did the *Herald*, under the second James Gordon Bennett, lift its ban on display.

In a more dignified field, the struggling *New York Times* had been setting its face against the disreputable advertiser. By 1896, when Adolph S. Ochs secured control, the newspaper seemed doomed. Yet, in face of many tempting offers, Ochs extended his slogan 'All The News That's Fit To Print' to cover advertisements. Determined that no one should be able to accuse the *Times* of being influenced by advertisers, he turned down a big Tammany Hall contract, even though assured that no attempt would be made to pull strings if it were accepted. He also rejected lucrative advertisements advocating schemes which he regarded as a waste of public money.

American newspapers did not enjoy, and never have enjoyed, circulation over wide areas. No advertiser could insert his message in one given newspaper and know that it would reach the whole nation, as in Britain. Popular magazines, however, did sell across the continent, and for that reason their advertising revenue began to build up on an impressive scale in the latter part of the century. The volume and standard of advertising in such magazines as *Scribner's*, *Harper's*, *Munsey's*, *The Ladies' Home Journal*, and the *Saturday Evening Post* was noticeably higher than in any periodical publications in Britain. Mr W. E. Gladstone was a great admirer of the advertising pages in these magazines. Even when English editions were available he sent to America for his copies: it was the advertisements which fascinated him. Several of these magazines were active in the campaign to clean up disreputable advertising. The *Farm Journal* announced in 1880 that it would make good any loss sustained by a reader as a result of buying an article advertised in its pages.

The last decade of the century saw much talk about the 'science' of advertising. There were several journals devoted to the subject, one of them being George P. Rowell's *Printer's Ink* (1888). In this organ, in 1895, appeared a significant sentence: 'Probably when we are a little more enlightened, the advertising writer, like the teacher, will study psychology.' There were numerous clubs at which advertising men met to talk shop, to convince each other that they were men with a mission, and to discuss ways of creating goodwill for advertising. Already there existed schools, postal and otherwise, which undertook to teach copywriting; and the subject was beginning to clamour for recognition in colleges and universities.

In one venerable New England college, so the story goes, a harsh surprise befell a Commemoration Day audience when a young prize-winning student, nominated to address the assembly, bowed and said with innocent amiability: 'Good morning! Have you used Pears' Soap?' After a harrowing pause, during which the Faculty writhed, the parents avoided each other's eyes, and even the students showed distress, the speaker went on: 'This is the advertisement that stares us in the face, turn where we will. Do you read the advertisements in the daily paper? You ought to.' He then went on to deliver an eloquent and well-informed address on the economics of advertising, and in the end was much applauded.

Many American advertisements of the nineteenth century, especially of the personal type, were marked by an engaging frankness of expression. Others oozed with idiosyncrasy, naïveté, and homespun humour (conscious or otherwise), all in piquant contrast to the often unctuous announcements to be found in many English newspapers. A good example is the following wedding notice which appeared in an American newspaper in 1877:

Millos–Fisher. On the 11th inst. by Rev. A. Vincent Group at his residence 136 Congress Street, Philadelphia, Mr Frank Millos and Miss Julia Fisher. No cards. No cake. Nobody's business.

The Barnum example was responsible for much cheerful ir-reverence. An English ecclesiastic, arriving in America to under-take a lecture tour, left the task of engineering publicity to an agent, not without misgivings. In due course he found himself being billed with great prominence as follows:

COME AND HEAR A

RARE old English DEAN

The reverend gentleman professed intense annoyance, but his lectures were packed.

There was a good deal of petty fraud, often of a good-humoured kind, in the advertising of the day. Persons sending money for an advertised 'Potato Bug Eradicator' received two slivers of wood, with the instructions: 'Place the potato bug between the two sticks of wood and press them together.' Telling this story in the *Atlantic Monthly* (1904), Macgregor Jenkins said that a victim's first reaction would be one of indignation, then of wry laughter; soon afterwards he would be urging all his friends to write to the advertiser. So it would go on, until the postal department, notoriously unable to see a joke, would step in. Commented Jenkins:

The seeming indifference [to abuses] is due to a curious American toleration of a fraud or an injustice. . . . To be good-naturedly imposed upon is a positive pleasure, provided the cost of it is not too great.

A censorious view of contemporary American advertisements is to be found in Henry Sampson's *History of Advertising*, which was published in 1874. With very few exceptions, said Sampson, the family papers arriving from the United States 'contain advertisements which would be rejected by the gutter journals of this country'. In course of time, he said, 'the American Press may adopt the plan now in use here . . . that of having an outward and visible show of decency in the advertisement columns, no matter what darkness or danger lurks beneath'. The great majority of American publishers, said Sampson, were too obsessed with making money to worry about what was said of their methods. 'Indeed there are many who exult in the notion of making capital by all kinds of advertisements, from the puff preliminary to the nauseating display of vile quackery or undisguised immorality, and vary this with agreeable little interludes in the way of black-mail.' Such blackmail, he indicated, consisted of publishing attacks on firms or corporations until they chose to take advertising space. Sampson was human enough to admit that the application of a stricter code of morality in American advertising would 'lead to a vast increase of dullness'. He said nothing about the disreputable advertisements of abortifacients and 'cures' for venereal disease which disfigured the British Press.

The type of 'immoral' advertisement which Sampson had in mind was that to be found in the notorious 'Personal' column of the *New York Herald*. Although the story of this column overlaps into the next century, it may as well be told here. The 'Personal' feature was at its spiciest on Sundays, when it covered the whole front page at a dollar a line and overflowed on to the next. From quite early days it had been a place for making simple assignations, like: 'Harry. In Town. ABC.' As the century reached its end the announcements became increasingly brazen. 'Jolly sports' began to advertise for 'witty, affectionate ladies'; 'young masseuses' offered 'special disciplinary treatment' to select clients; 'highly magnetic' Parisiennes promised 'very interesting conversation' in 'chic suites'. Many of these announcements, couched in the *lingua franca* of vice, came from organizers of brothels who had been forced under cover as a result of purity drives. Here are a few typical items from issues of June 1905:

BRIGHT unencumbered woman, pleasing personality, seeks work afternoons, evenings by hour. – ADAPTABILITY. – 236 Herald.

CONFIDENTIAL work for wealthy ladies by refined, discreet, well-appearing gentleman. EXCLUSIVE. Herald, Brooklyn.

COURTEOUS and discreet gentleman will oblige ladies in any confidential capacity. – 'College-Bred'.

AN ADAPTABLE, handsome girl of Bohemian tastes can find exclusive board with liberal-minded woman. SMART WIDOW 324 Herald.

AFFABLE trained nurse would like patients; massage; baths. Alys, 42 West 66th.

ACCOMMODATIONS for refined parties in private flat, convenient to subway, reasonable. SELECT 135 Herald.

So it went on, column after column – unobtrusive service, absolute privacy, complete discretion. Occasionally the mixture was leavened by invitations to adopt twins, by offers to buy pawn tickets or to banish pimples.

The second James Gordon Bennett was warned of the risks he ran in publishing this feature, but he said that it had always

E

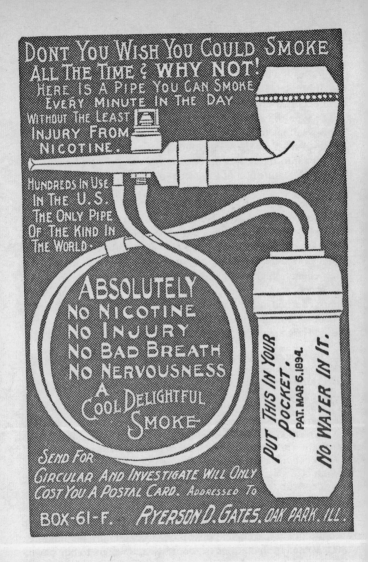

For non-stop smoking 1898

appeared in the *Herald* and would continue to do so. It was, in any case, a lucrative source of revenue. Even when William Randolph Hearst began to crusade against the column in 1899, Bennett refused to alter his decision.

The 'personals' might have gone on indefinitely had not Bennett in 1906 ordered the *Herald* to oppose the candidacy of Hearst as Governor of New York. Hearst held Bennett responsible for his defeat and had little difficulty in devising his revenge. His investigators rented a postal box under assumed names and clearly established the true nature of the traffic for which the front page of the *Herald* was being used. Before a New York court Bennett pleaded guilty to using the mails to circulate improper reading matter, and was fined $25,000. The firm was ordered to pay $5,000 and the advertisement manager $1,000. A *Herald* employee who had come to court suitably prepared peeled the notes from a fat wad. Thereafter Bennett rarely visited New York and Hearst's name was excluded from the *Herald* for many years.

A Hearst executive boasted that the judgement would cost Bennett $250,000 a year. Significantly, the Sunday circulation of the *Herald*, which had been the highest in New York, now dropped to third place.

It remains to add that vice advertisements of this type were to be found in the windows of numerous shops in the heart of London in the mid twentieth century. The problem of how to eliminate them seems to have defeated the legislature.

6   The Pace Quickens

The dying years of the nineteenth century have been called 'the golden age of advertising' – in the sense that an advertiser, unhampered by codes of ethics, scarcely restricted by legislation, unconfused by market research theorists, could pit his wits against the world and score spectacular successes. He had little to guide him save his own judgement of human nature. The leading showmen did very well at the game, but lesser men spent huge sums of money on badly orientated advertising which produced no dividend except public exasperation. Rather was it 'the brazen age of advertising'.

By the nineties, the spectre of over-production, *alias* underconsumption, was beginning to grimace at the factory windows. In this decade, the scale of advertising expanded, the tempo quickened. It was the period when modern advertising began.

In 1892, it will be recalled, a hostile critic of advertising wrote to *The Times* to point out (rightly or wrongly) that 'the colossal and flourishing biscuit works at Reading have never advertised'. At the turn of the century it was less easy to find a colossal and flourishing firm which did not trumpet its wares. Unless a manufacturer had a monopoly of some essential product, or enjoyed the perennial and indestructible goodwill of a specialized public, he had to fight for a market.

Many firms resorted to advertising only with the deepest reluctance and misgivings. They feared that, to their business associates, an advertisement would be interpreted as a flag of distress, and the bigger the flag the graver the distress. Hence, possibly, the determination of these firms to spend no more than they could help on the preparation of their announcements. There is also evidence that the heads of some businesses secretly sighed for a ban to be imposed on advertising, especially out of doors, to save the drain on their purses.

Henceforth, said the cynics, the country would see the survival of the loudest. Probably the fiercest competition was in soap. Surely, it was argued, no soap manufacturer could hope to persuade the public to use more soap (the Englishman's passion for washing himself was already a joke in many parts of the world). All the advertiser could do was induce people to buy more of his soap at the expense of somebody else's. Many of the public had began to wonder whether soap might not be cheaper if it was not so wastefully advertised. They were never entirely reassured when told that it was advertising which made their tablet of soap as cheap as it was, by enabling raw materials to be bought in bulk. In fact, there is little doubt that the soap war *was* wasteful. Lord Leverhulme's purpose, or one of his purposes, in bringing about mergers of soap firms in the early years of the twentieth century was to reduce the costs of competitive advertising; an aim which inspired the savage attacks on his enterprises by the Northcliffe newspapers in 1906, for which Lord Northcliffe had to pay damages of £141,000.

Those manufacturers to whom advertising was a faith rather than a vulgar necessity refused to believe that they were straining the public's goodwill. They accepted that, in the new conditions, the mere manufacture of an article was only the tenth part of success; the selling of it was the task that would call for the sharpest brains and a heavy budget. There were, after all, encouraging signs. Newnes, Pearson, and Northcliffe were widening the reading public, and hence the buying public. If readers of the popular sheets were uncovetous of material goods, then they must be made covetous. If supply really was treading on the heels of demand, then demand must be stimulated. From this conclusion was to evolve, by slow degrees, the next stage in advertising: the stage of persuasion, as distinct from proclamation or iteration. Lord Leverhulme was one of the first to see that whereas it had once been enough for an advertisement to be 'pithy, bright, original, and humorous', the public now needed 'logical and considered arguments'. More and more there was a vogue for what came to be called 'reason why' copy. Even Thomas J. Barratt had begun to explain *why* Pears' Soap was the best. By the turn of the century the cocoa firms had discovered that their product had other virtues besides purity. A Cadbury's advertisement said:

For the INFANT it is a delight and a support; for the YOUNG GIRL a source of healthy vigour; for the YOUNG MISS in her teens a valuable aid to development; for the YOUNG WOMAN a reliable and always beneficial influence; for the WIFE a solace and a stay; for the MOTHER a beverage that gives endurance; and for the ELDERLY DAME a never-failing help to the enjoyment of a vigorous old age.

There was even a Sunlight advertisement which foreshadowed the fashion of proclaiming, not the intrinsic functions of a product, but its possibilities as a generator and guardian of marital bliss. The illustration showed a harassed wife perspiring over the wash-tub, with an offended husband, newly returned home, in the background. 'Don't let steam and suds be your husband's welcome on wash days,' said the heading. Today this would be criticized as showing the 'negative' side of the picture; far better to show a pert-bosomed, carefree, *soignée* wife, all her washing completed hours before, greeting her husband with a smile.

Luckily, a large section of the public was quite willing to be stimulated into adding to its material possessions, a process variously described as raising the standard of living and keeping up with the Joneses. To the manufacturer it did not matter what the process was called so long as the household with a pound or two to spare opened its maw and allowed it to be stuffed with encyclopedias and sewing machines.

So bigger and bigger advertising campaigns were mounted, and instead of one firm stealing the market from the others it frequently happened, to everyone's surprise, that after a more than usually frenzied battle all the participating firms sold more, even though the market was supposed to be saturated. Sometimes a small firm benefited from the advertising of its big competitors, just as a 'flea pit' cinema sometimes takes in the shillings of the persons unable to gain admittance to the over-advertised attraction at the luxury cinema across the street. All too often, however, the little firms which did not advertise were squeezed out, or bought out.

In the nineties the first motor-car advertisements began to

appear. Because of the 'red flag' law the British industry got away to a late start, but the lyricist who drew up the advertisements of the Great Horseless Carriage Company in 1896 did his best to force the pace. 'Vehicle Revolution! A New Industry!' he cried, and stressed the need for a parent company to take up, work, and develop 'this immense industry'. In the prospectus were quoted Press opinions. The *Engineer* said: 'It seems that a great sale is found in France for the vehicles to country doctors, who are able to do from 40 to 50 miles a day, and in some cases the Motor has taken the place of four Horses, which had to be kept previously in order to obtain a satisfactory service.' The *Glasgow Evening News* thought the life of the draught horse not worth thirty years' purchase. And the *Freeman's Journal* said: 'Carlyle's method of testing respectability by the keeping of a gig will disappear when every man has his motor-car in his backyard and has only to light his petroleum lamp when he wishes to go out for a drive.'

The Great Horseless Carriage Company was ahead of its time, and disappointed its promoters. Development in the motor-car field was strictly individual and competitive. There is much fascination in the early car advertisements. For instance, the Daimler Company in 1901 said:

> Kindly write to us, stating your requirements, and let us know:
> 1st. At what speed you wish to travel.
> 2nd. Number of persons to be carried.
> 3rd. Whether your district is flat or hilly.

In the popular newspapers and magazines, however, motor-car advertisements were infrequent until Henry Ford began to attack the British market. The first Ford was driven to the top of Ben Nevis in 1911; a year later the Morris-Oxfords began to stream on to the roads.

The new century brought an extension of the rule: 'Advertise or go under.' Not only must a firm advertise for its own salvation, but British firms must advertise overseas for their country's salvation. Already the emissaries of more energetic countries – notably the Germans – were peddling their wares under palm and pine, while British salesmen slumbered. His Majesty's consuls complained of the 'take it or leave it' way in which British goods were offered; often there was no attempt to adapt a product for local needs, or even to translate the instructions that went with it. In 1901 the Prince of Wales (later King George V) made this point, modestly enough, in a speech at the Guildhall:

> To the distinguished representatives of the commercial interests of the Empire, whom I have had the pleasure of meeting here, I venture to allude to the impression which seems generally to prevail among their brethren across the seas, that the Old Country must wake up if she intends to maintain her old position of pre-eminence in her Colonial trade against foreign competitors.

To the Prince's surprise, this solitary, diffident sentence caused the speech to be loudly hailed as a 'Wake up, England!' call. In succeeding years, the Prince pressed home the charge whenever possible, urging British firms to display their wares arrestingly at international exhibitions. This, he said, was in accord with the principle of advertising which they already accepted. They knew that if a firm ceased to advertise its sales fell away. What if Britain herself ceased to advertise?

The 'Wake up, England!' speech came as a timely rallying-cry for one group of manufacturers who were fighting a stern battle against foreign rivals – on British soil. Leading cigarette firms had long been trying to frustrate a skilful and determined invasion from the other side of the Atlantic. The American Tobacco Company, selling in particular Richmond Gem and Sweet Caporal, took half-pages in the newspapers to proclaim 'Genuine Imported Cigarettes at Popular Prices'. Usually these advertisements were followed, and sometimes accompanied, by sneering announcements from British manufacturers. Ogdens cried:

> Don't be gulled by Yankee Bluff.
> Support John Bull with every puff!

and to press the point home, a large picture of a gull was incorporated in the advertisement, with sportsman John Bull discharging both barrels at it. Godfrey Phillips showed Uncle Sam plunging a dagger into the back of John Bull. The same firm had a picture of the British lion crouched defensively over a display of the firm's Guinea Gold cigarettes, and snarling at a top-hatted and star-spangled octopus which had swum up to give battle. In the background was the Statue of Liberty, with the sinister word 'TRUSTS' radiating across the sky like the Aurora

Borealis. In common with most of the British firms' advertisements, it was indifferently drawn and badly laid out. By contrast, the American advertisements, though there was more than a touch of billposting about them, were intelligently displayed and showed some regard for the rules of typography.

In the London evening newspapers, at the end of 1901, the rivalry culminated in a frenzy of knockabout, which delighted the public no less than the advertisement managers of the newspapers. Ogdens printed a large drawing of their factory, which was said to employ 3,000 British workers. Then, perhaps because the sight of rows of roofs lacked emotional appeal, they depicted the 3,000 workers whose happiness was in the hands of the British smoker. The American companies retaliated with drawings of healthy, upstanding workers in plantations, nobly dedicated to the task of selecting the best of the leaf for Britain. Steadily, the American advertisements grew bigger, and the British firms were goaded to new heights of patriotism. By now Ogdens were running an ambitious project whereby they undertook to buy every month from members of the public, 10,000 albums filled with the firm's cigarette cards, at 10s. an album. One day in November 1901 they took more than four pages of the London *Evening News*, ordinarily only a four-page paper, to print in small type the names of those to whom they had paid ten shillings. Godfrey Phillips also had a four-page advertisement – in the *Star*. 'We offered a fabulous sum for the entire eight pages of the *Star*,' said the announcement, 'but the proprietors decided otherwise.'

The pace was too hot for individual firms. On 2 December leading newspapers carried a full-page advertisement which announced the banding together of several leading firms as the Imperial Tobacco Company. The result of this hard-fought war was the now familiar one: both sides prospered. Whether the rush of orders received by British firms was inspired by patriotism will never be known. Little or no attempt was made during the campaign to tell people why they ought to smoke, or what benefits they might expect to derive from so doing. Like the cocoa firms, the tobacco lords contented themselves with stressing the purity of their products.

The early years of this century saw many other well-planned and determined advertising campaigns launched in Britain by foreign countries anxious to dispose of surplus foods. The Greeks unloaded their unwanted currants in this way. Then the State of São Paulo, Brazil, faced with serious over-production of coffee, launched a big and successful campaign on behalf of 'Fazenda' coffee. At that time Britain consumed only half a pound of coffee per head, against ten pounds consumed in many other countries.

How could Britain counter-attack? Only by means of better-planned advertising campaigns overseas, said the leading agents; and they pointed to their specialized knowledge of foreign markets, foreign tastes, foreign wiles.

Flattered, perhaps, by cordial words from the royal house, some of the advertising agents were seeking to band together in order to improve the status of their calling. Already the word 'ethics' was being used in conjunction with advertising, but no ethical code could be set up until there was some measure of co-operation among advertisers, who for the most part were cut-throat individualists. The young firms were willing to go to any lengths to outshine the old ones; respectability was a thing which could come with riches.

A serious obstacle in the agents' path was the assiduity with which all but the most triumphant publications concealed their net sales. By their own rough tests, agents could discover that certain newspapers brought better results than others, but much wasteful trial and error was necessary. To old-fashioned publishers, this demand for audited circulation figures was only the latest in a long string of impertinences from the advertising fraternity. Freedom of the Press, they felt, ought to include freedom to sell the advertiser a pig in a poke. It was to combat this attitude that the Advertisers' Protection Society (later the Incorporated Society of British Advertisers) was formed, in 1900.

It is time to trace briefly the rise of the new popular papers and periodicals, in which advertisers were to be allowed much greater liberties than ever before. Sir George Newnes, Sir Arthur Pearson, and Lord Northcliffe, who had been so quick to extend their sway over the new Board School generation, were themselves advertisers and 'stunt' men of no mean order. Sir George Newnes, who launched *Tit-Bits* in 1881, was the first to offer the bait of free

The World's Record. One Firm Takes Four Pages.	**The** ☆ **Star** THE BIGGEST ADVT. EVER ISSUED.	The World's Record. One Firm Takes Four Pages.

No. 4,352. LONDON, TUESDAY, 12 NOVEMBER, 1901. ONE HALFPENNY

THE
MOST COSTLY
COLOSSAL & CONVINCING
ADVERTISEMENT
Ever Used in an Evening Newspaper the Wide World O'er.

THE DEAREST ADVERTISEMENT AND THE CHEAPEST CIGARETTE.

GODFREY PHILLIPS'
GUINEA GOLD CIGARETTES

ARE THE ONLY GUINEA GOLD CIGARETTES NOT MADE BY AN AMERICAN TRUST.

FIVE		FIVE
A		A
PENNY.		PENNY.

THE ENGLISHMAN'S TOAST.

"Don't be galled by Yankee bluff,
Support John Bull with every puff."

And always Smoke the Real Old fashioned and Original English Cigarette.

GODFREY PHILLIPS' GUINEA GOLD.

This is only one of the 4 Colossal Advertisement Pages comprised in this day's issue of "The Star." Read them all. Each is more interesting than the other. We offered a fabulous sum for the entire 8 pages of "The Star," but the Proprietors decided otherwise.

American competition stimulated this British tobacco firm into taking four pages in the Star *on 12 November 1901. This was page one.* The Times *had already carried a four-page advertisement on 29 December 1834*

insurance against railway accidents, a form of bribe which was to lead his later imitators into deep waters. At one time he offered to pay £10,000 to hospitals if his readers would lift the circulation of his paper to a million; after much exhortation they raised it to 850,000 and he made a gift in proportion. Sir George Newnes's proudest publication was the *Strand Magazine* (1890), which in its heyday carried 100 pages of advertisements.

Lord Northcliffe (Alfred Harmsworth) started *Answers* in 1888. The trick which brought him prosperity was the famous contest in which readers were invited to earn £1 a week for life by guessing the total amount of gold and silver in the Bank of England on 4 December 1889. Each entry had to have five supporting signatures, and there were more than 700,000 entries. Originally Northcliffe had hoped to run *Answers* without advertisements, but he rapidly changed his mind. Many of the other publications which he founded in the nineties were boys' papers, which could never hope to carry more than a few announcements about stamps and stink bombs (certainly this was not the medium in which to advertise soap). In 1896 he launched his most ambitious venture, the *Daily Mail*, which was to be the pace-setter in newspaper advertising for the next generation.

The third member of the trio, Sir Arthur Pearson, started his *Pearson's Weekly* in 1890 (he had earlier won a prize of a £100 a year post on *Tit-Bits*). He too showed himself a fertile stunt-monger. Once he had the entire issue of his paper soaked in eucalyptus during an influenza epidemic; any copy, if waved about sufficiently, was supposed to ward off germs. Pearson and Northcliffe also sponsored contests which involved such monumental futilities as counting how many times a certain letter occurred in a given book of the Bible, or supplying missing words in poems. Some competitions were so much of a gamble that the law intervened.

These frivolous yet undeniably lucrative stunts went on year after year. One which rocked the country was the treasure hunt organized by the Northcliffe *Weekly Dispatch* in 1904. It was not an original idea, for *Tit-Bits* had already run a similar contest. Tokens representing various amounts in cash were buried up and down the country, and clues to their whereabouts printed in the newspaper; the whole scheme was then vigorously publicized in the *Daily Mail* and the *Daily Mirror*. Soon the *Weekly Dispatch* was obliged to print this warning in bold type:

It cannot be too clearly understood that *the treasure is only to be sought in public places*, none of it having been hidden in private grounds. . . . Some over-enthusiastic treasure hunters have sought the medallions in flower beds, under paving stones, in chinks of walls and in such-like places, but they have in every case been altogether off the track. *Persons who trespass or who do injury to private property may rest assured that they do not stand the slightest chance of finding the buried treasure. . . .*

No spades or pickaxes are required.

Gloatingly, each week the *Dispatch's* reporters described the activities of the treasure hunters. Hundreds were seen digging in 'the most extraordinary places' in Islington and Holloway. Because one clue had indicated that a token was concealed near a spot 'where people went against their will', ten constables had to clear destructive crowds from the vicinity of Pentonville Prison and a nearby fever hospital. 'This was not the fault of the *Weekly Dispatch*, the too energetic seekers having altogether mistaken the published clue.' In Lower Clapton was to be seen 'a vast crowd of men and boys digging up every soft piece of ground in the road . . .' A stretch of waste land in Canning Town was being turned over by 'hundreds of men and boys using knives, shovels, sticks, pick-axes, iron bars, and every imaginable implement'. In this area a man believed to have unearthed treasure was chased by the mob. Elsewhere a joker who planted misleading discs of his own manufacture had to flee for his life. In their excitement women fell into rivers. On Sunday mornings the newspaper offices were invested by such large crowds eager for clues that the wholesalers could not be supplied. In the provinces hundreds waited at the railway stations for the arrival of the newspaper trains. After six weeks, during which the equivalent of £3,790 was buried and £2,935 paid out, the contest was called off because of the heavy volume of complaints, presumably from angry property owners. The contest had served to raise the circulation of the *Weekly Dispatch* from a modest total to nearly a million.

In appearance the *Daily Mail* did not greatly differ from its more sedate contemporaries when it first appeared. But standards were fast changing. At long last the advertisers had successfully raided the big black type. In 1897 a writer in the *Nineteenth Century* had much to say about the 'typographical impropriety' of the advertiser.

Today *The Times* itself is ready, subject to certain conditions, to clothe advertisements in type which three years ago would have been considered fit only for the street hoardings, while even that once intolerable monstrosity, the picture block, is now cheerfully accepted by journals of the highest standing to emphasise a full-page advertisement.

The debauching of *The Times* evidently caused much distress among the priesthood of Printing House Square. According to the advertising journal *Fame* in 1892 'one man in the office was struck dumb and another had his hair turn grey in an hour when the proposal was made to put a block into the sacred pages'. This illustration was nothing more than a map illustrating a railway prospectus. Another decade was to pass before *The Times* suffered illustrations to appear regularly in its advertising columns. Even then readers rebelled. Surely there should be one sheet in which the eye was not confronted with the hirsute head of George R. Sims, 'donor' and popularizer of the hair tonic 'Tatcho'.[1]

Like its rivals, the *Daily Mail* at the outset leaned heavily on classified advertisements. Then the day came when Northcliffe decided that advertisements were news. Peremptorily he sent for his £3 a week advertisement manager, a young man called Smith, who had begun to call himself Wareham Smith. The dialogue, as recorded in the latter's *Spilt Ink*, went like this:

Your name is Smith, isn't it?
Yes, sir.
You are in charge of the advertising department?
Yes, sir.
When are you going to start thinking? When are you going to *do* something? The advertisement columns all look alike. They are the same today as in the first issue. I want to see something different. Start thinking. I'm busy now. Good day.

Northcliffe had only himself to blame for what followed. Wareham Smith was a young man of ambition, and hardly needed

1. No mention is made in Sims's obituary notices of his association with 'Tatcho', but to the masses he was as well known for the vigour of his hair as for the vigour of his Sunday writings.

this stimulus to action. Soon the rider who had so callously applied the goad was tugging madly on the reins.

It seemed to Wareham Smith that the big stores were the greatest source of advertising riches, as yet not properly tapped. Only within quite recent years had the stores been persuaded (or permitted) to take extensive advertising space. It was the lifelong rule of William Whiteley, founder of London's first department store, never to advertise in the newspapers, though he went out of his way to engineer free editorial publicity. Old and respectable stores had long cherished a hallowed advertising formula. This began with an expression of thanks to all patrons who had so liberally supported the establishment in the past followed by a deeply respectful invitation to inspect a new range of calicos, bombazines, silks, and taffetas, all unpriced. The less respectable firms also had their time-honoured formula; this was to placard their shop fronts with concussive posters, 'AWFUL SACRIFICE!' 'SOLD AT FEARFUL LOSS!' and so on. Hardly a window but held, allegedly, the fruits of bankruptcy, mergers, shipwreck, inundation, and fire (sometimes goods were specially singed). After a hundred years or so, this joke had begun to wear thin, but it is not extinct yet.

Those stores which took space in the Press had concentrated their advertising in the latter part of the week. Under the prodding of the *Daily Mail*, they consented to insert their announcements also on Monday, Tuesday, and Wednesday. In return they demanded concessions in the use of ever bolder type and illustrations, to the open wrath of Northcliffe. Wareham Smith tells how the 'Chief' denounced the *Daily Mail's* advertising displays as 'bludgeoning', 'shocking', and 'disgraceful', assured him 'You are a damn nuisance to everyone who is trying to produce a good-looking paper', and persuaded the rest of the staff to 'freeze' him. And yet, comments Wareham Smith, 'he plastered the sides of houses and railway bridges and the sky with hideous advertisements of the *Daily Mail*'.

There were other pitfalls in the way of progress. One of the early drapery advertisements showed a woman in combinations, and from valley and plain 'a howl of execration went up'. Northcliffe told his advertisement manager: 'You are ruining the paper with your vulgar advertisements. Stop it at once.' Wareham

Smith argued that drapers could not illustrate combinations properly without putting a woman's body inside them, and that 'millions sterling' were involved in the principle.

Alfred bullied. I urged a fight with the reader. We compromised. 'Give combinations a rest.' I did for a time, and then let them through gradually. But it was a near thing.

At this period and for long afterwards the big drapers seemed to have only one idea: to pack the front page of the *Daily Mail* with as many drawings as possible of simpering women in unerotic undress. How morals could conceivably have been imperilled by these studies of bosomless matrons posed in forbidding knickers and shroud-like nightdresses, all as sexless as the heroines in schoolgirl stories, is difficult to conceive. Day after day the advertising pages of the *Daily Mail* and other newspapers showed parades of crudely drawn female figures in row after row, like monstrous parodies of classical figures on a Grecian urn. Some of the distaste which the *Daily Mail* aroused in politer breasts may well have stemmed from the first glimpse of its front page as disfigured by drapers. How much more seemly, by contrast, the front page of *The Times*!

No one who turns through the files of the *Daily Mail* for the early years of this century will deny that Northcliffe at times suffered grave provocation from his advertisers. It had not yet occurred to the big stores – or indeed to any but a handful of advertisers – to spend money on effective layout. Too many of the store advertisements, as the *Advertising World* pointed out, looked like the work of office boys. The new halftone blocks which came into general use in the newspapers from 1904 onwards did not always make for a more elegant appearance; often the subjects of them were barely recognizable.

A shake-up came in the spring of 1909 when a retired American businessman, H. Gordon Selfridge, opened his new store in Oxford Street. Selfridge was no stranger to the ways of advertising. He once told how in his youth, as a space seller, he had tried to collect the price of an advertisement from a hard-up dentist and finally had allowed one of his teeth to be pulled out in settlement. His London venture was supposedly inspired by Blücher's verdict on London: 'What a city to sack!' It was a great gamble. If this new store, at the end of seven days, was not accepted by the public as of equal status with any other big store, then, said Selfridge, he was lost.

Preliminary announcements were couched in the then unfamiliar prose of High Commerce, with many capital letters:

The Great Principles upon which we will build this Business are as everlasting as the Pyramids. These Principles are Integrity, Truthfulness, Value-giving, Progressiveness, Dignity, Liberality, Courtesy, Originality, a daily presentation of what is New, coupled with a determination to Satisfy.

As the day of the opening neared, the old-established stores responded in a way which must have warmed the Wareham Smiths. Harrods opportunely discovered that their diamond jubilee coincided with the Selfridge opening week, and planned to celebrate it with grand afternoon concerts, floral galas, and special fashion displays. Waring's announced that they had redecorated all their model houses; Derry and Toms took full pages to boast of a special display of hats; D. H. Evans cried 'Paris in London!' Through it all the Selfridge trumpet sounded portentous and daily louder. 'We have issued 600,000 personal invitations to the opening,' said one advertisement, 'but if you haven't received one, come anyway.' On the night before the opening, hotels in London were heavily booked; in the morning enormous shopping crowds descended on Oxford Street from suburbs and provinces. At the stated hour a bugle blew and the curtains on the windows were pulled back like stage curtains. Sixty police were called out to control the crowds in the store.

In six days Selfridge filled ninety-seven newspaper pages with advertising. He had hired a number of artists to draw 'cartoons' in which bearded or bosomy classical figures represented Courtesy, Liberality, Integrity, and so on. These appeared as full-page advertisements in all London daily newspapers, with one exception, every day for a week, and also in certain provincial and overseas papers. The scale of this advertising was so overwhelming that it became news whether editors liked it or not, and Selfridge became a household word quicker than he dared to hope.

Critics were not lacking. The *Advertising World* congratulated

F

Selfridge on infusing new vitality into the columns of the Press, and noted that the responses of rival stores were 'like the feeble attempts of a few small boys to arrest the legions of an invading army'. But it complained that the announcements contained much 'high-falutin' nonsense', not to mention bad English. There was 'an apparent attempt to be more British than the British themselves'. Nobody held it against Selfridge that he was an American, hence 'the pouring out of a soothing balm for the cure of a quite unwounded national susceptibility was as graceless as it was unnecessary'.

Selfridge paid no attention to these objections, and continued to sprinkle capital letters through his rich prose. On top of it all, he hired 'Callisthenes' to laud the commercial virtues in a daily half column in the more serious papers. (John Wanamaker's store in New York had long been famous for its daily talks.) Those advertising agents who had shaken their heads at the extravagance of the opening campaign were now quick to use the Selfridge example as a stick to beat their pinchpenny clients.

Advertising had reached the stage at which writers were beginning to discuss not only its ethics but its psychology. The leading pundit in the latter field was an American, Professor Walter Dill Scott, Director of the Psychological Laboratory at Northwestern University, Chicago, whose book *The Psychology of Advertising* was issued in Britain in 1909. In the previous century psychology had been an abstract study, couched in intimidating jargon. In order that practical use might be made of its conclusions, 'psychological laboratories' like the one at Northwestern University had been set up, and those psychologists who could pass on their knowledge in simple terms had begun to address advertising clubs. Many of the truths they announced had been discovered empirically generations ago. It is open to argument whether the psychologist gave the advertiser new ideas, or whether he merely told the advertiser which of his ideas were good ones.

At this distance, many of Professor Scott's maxims now seem elementary enough. One of them was the principle of 'association'; an advertisement should be presented in such a way that a reader would associate it with his own experience, which was best done by appealing to his ruling interests and motives. These included the desire to be healthy, to hoard, to possess, to wear smart clothes, to get something for nothing, to be like the more privileged and successful classes. The instincts were there to be played on. A picture of a mother dosing a child would appeal to the 'maternal instinct' – but scores of advertisers knew that already. (In 1843 the *Edinburgh Review* had noted how Atkinson's Infant Preservative was 'forced on the public attention by the portrait of a female, far gone in the family way, in the act of pouring the anti-Malthusian fluid down the throat of a struggling baby with a spoon'.)

Professor Scott stressed the need for cheerful advertisements. Patent medicine manufacturers were fond of portraying ugly consumptive-looking women coughing their heads off or sneezing in the reader's face. While these pictures made an appeal, possibly, to consumptive women, they frightened away healthy readers from the neighbouring advertisements. It was better, he said, to draw pictures of men and women in sparkling health. Eventually even those who marketed rupture appliances caught the idea and instead of depicting anguished men clutching their vital regions they showed laughing (and presumably unruptured) fathers tossing infants in the air.

The Professor criticized those advertisers who linked their products, even in jest, with bulls, pigs, frogs, squids, and even less engaging creatures. He could have found a distressing example in the *Daily Mail* in 1900 – 'Have you ever seen a Dead Donkey? Good sauces are just as rare.' It was also a bad mistake, he pointed out, to associate the product, even in jest, with tramps or other unprosperous-looking characters. (Yet Pears' poster of the tramp writing his ambiguous testimonial was generally held to be a triumph.) The Professor's hint was taken by manufacturers of cheap bagatelle tables, who showed their product being enjoyed by aristocratic young men in evening dress, with lovely patrician women looking on.

Professor Scott distrusted humour. 'Advertising is a serious business, and unless the advertisement is extremely clever it is unwise to attempt to present the humorous side of life, although it is highly valuable when well done.'

Among other recommendations were these: do not appeal to men when selling goods like boys' stockings which are bought by women; do not caution the public against substitutes – write the advertisement in such a way that it will not occur to the reader that there can possibly be a rival product.

A few of the criticisms voiced by Professor Scott seem a little baffling, but no more baffling than some of the criticisms of advertisements to be found in professional journals today. For instance, he criticized a Packard advertisement on the grounds that it did not contain 'directions for securing the product'. It might be thought that anyone successful enough to be able to afford a luxury limousine would know how to set about buying one.

As a period piece, the article on advertising in the eleventh edition of the *Encyclopedia Britannica* (1910) is not without interest. The writer of it holds his subject at arm's length, but is quite willing to theorize about it. He enunciates what he calls 'a curious and obscure principle' at the back of advertising: 'The average man or woman who goes into a shop is more or less affected by a vague sense of antagonism towards the seller,' he says. The potential buyer entertains a powerful suspicion that the shopkeeper is out to give him the worst of the bargain. The customer, however, can rapidly disarm the shopkeeper if he asks for the article he wants by its trade name, 'not because he has any reason to believe it to be better or cheaper than others, but simply because he baffles the shopkeeper and assumes an authoritative attitude by asking for some specific brand'.

If shoppers ever thought along those lines, they would appear to have ceased to do so today; for the modern shopper has now cheerfully and unthinkingly swallowed the proposition that if an article is advertised widely enough, it must be a good one, or at least a reliable one. Probably more citizens enter a shop in a mood of diffidence and indecision than in a state of antagonism.

The writer in the *Encyclopedia Britannica* forebore to touch on one interesting aspect of his subject: the attacks which for some years had been levelled at advertising by socialists. To the Marxist, the advertiser was one of the more pernicious lackeys of capitalism. His role was to persuade the public to mis-spend money on inessentials instead of on goods or services produced by common agreement for the common good. The advertiser, it was argued, should serve the community, not the rapacious elements in that community.

In 1914 Sidney Webb elaborated socialist criticisms in an introduction which he wrote to G. W. Goodall's *Advertising: A Study of a Modern Business Power*. Was it in the public's best interest, he asked, that rival capitalists should go on squandering huge sums on advertising until the weaker went to the wall? Did the three million pounds which Thomas J. Barratt had spent on the promotion of soap represent 'the value of the wrecks to which the competition of this giant soap manufacturer has reduced so many old-fashioned soap boilers'?

When each branch of industry falls into the hands of a single monopolistic trust, these cannot pretend to effect any further economies in the cost of production by further increasing their business. The cost of advertising would then represent their struggle one with another for the largest share of the consumer's income.

How much more alluring, thought Sidney Webb, to consider the way in which advertising might be employed in a 'cooperative commonwealth'. There was no question of eliminating advertising completely, only of eliminating motives of personal self-interest. He was willing to concede that even a socialist state might 'find it convenient to publish a catalogue of its productions, so as to allow the customers freedom of choice in the outlay of the incomes received by them in cash'. He recognized the value of advertising as an educational force – 'However great may be the common improvement in intelligence, farmers, we may presume, will continue to be relatively slow to move.' The United States Department of Agriculture had been bombarding farmers with good advice, and that, Webb noted, 'may be the type of much advertising of the future'. He also admitted: 'Unless our freedom of choice is to be a mockery, all novelties must up to a certain point be actually forced on our attention. This means advertising.'

What kind of advertising would the cooperative State adopt? Webb explained:

Even when all our various manufactories and stores have become public services, and when no capitalist levies a toll upon our supplies, we can easily imagine the various public health departments advertising their baths and other hygienic opportunities; the educational authorities importuning every young man and maiden to try their attractive lecture courses and organized games; the municipalities of the various pleasure resorts commending their holiday attractions; the national

railway and steamship administration tempting us to enlarge our minds
by travel; the State Insurance Department urging us all to insure for
allowances in old age or sickness, supplementary to the common pro-
vision; in short no end of advertising intended to influence our decision
as to how to spend our incomes in the ways that the 'general will' of the
community felt to be good.

This was written in May 1914. The next four years were to see
enormous developments in state advertising, but on very different
lines from those envisaged by Sidney Webb.

AMERICA: TRUTH IS SUGGESTED

In America, at the end of the nineteenth century, the technique of
advertising was being studied far more seriously than in Britain.
One of the hottest pace-setters turned out to be a young man from
Galveston, Albert Davis Lasker, who in 1898 joined the Chicago
agency of Lord and Thomas. Lasker, having been persuaded that
advertising was 'salesmanship in print' – as distinct from mere
description, or reiteration of a brand name – helped to establish
the fashion for 'reason why' copy, which preceded the strategy of
appealing to the public's hopes and fears. In the process, says
John Gunther, 'he took more money out of the advertising
business than anybody who ever lived – more than $45,000,000 –
or anybody who ever will live'.[1]

In 1903 an advertisement of Lord and Thomas – by then 'the
third biggest advertising agency in America' – showed a picture
of a file stocked with the arcane wisdom of over twenty years of
advertising research. 'It is to us, and indirectly to our 527 clients,
what the compass is to the mariner at sea . . . The precise *knowledge* this $100,000 cabinet affords is what *compels* us to pay
$72,000 yearly for a staff of Copy Writers . . .' This was mere
window dressing; the agency's greatest asset was the $45,000,000
cabinet of Lasker's brain. One of his first copywriters was the
man who convinced him that advertising called for aggressive
salesmanship – John E. Kennedy, a former Royal Canadian
Mounted policeman in the service of Dr Shoop's Restorative. It
is, of course, nonsense to suppose that at this date no one had
tried out aggressive salesmanship in print; but most firms and

1. *Taken At The Flood.*

their agents were content to rely on repetition, picturesque exaggeration, or slogans. Lasker's notion of salesmanship was to seize on the 'news' in a product and then tell people *why* they should buy it. In this, he was long and brilliantly served by that other graduate from Dr Shoop's Restorative, the copywriter Claude C. Hopkins, a legendary figure who was able to boast in his autobiography that he had made one million dollars out of Pepsodent alone.

Hopkins, a man of the people, who had done door-to-door canvassing, put much faith in what would now be called product research. Before he could boost the sales of canned pork and beans, he had to find *why* they were better than the home-made dish, and then ram home the reason in simple words. He also believed in giving away food samples, by the million if necessary, before loosing the heavy artillery of advertising. And long before the days of 'copy laboratories' he tested the pulling power of different headlines by means of keyed coupons.

The difficulty with seeking the 'news' in a product was that many of them contained nothing to distinguish them from those of rival firms. This did not deter men like Hopkins and Lasker, who were content to play up some aspect which might well be common to all products in the range, but which nobody else had considered to be worth stressing. If the rivals then played up the same aspect, they merely helped to sell the other man's goods. This policy, soon widely imitated, resulted in one of the follies for which advertising has been, and still is, roundly criticized: an obsession with trivial, imperceptible, and even non-existent advantages.

One of Hopkins's more spectacular campaigns was that in which he proclaimed Puffed Wheat and Puffed Rice to be 'food shot from guns'. In this there was an element of 'reason why' – puffing made the food easier to digest – but perhaps not everybody noticed it. 'The idea roused ridicule,' says Hopkins, 'and one of the greatest food advertisers in the country wrote an article about it. He said that of all follies evolved in food advertising this certainly was the worst. But the phrase was such a curiosity-rouser that it proved itself the most successful campaign ever conducted in cereals.'

Hopkins, like Professor Scott, scorned the use of humour in advertising. 'People do not buy from clowns,' he said, and Lasker agreed with him. For this reason, both men thought little of the big campaign to popularize the cereal 'Force', with its buoyant character 'Sunny Jim.' Nevertheless, Edward Ellsworth worked up immense popularity for his product, with the aid of a series of jingles, the first and best-known being:

> Jim Dumps was a most unfriendly man,
> Who lived his life on the hermit plan.
> In his gloomy way he'd gone through life
> And made the most of woe and strife,
> Till Force one day was served to him.
> Since then they've called him Sunny Jim.

Verses like these were breakfast reading for hundreds of thousands of children, to whom Sunny Jim was a better-known character than Hiawatha or Robinson Crusoe. Sunny Jim began to appear at fancy dress balls, on the stage, in newspaper cartoons. The name of the food also helped to inspire free publicity of this kind:

I can't coax my husband to eat any breakfast.
Have you tried Force?
Madam, you don't know my husband.

America was ahead in the car race. In 1901 Ransom E. Olds was turning out four hundred cars a year, which put him ahead of all rivals anywhere in the world. But in 1903 selected American magazines carried the announcement of a Fordmobile:

It is positively the most perfect machine on the market, having overcome all drawbacks such as smell, noise, jolt, etc. common to all other makes of Auto Carriages. It is so simple that a boy of 15 can run it.

Nevertheless, Henry Ford continued to perfect perfection. By 1906, when he was building 10,000 cars yearly, he began to enunciate his mass-production economics:

Such quantities were never heard of before. If we made as a profit one-fifth as much on each car as is usually figured as a proper profit, we would make as large a gross profit as a manufacturer who builds 2,000 cars.

Ford did not encourage the romantic, adventurous note in his advertising (though in later days his copywriters grew lyrical enough). He left it to other manufacturers, like Jordan, to hint at the joys of roaming the wide open spaces. To Ford, at this stage, a motor car was a means of transportation, not a subject for transports. One early advertisement read:

Our purpose is to construct and market an automobile specially designed for everyday wear and tear – business, professional, and family use; an automobile which will attain to a sufficient speed to satisfy the average person without acquiring any of those breakneck velocities which are so universally condemned.

Later, however, a Ford announcement said that a person could either drive slowly 'or press down the foot lever until all the scenery looks alike to you and you have to keep your eyes skinned to count the milestones as they pass'.

'We never bothered with a sporting car,' said Ford in *My Life and Work*; but he entered Fords in many races and reliability trials. In 1909 he decided that perfection had again been reached. There would now be only one car: the Model T, or 'Tin Lizzie'. And he proclaimed: 'Any customer can have a car painted any colour he wants, so long as it is black.' Nor did he abandon his stand until eighteen years and 15,000,000 cars later.

The vogue for 'Tin Lizzie' jokes was encouraged by Ford himself, against the earnest advice of his executives. An old lady was supposed to have sent a consignment of tin cans to Detroit; by return she received a Ford car and a letter saying that a few tins were left over and these would be credited to her. It did not matter how silly the stories were, so long as Ford became a household word. As will be seen, a vogue for 'ribbing the product' developed in advertising on the radio, but in Ford's early days few manufacturers were willing to laugh at themselves. (In 1904 the comedian Courtice Pounds, appearing in *The Cherry Girl* in London, said of some hypothetical horses, 'Alas, they are Bovril now!' He received a peremptory demand for a public apology by the Bovril Company.)

There was no slackening in the pace of invention, and each new device brought its advertising challenge. Not the easiest device to popularize was the vacuum cleaner, the brainchild of H. Cecil Booth, an English inventor. Booth watched a railway cleaner blowing the dirt out of a carriage with compressed air. How much tidier, he thought, to reverse the process, and suck in the dirt. His first vacuum cleaner was considerably larger than a heavily laden railway trolley, and ugly to a degree. Even when it was reduced to more comely proportions, the housewives of two hemispheres needed a good deal of persuasion to try it.

Then came the safety razor boom. King C. Gillette, a young American eager for fame, had been advised by one of his employers to invent 'something that can be used and thrown away'. One morning, so the story goes, he gazed disgustedly at the dull blade of his 'cut-throat' razor. It was a lump of expensive steel, of which only a tiny sliver did any useful work. Why not manufacture just that sliver of steel, to be thrown away when blunted? Experts said that wafer-thin metal could not be given an effective cutting edge. Gillette's idea, which 'changed the face of the world', was perfected only after many disappointments. From the advertising point of view it was not enough to persuade men to use safety razors; it was necessary to persuade them to use razors. Perhaps Gillette's assurance that his safety razor could be used as freely as a knife and fork was not the happiest of inducements. Nevertheless, the idea caught on. Rival manufacturers saw in Gillette's five-dollar razor a target to be shot down with all speed. Soon there were two-dollar and one-dollar razors on the market; then razors at fifty cents and at twenty-five cents; and finally came the ten-cent razor, complete with blades. Gillette opened a British factory in Leicester in 1905, pricing his British model at a guinea, and again rivals brought the price down with a rush.

Another American whose name figured largely in the advertising of this period was Robert H. Ingersoll, the man who put a watch in the pocket of millions of schoolboys. Obstinately convinced that a sound watch could be marketed at a dollar, Ingersoll wore down opposition and made his fortune. After many years' success in America, he began to advertise his five-shilling watch in Britain, in 1905. Jewellers were hostile. Why sell a five-shilling watch with a year's guarantee, when a bigger profit could be made on the sale of a non-guaranteed watch, with lucrative repairs to be charged over and above? But Ingersoll advertised his watch to such good purpose that the jewellers *had* to stock it, if only to keep the cheap watch trade out of the hands of drapers and newsagents. Not for the first time, or for the last, advertising was used as a flail to break down not the consumer but the retailer.

It was in this decade, also, that William Wrigley Jr, who once sold his father's soap from a basket, popularized his now universal cud. Back in 1866 one Thomas Adams Jr had brought a lump of chicle back from Mexico. He tried to vulcanize it in order to make dental plates, but was unsuccessful. Nobody could suggest a use for it, except as a substitute for chewing tobacco. The early addicts chewed it almost unflavoured, and it was left to Wrigley, who knew an expendable when he saw one, to introduce such flavours as spearmint. Even so, the habit was slow to catch on; but in 1907 Wrigley began to advertise on what seemed a reckless scale, and another addiction was born. Wrigley is credited with the saying that even if the whole world chewed gum it would still be necessary to advertise it, in case people began to slacken off. The idea of calling a halt to advertising, he thought, was as foolish as detaching the locomotive from an express train and expecting it to retain its momentum.

Occasionally British firms were to be found counter-attacking with vigour in the American Press. The face of John Mackintosh looked out from many a printed page, with variations of this message:

I AM THE TOFFEE KING

I have given to England a great national candy and I am now offering to America the same toffee that has made me famous abroad. Does America propose to welcome me – to welcome a candy that is so pure that any mother can recommend it to her child? The answer is: 'Yes, by all means.'

John Mackintosh's advertising owed rather more to Barnum than it did to Professor Walter Dill Scott. It is possible to do much research in American newspapers and magazines of this period and find very little evidence of the 'psychological attack' which the pundits were advocating; this did not become a widespread weapon until the twenties. It is true that American canned meat firms now refrained from showing bulls and carcases and were illustrating their advertisements with plates of succulent slices of meat tastefully arrayed and carried by pretty girls – the first move towards the mouth-watering appeal so chromatically cultivated today. In view of Upton Sinclair's disclosures in *The Jungle* (1906) it was undoubtedly good policy to overlook the animal origin of meat.

An interesting example of 'scare' selling was an advertisement by a school of memory training. It showed a railway signalman clapping his hand to his brow, and exclaiming 'I forgot!'; in a 'balloon' above his head two express trains were crashing, magnificently, head-on. The advertisement continued: 'How much is expressed in those two words "I forgot!" Thousands of human lives and millions of dollars worth of property have been sacrificed to a faulty memory.'

This was an exception, however. In an American magazine chosen at random – the October 1905 issue of *Munsey's*, a *Strand*-type magazine with 138 pages of advertisements – very few announcements attempt psychological warfare. First in the magazine, inevitably, was Pears Soap, with a challenging sentence attributed to Bacon:

Cleanliness of body was ever esteemed to proceed from a due reverence to God, to society, and to ourselves.

Sapolio's variation on this theme was: 'You can't be healthy, or pretty, or even good, unless you are clean.' A full-page advertisement by Otis Elevators showed a grandmother sitting confidently in a lift while her granddaughter, aged about two, pressed the appropriate button, just as confidently. 'Now Grandma, no more stair climbing,' said the caption. The advertisement of the Victor Talking Machine Company cried 'Loud enough for dancing!' It incorporated the picture of the dog listening to 'his master's voice' – a trade mark which was to inspire a change of name by the firm. The Columbia Phonograph Company proclaimed that their new model was 'sixteen times louder than all other talking machines'. Electric broughams were competing with petrol-driven cars. 'Coca-Cola' was content with a mere quarter-page. A notable feature of the issue was the number of firms anxious to sell diamonds on credit. But the prize went to the advertiser who offered 'ball-bearing garters' for men – 'assures ease of movement'.

In this issue of *Munsey's* almost the only unillustrated advertisement was by Kodak. Yet it was during this decade that the Kodak girl laid the foundations of her considerable popularity, rivalling even Sunny Jim and Johnnie Walker. The public regarded her as a 'nice girl', and were concerned that she should remain so. Her striped skirt is said to have had its influence on popular fashion.

American advertisers had mastered the technique of the positive approach. This tendency of the day was remarked by the *New York Evening Post* in 1909:

The hypothetical and somewhat overworked visitor from Mars who should pick up a copy of one of our magazines could not help being struck at the difference in spirit between the literary and advertising sections. If he concludes that the earth is inhabited by two races of men, a race of stumbling, bungling, unhappy failures and pessimists, and a race of vigorous, successful, radiant optimists, we can scarcely blame him. In the literary pages the world is the worst of all possible worlds; in the advertising supplement it is the best of all conceivable worlds. In the magazine proper everything goes askew. The railroads cheat us and kill us. The food manufacturers poison us. The liquor dealers destroy our moral fibre. The army is depleted. The navy has its armour belt in the wrong place. Workmen go about without work. Lack of sanitation kills its thousands. Automobiles do their share – the list is endless. But what a reconstructed world of heart's desire begins with the first-page advertisement. Here no breakfast food fails to build up a man's brain and muscle. No phono records fail to amuse. No roof paint cracks under the cold or melts under the sun. No razor cuts the face or leaves it sore. Illness and death are banished by patent medicines and hygienic shoes. Worry flies before the model fountain pen. Employers shower wealth upon efficient employees. Insurance companies pay what they promise. Trains always get to Chicago on time. Babies never cry; whether it's soap or cereal, or camera or talcum, babies always laugh in the advertising supplement. A happy world indeed, my masters!

Even the manufacturers of automatic weapons tried to raise no more fears than were strictly necessary. This advertisement appeared in *Collier's* in 1910:

Is Your Home An Eggshell Home?

Suppose your wife, mother or sister left alone in the house should wake up tonight and find a burglar in her room. What would she do? Suppose she were left alone and a tramp, drunk or vicious person should come to the house and attack her. What *could* she do by way of resistance? Nothing. Absolutely nothing. She would be helpless – helpless as a little child. Get her the new 'human arsenal' – new Savage automatic . . . it converts your home from a defenceless shell of a place into an arsenal . . . gets in the first (vital) shot. Please send us the name of the retailer from whom you buy your firearms . . .

In 1911 the visionaries who were striving for a code of ethics in advertising scored their first success. They persuaded the Associated Advertising Clubs of the World, meeting in America, to adopt the slogan, if not the policy, of 'Truth in Advertising'. It was, and is, an almost impossible goal; if it were necessary to proclaim 'the truth, the whole truth, and nothing but the truth', advertising would stop abruptly. Some advertisers did try, honourably, to live up to the ideal. Many others were content with an unvoiced slogan of 'Half-Truth in Advertising'.

WAR ON THE QUACKS

On both sides of the Atlantic, the period 1890–1914 saw the mounting of vigorous attacks on the more presumptuous of the medicine men. If advertising were to be made respectable, it was necessary to dissipate two centuries of distrust created by cure-mongers. Today the advertising world claims to have cleaned up the major abuses by its own efforts and on its own initiative; which is by no means wholly true.

Certainly a powerful motive for reform was that until late in the nineteenth century reputable firms refused to advertise in the same columns as the medicine vendors. Not only did the quacks' advertisements create an atmosphere of mendacity, but their pictures of warty women and consumptive adolescents were so repellent that the healthy reader's eye forebore to linger in their vicinity.

Already it has been seen that certain leading agencies in America dropped their patent medicine accounts as soon as they could afford to do so. It required moral courage to give up a contract worth hundreds of thousands of dollars a year in the knowledge that it would forthwith be transferred to a rival agency, which would not even attempt to discourage the impudent claims of the client. Sometimes an agency was in the position of the girl who, finding that her fine dress was leading her to perdition, gave it to her young sister.

In America it was the *Ladies' Home Journal*, under the militant Edward Bok, which made one of the first stands against patent medicine advertising. In 1892 it refused to carry any medicinal announcements whatever. By contrast, some of its contemporaries continued to publish announcements which would have aroused suspicion even in Steele's *Spectator*. One of them, in a popular magazine of 1895, read:

BE BRILLIANT AND EMINENT. The new physiological discovery Memory Restorative Tablets quickly and permanently increase the memory two or ten-fold and greatly augment intellectual power; difficult studies etc. easily mastered; truly marvelous; highly endorsed. Price $1.00 post-paid. Send for circular. MEMORY TABLET COMPANY, 114 Fifth Avenue, New York.

In 1904 the *Ladies' Home Journal* opened a vigorous campaign, extending over two years, exposing dishonesty and chicanery by the medicine men. *Collier's* joined in the attack in 1905, Samuel Hopkins Adams conducting scathing exposures under the title 'The Great American Fraud'. The public learned for the first time that its favourite catarrh powders contained cocaine, that the soothing syrups with which it dosed its children were composed of laudanum and morphine. The Women's Christian Temperance Union was invited to take note of the fact that some medicines were forty per cent alcohol (it was unlawful to sell a certain widely advertised pick-me-up to Red Indians, for this reason). One article by Adams began with a list of names and addresses of persons who had died from the effects of a named medicine. Numerous scare advertisements were reproduced, of the kind which listed common, trifling ailments and represented them as the symptoms of grave disease. One of them read:

Does Your Back Ache?

Thousands of men and women have kidney disease and do not know until it has developed into Bladder Trouble, Rheumatism, Diabetes, or Bright's Disease, which will prove fatal if not attended to at once.
IT'S YOUR KIDNEYS!

The advertisement was accompanied by a picture of a man turning over in bed, holding his hand to his back in pain.

Another advertiser who said 'I will give $1,000 if I fail to cure any cancer or tumour' proclaimed in black type:

ANY LUMP IN WOMAN'S BREAST IS CANCER.

Readers were told how the medicine firms handled those confiding letters beginning 'Dear Doctor . . .' which they received in shoals by every post. The letters were rough-sorted by clerks according to whether the symptoms seemed to indicate tuberculosis or cancer, and an appropriate routine letter was sent in return. If there was some unusually intimate passage in a letter, it was handed round so that a good laugh might be enjoyed by all. When the replies had been sent out and the medicines dispatched to the victims, their letters were sold for five cents each to other firms seeking an outlet for their rubbish.

'Unsolicited testimonials' to medicines could be obtained from a bureau in Washington which existed solely to supply them. Nor was that the only source. Adams told how the representative of a celery-compound firm called on the editor of a Chicago newspaper, flourishing a proof of a full-page advertisement for his firm's product. It contained some blank squares. 'We want a few testimonials to fill out with,' explained the representative. When the editor replied, 'You can get all of those you want, can't you?' the representative slapped the proof and said, 'Show me four or five strong ones from local politicians, and you get the advertisement.'

Some newspapers, it appeared, were coerced into signing agreements to the effect that the advertising contract was void if the editor published any material hostile to patent medicines. But newspapers were not always the innocent victims; there were instances in which quacks were blackmailed into advertising by threat of exposure if they did not.

These campaigns in *Collier's* and the *Ladies' Home Journal* were first-class journalism. They had the backing of the American Medical Association, which was conducting vigorous exposures on its own account. As a result, many publications, usually the more prosperous ones, were persuaded to ban or to censor patent medicine copy. More important, the attacks inspired the passing of stringent food and drug regulations.

In Britain H. G. Wells, who in his apprentice days had rolled many a pill, published in 1908 his novel *Tono-Bungay*, in which that ambitious humbug, Uncle Ponderevo, debauches the population with his 'mischievous trash' at 2s. 6d. a bottle. The plot is not extravagant by comparison with the success stories of real-life Ponderevos of that day. Wells neatly sums up the philosophy of quackery. One of his characters has the idea that it would be profitable to adulterate mustard with horse radish, but baulks at the thought of adulteration. He is assured that adulteration is unnecessary. Far better to concoct a mixture, three-quarters horse radish and one-quarter mustard, give it a fancy name and sell it at twice the price of mustard. Then the question is frivolously raised: Could cinders be turned into biscuit? 'Why not?' argues the Devil's advocate. 'You might advertise "Why are birds so bright? Because they digest their food so perfectly. Why do they digest their food perfectly? Because they have a gizzard! Why hasn't man a gizzard? Because he can buy Ponderevo's Ashpit Triturating Friable Biscuit – which is better." '

Tono-Bungay let some much-needed light into the underworld of patent medicines. A more calculated attack, deadly and skilful, was loosed by the British Medical Association, which published two pamphlets, *Secret Remedies* (1909) and *More Secret Remedies* (1912). These contained laboratory analyses of some of the most widely advertised specifics of the day; analyses which made it all too clear that the public were paying heavily for rubbish. The first pamphlet had much of the effect on the medicine-mongers that Samuel Plimsoll's *Our Seamen* had on the shipowners. There were attempts to impugn the motives of the British Medical Association, and even to put the pamphlets out of circulation; some newspapers refused to carry advertisements of them. At least one action was brought against the Association, only to fail.

There is no doubt that these pamphlets prepared the way for the House of Commons Select Committee on Patent Medicines, which sat from 1912 to 1914. The Report of this body inspired Lord Bledisloe to say: 'Never has such a tissue of fraud and falsehood been disclosed to any Parliamentary Committee in either House.' It is one of the most disillusioned documents of the century and contains enough criminal plots to last a novelist a lifetime. Since it mentions the products of several firms which enjoy high eminence today, and which have lived down their pasts, it must be quoted with a certain reserve.

In one heavy-laden but devastating sentence the Committee summed up their conclusions:

G

For all practical purposes, British law is powerless to prevent any person from procuring any drug or making any mixture, whether potent or without any therapeutical activity whatever (so long as it does not contain a scheduled poison), advertising it in any decent terms as a cure for any disease or ailment, recommending it by bogus testimonials and the invented opinions and facsimile signatures of fictitious persons, and selling it under any name he chooses on the payment of a small stamp duty for any price he can persuade the credulous public to pay.

It was possible, the Report pointed out, for a single drug to be sold under an infinite number of trade marks. For example, phenolphthalein appeared under the following names: Aperione, Laxans, Laxatin, Laxatol, Laxatoline, Laxiconfect, Laxoin, Laxophen, Paraphthalein, Phenolax, Proliclin, Purgen, Purgo, Purgolade, Purgella, and Purgylum. There were firms which did nothing else but buy well-known chemical substances, invent fancy names for them, and advertise them as remedies for freckles, falling hair or spots before the eyes.

For generations it had been the custom to proclaim that the recipes of medicines had been secretly handed down by Old Mother This or Nurse That, in romantic and implausible circumstances. The Committee set out to trace the origins of an American soothing syrup, the makers of which boasted having sold ten million bottles. Originally these bottles had borne a legend telling how 'an old woman . . . on her last legs with dyspepsia, was given up by her relatives and was allowed to wander in the lanes about her native village in Germany. One day she chewed a leaf of a herb only found in those parts and found immediate relief.' In the course of 1,607 questions, the firm's representative admitted that this story was a piece of fiction. Another product was 'composed of the active principles of certain rare plants which flourish in the valleys situated on the southern slopes of the Himalaya, between the immense gorge separating Nepaul from Bhutan on the East and Almorah on the Bhangulpore, India. . . .' Any rival manufacturer seeking to raid these happy valleys would have been frustrated at the start by being unable to find the word Bhangulpore in the gazetteer. A certain purge was said to have been inspired by Captain Cook, who had seen the beneficent results obtained by natives after eating the local vegetation. A drug to ease childbirth had been devised 'as a result of patient investigation of a minister of religion ... profoundly impressed by the death of a young wife'.

As in America, there was a brisk traffic in nominal rolls of sufferers:

We were informed that there exist today agencies, one in Leeds which advertises frequently, and one or two in America, selling lists of names of sufferers from various diseases at so much per thousand. That is, a person about to put on the market a 'constipation cure' or a 'rupture cure' or a 'cancer cure' can buy a list of a thousand persons suffering from tuberculosis or rupture or cancer, these lists containing the names of persons who have at some time answered advertisements regarding those diseases, and whose names and addresses thus possess a monetary value.

Lists of sufferers from consumption were more highly priced, according to one witness, because this class was regarded as the most profitable.

The Report named various individuals – some of them well-known – who had exploited one class of sufferer after another, changing their names when they judged credulity to be exhausted. '—, a well-known swindler, is believed to have spent £20,000 a year in advertising an "alcohol cure" – at his death he left £80,000.'

From this disreputable trade, the country derived an appreciable revenue in the shape of stamp duty. Often, to the innocent, the presence on a bottle of a Government stamp appeared to be an endorsement of integrity. Some manufacturers even went so far as to indicate on their labels, and in their advertisements, that the stamp was a guarantee of excellence. The regulations were riddled with loopholes, and a manufacturer could avoid paying tax altogether on his 'cough mixture' if he renamed it 'chest mixture'.

Manufacturers of 'tonic wines' were heavily raked by the Committee. Many of these products – including one which claimed a testimonial from the Pope – were 'about twice as intoxicating as ordinary claret'. There was no doubt, the Report said, that many persons acquired the drink habit from taking these wines, 'either knowing that they are alcoholic, since they can be purchased and consumed without giving rise to the charge of drinking, or in ignorance that they are highly intoxicating liquors'. One wine firm was said to have obtained the signatures of six thousand doctors by offering to send a free bottle to any person the doctor cared to name. The president of the British Medical Association said that the profession had since learned its lesson.

Some newspapers, the Committee noted, exercised their own censorship over patent medicine advertisements, but it was probable that a number of small provincial papers would be unable to exist without them. The 'so-called religious Press' – which had been criticized by the jury in the Chrimes case – showed wide hospitality to quack announcements, especially 'in the sexual class'. Dr Alfred Cox, of the British Medical Association, quoted the Association journal as saying: 'It is a fact that quack medicines have more vogue among Nonconformists than among sects of a different theological shade.' Apparently contempt for the established clerical order was extended to include the established medical order.

Cheap 'home' papers were said to contain many advertisements of 'a grossly improper nature'. A single issue of a Sunday newspaper carried nineteen announcements of drugs intended to be used as abortifacients. One prosperous witness, who showed resentment when asked how many tons of soap he used annually in his pills, tried to convince the Committee that the phrase 'for any unusual delay' employed in his advertisements was directed at the costive; but by this time the Committee were incurably sceptical.

As unscrupulous as any of the medicine men were the makers of useless appliances, which ranged from electric belts to artificial ear-drums. The assistant editor of *Truth*, G. Sidney Paternoster, who had exposed many frauds in his journal, told of the curious principle of 'gas pipe therapy' as displayed in a device of American make. 'It consists of a piece of tubing which may have some charcoal or something else inside to which two pipes are attached, and discs. You are supposed to put the piece of pipe in a bucket of water and attach the discs to your ankle, and by this means your blood becomes oxygenated and you are cured of anything that is the matter with you.' The device, which was 'merely a piece of pipe nicely polished and got up', sold at between £3 and £5. An American 'sight restorer' consisted of a cap fitted over the eye; by squeezing a rubber ball, the victim gave himself 'a mechanical massage with air pressure'.

At any given moment, up and down the country deluded citizens were sitting down in the privacy of their homes seeking to woo back the faded senses with the aid of preposterous engines, expensively bought. It was a grim jest played by the New World on the Old. Before sailing for Britain, some of these adventurers secured flattering headlines in their own towns. 'Anti-Fat Missionaries to Reduce London' had run a headline in the *Denver Post*.

The Assistant Director of Prosecutions told the Committee some of his difficulties. As the law stood, manufacturers could say what they liked in their advertisements so long as they avoided gross impropriety. If their products were criticized, they could always produce a string of witnesses, many of them voluntary, to say the medicine in question had saved them from an untimely grave. On the other hand, the prosecution had great difficulty in persuading a woman who had bought an abortifacient or a man who had been trying out a cure for sexual weakness, to go into the witness-box.

The Committee strongly urged that the sale and advertisement of cures for cancer, consumption, deafness, diabetes, paralysis, fits, locomotor ataxy, Bright's disease and abortifacients should be banned – a recommendation which did not become law until twenty-seven years later.

Not the least reason for the Government's failure to follow up the recommendations of this Select Committee was that the Report – by a grim coincidence – was issued on 4 August 1914. Even so, it sold out rapidly. It has been alleged that those whose activities were described in its pages bought up copies by the hundred.

7   The Technique Changes

During the First World War the technique of advertising ripened under fierce stimulants. It fell to the Government to initiate, or at all events to endorse, the outright appeal to the emotions – to pride, to shame, to fear, to vengeance.

The detailed story of the great recruiting campaigns need not be told here, but it is important to see how the psychological attack – which was to be followed up, nervously at first, in commercial advertising after the war – was sharpened in the days of peril.

In 1914 the Government had planned to pull in 35,000 Army recruits by advertising. Then Kitchener asked for 100,000. Sir Hedley le Bas, who was concerned with the ensuing publicity campaign, has told how Kitchener was 'sometimes startled', as indeed many were, by popular appeals which 'departed so drastically from traditions he had respected all his life'. The appeals were of a brutal simplicity. One of them was the famous 'Five Questions to Men Who Have Not Enlisted':

1. If you are physically fit and between 19 and 38 years of age, are you really satisfied with what you are doing today?
2. Do you feel happy as you walk along the streets and see *other* men wearing the King's uniform?
3. What will you say in years to come when people ask you – 'Where did *you* serve in the Great War?'
4. What will you answer when your children grow up, and say, 'Father, why weren't you a soldier, too?'
5. What would happen to the Empire if every man stayed at home *like you*?

Your King and Country Need You

ENLIST TODAY

God Save the King

Daddy, what did YOU do in the Great War?

Imperial War Museum

*Psychological Warfare: this famous poster of the First World War
pointed the way to commercial advertisers*

This was only one of a series of posters on similar lines. There were five questions to those employing male servants:

1. Have you a Butler, Groom, Chauffeur, Gardener, or Gamekeeper serving *you* who at this moment should be serving your King and Country?
2. Have you a man serving at your table who should be serving a gun?
3. Have you a man digging your garden who should be digging trenches?
4. Have you a man driving your car who should be driving a transport wagon?
5. Have you a man preserving your game who should be helping to preserve your country?

A great responsibility rests on you. Will you sacrifice your personal convenience for your Country's need?

Ask your men to enlist TODAY

Hence the sonnet by Siegfried Sassoon which begins 'Squire nagged and bullied till I went to fight. . . .' Certainly many employers needed to be jolted into a sense of reality. An advertisement by a provincial firm of drapers on 29 August 1914 began: 'The War and the Drapery Trade. The present problem of the moment to all employers, particularly those in the Drapery Trade, is how to keep their assistants fully employed . . . we shall endeavour to retain our entire staff. . . .'

There was a third line of attack. The women of England were asked, *inter alia:*

When the war is over and your husband or your son is asked, 'What did you do in the great War?' is he to hang his head because *you* would not let him go?

It was also hinted that a man who let down his country by not volunteering was the sort of man to let down his sweetheart or wife.

The advertisements of commercial firms in the early months of the war showed ingenuity in giving the product a patriotic glow – an art already practised in the South African War. 'British eau-de-cologne for British people,' cried Boots. 'The Pianola piano enables you to play the national anthems of all the leading nations,' cried another headline. 'If you owned a Pianola Piano you could render the Marseillaise with all the fire and vigour that has made it famous.' A fountain-pen firm exposed a rival which, it asserted, had ninety-nine per cent of its shares owned by Germans.

'Would you not like to talk to the wounded Belgians in their own language?' asked the proprietor of a French course. A clothing firm promised that if a person bought three pairs of socks it would send a fourth pair free to the Belgians. Nurses were called upon to use Palmolive – 'They know that hard rough skins would irritate and often cause pain to the sufferers whom they have to tend and care for.' The Y.M.C.A. took full pages, well laid out, to proclaim: 'Queen Alexandra herself gives a building. Will you also give one?'

As the war progressed, the commercial advertisers sobered down. Lord Northcliffe at one stage had his qualms about the corset displays which his newspapers were accepting. Might not the paper control condemn this as a frivolous use of paper in war time? His underlings were able to assure him that corsets were now regarded as an essential for women.

During the war entirely new feminine garments began to be marketed: the brassière, dating from about 1916, and cami-knickers, shortly afterwards. The brassière of those days was designed to flatten rather than to flatter, and it bore no visible resemblance to the uplifting, bifurcating garment which was to dominate the advertising pages a generation later. The war also stimulated the fashion of pyjamas for women. Those who had been shocked by pictures of families romping in their combinations now turned the pages shuddering.

One long-notorious type of advertiser encountered a permanent setback during the war: the quack peddler of 'cures' for venereal disease. In 1917, according to a Government spokesman, there were 5,000 men calling themselves herbalists who offered treatments, and who prospered only because victims of the disease – which through wartime laxity was rapidly spreading – were afraid to go to their doctors. The Venereal Diseases Bill putting the quacks out of business was not passed without the expression of fears that the liberty of the subject was being jeopardized. One Member pointed out that 'a quack may be, and very often is, a man who has definitely studied this disease and is an honest, straightforward, and an honourable man'. So, under pressure of national emergency, ended a type of advertising which had disfigured newspapers for more than three centuries.

When the peace treaties were signed (and blotted with Ford's blotting-paper) those leading advertising men who had been called on to spend millions of the taxpayer's money felt that they had done their bit; and the subsequent award of a knighthood to Charles Higham, who had been associated with most of the big wartime campaigns, was considered no more than his due.

The 'buy bonds' campaigns ended on an unhappy note. Some tens of thousands of patriotic citizens had risen to the lure seductively offered by Horatio Bottomley, who invited the public to buy one-fifth portions of the £5 Victory shares, with the prospect of winning £20,000. 'The British Empire is your security. You cannot possibly lose your money,' said Bottomley. But they did, and Bottomley went to serve seven years' penal servitude.

In 1920, to mark an international advertising exhibition at the White City, an advertising procession a mile and a half long wound through the streets of London. The public were invited to applaud 'Bubbles', the Kodak girl, the Michelin man, the Monkey Brand monkey, and other characters from the advertisers' mythology. The biggest exhibit possibly aroused the least fervour in the public's breast; it was a banner reading 'Advertisers Demand Net Sales'. This cry was being raised ever more loudly. The Advertisers Protection Society had drawn up its own estimates of newspapers' circulation and usefulness, for the benefit of its members. This enterprise brought upon the Society a writ for libel by Lord Northcliffe, who complained that the Society's assessment of the *Observer* had done that newspaper less than justice. Lord Northcliffe lost his case.

Even Whitehall was now advertisement-minded. Some indignation was aroused when the Postmaster-General, in 1922, proposed to lease the backs of stamps for advertising. 'A great shock,' said a reader of *The Times*. 'I wince at advertisements on stamps as much as I should wince at an advertisement on a cathedral or on my wife's forehead.' That same year there were complaints that income-tax forms (on which Thomas J. Barratt had once sought to advertise) carried offers of plots of land in Canberra.

In the newspaper field, the *Daily Mail* was still the pace-maker, but its competitors, notably the *Daily Express* under Lord Beaverbrook, were beginning to press hard. Still protesting about bludgeoning headlines, Lord Northcliffe in 1921 took a step which some regarded as just another sign of increasing unbalance, though others have since wondered whether the 'Chief' was perhaps saner than they thought. Out of the blue, he summoned his head hall porter, Robert Glover, to Carlton House Terrace and told him that henceforth he would be censor of advertisements. Glover was a forthright, sensible, and level-headed man, as befitted a head hall porter, and Northcliffe's idea was that he should bring the judgement of the average man to the subject of advertisements. For three hours or so Northcliffe briefed his censor in the rudiments of typographical decency. Then he sent for his advertising staff and instructed Glover to lay down the law, first pointing out that Glover weighed eighteen stone and had a reach as long as Jack Dempsey. Glover appears to have risen to the occasion commendably. Daily until Northcliffe's death in 1922 he submitted a report on the appearance of the day's advertisements, earning an extra £2 a week for so doing.

A periodical feature of the *Daily Mail's* pages was the composite advertisement, in which perhaps a dozen firms were persuaded to band together. One of the more ambitious of these was a full-page advertisement on 1 June 1922 entitled 'A Page of Robey'. It had twelve pictures, in each of which Mr George Robey was intimately involved – drinking health salts, shaving, flying to Paris, pumping up his motor tyre, buying batteries for his radio, listening to the gramophone, and so on. The practice of endorsing goods could not go much farther than this.

As before the war, Britain once again became a dump for overseas food growers, who were willing to spend huge sums on advertising in order to rid themselves of their surplus crops. California led the attack. Over a span of five years the Walnut Growers Association of that state increased their sales in Britain by 200 per cent, and the British public, instead of cracking walnuts in only two months of the year, were cracking them in six. Even more successful were the Sun-Maid raisin growers, also of California. Although they had taken energetic steps to increase their sales at home, they nevertheless found themselves in 1920 with an immense glut of raisins. On their behalf, Stanley Q. Grady spent half a million dollars advertising Sun-Maid raisins in Britain. He 'won the British market in one of the quickest campaigns ever held in England', defeating vested interests which had maintained a bulk market for eighty years. Grady claimed that he saved the growers between seven and eight million dollars. He achieved his results by full-page newspaper advertisements and a big poster barrage. Consumption was stimulated by the popularizing of raisin bread, and by drawing attention to the iron content of raisins – 'Have you had your iron today?' Three years later a critic of advertising complained: 'People have stopped eating raisins because they are good and now eat them because they are fatigued at three o'clock in the afternoon.'

If the British public could be driven to eat raisins in such prodigious quantities, why not apples, pears, lemons, grapes? Late in 1923 the British Fruit Trades Federation launched their 'Eat More Fruit' campaign, a well-mounted broadside levelled at 12,000,000 people daily. Shippers and brokers contributed funds – many of them sceptically – at the rate of one farthing per package. More than one hundred different advertisements were put out, with slogans stressing the enjoyment and good health to be derived from eating fruit. Fortuitously, an influenza epidemic broke out, enabling the promoters to point out how fruit fortified the human frame against illness. A diet of fruit, it appeared from the advertisements, would make children sparkling eyed, good-tempered, and even clean-kneed, and girls eupeptic, graceful, and enchanting. The mixture of reasoning and 'charm' had gratifying results, and the fruit trade were left in no doubt whether to repeat the campaign. Thus the way was paved for rival 'eat more' and 'drink more' campaigns, of which the public eventually tired. There was a limit to its stomach capacity as well as to its purse.

America's assaults on the British market were not invariably successful. A big campaign to popularize chewing gum in Britain soon after the war made poor progress; but failures, on the whole, were few, and Britain acquired more and more American tastes and customs. By way of counter-attack, Sir Charles Higham tried hard to make America a nation of tea-drinkers.

Higham at this time was a powerful advocate of collective advertising. It had been shown time and again, he argued, that when many firms selling the same product advertised competitively, the result was that the sales of all of them increased. If firms adopted schemes for group publicity, the result would be to ripen the market for competitive advertisements. Moreover, a group could afford to buy full pages where a firm could rise only to a quarter of a column. 'It does not matter which firm gets the most orders,' he wrote, 'so long as all the firms composing that industry or service get more orders than are customary.'[1]

Sir Charles's writings suggested that he had accepted the teachings of American advertising pundits – never appeal to the conscious, only to the subconscious; never give the customer a chance to marshal rational objections. He argued that it was bad psychology for a manufacturer of cosmetics to hold out the lure of beauty, because most women knew they were plain; the association would only bring about reasoned resistance in a woman's mind. It was better, he said, to present the idea of improvement, of increased attractiveness.

The influential men in advertising were now to be found in the agencies. Hitherto the public's notion of 'an advertising man' had been someone like Thomas J. Barratt, whose function was to popularize his product alone; the new men handled a whole range of products. They staffed their offices with writers, artists, and photographers and offered specialized knowledge on markets and media (though as yet real market research had hardly begun). The leading agents expected the client to put himself almost unreservedly in their hands and accept whatever copy they prepared. If they thought the sight of his honest face in the advertisement did nothing to sell the product, then out it must come. If they decided the public was bored by references to the gold medals won in Brussels and Barcelona in 1875 and 1888, then the gold medals must be forgotten. If they thought it necessary to stress an aspect of the product which the manufacturer thought trivial, then he must give in gracefully.

The names of most of these agents were unknown to the public, but two much-publicized (and self-publicizing) exceptions were Higham and William (later Sir William) Crawford, both of whom indefatigably preached the mission and the *mystique* of advertising. Crawford, a Glasgow Scot, never doubted that advertising was a noble task. 'That old communities may be richened; that new communities may spring to life; that the deserts of the world may be made gardens – this is our work . . .

1. Charles Higham, *Advertising, Its Use and Abuse*.

The pens in our hands are the makers of a new earth.'[1] His fervour was backed by strong technical resources and he did much to improve the standards of layout.

It was Crawford who was instrumental in persuading the International Advertising Convention to hold its 1924 session at Wembley. The delegates reaffirmed the principle of 'Truth in Advertising' and adopted a Code of Ethics which ran:

We pledge ourselves:
1. To dedicate our efforts to the cause of better business and social service.
2. To seek the truth and to live it.
3. To tell the Advertising story simply and without exaggeration and to avoid even a tendency to mislead.
4. To refrain from unfair competitive criticism.
5. To promote a better international understanding based upon a recognition of our mutual responsibility and our interdependence.
6. To conserve for ourselves and for posterity ideals of conduct and standards of Advertising practice born of the belief that truthful Advertising builds both character and good business.

In the emotional fervour of a big convention it was easy to make resolutions like these. It was more difficult for a manufacturer to adhere to them when a competitor was seen to be stealing a march by making questionable claims; and it was difficult for an agency to refuse to make reckless claims on behalf of a client's product, knowing that refusal would simply mean the loss of a valuable account. In any event, the man at grips with his conscience would ask himself, what is truth in advertising? Nobody complained because Beecham's Pills were proclaimed to be 'worth a guinea a box', a statement never intended to be taken literally.

Slowly, however, the advertising industry began to put its house in order. That International Advertising Convention of 1924 had been promoted by the Associated Advertising Clubs of the World, on which the British representation was a very modest one, cloaked by the title 'District 14'. After the convention District 14 expanded rapidly, and in the following year established a vigilance committee to examine questionable advertising. At the end of that year the Advertising Association was formed, with the object of raising professional standards and efficiency.

1. G. H. Saxon Mills: *There Is A Tide*.

The year 1924 is still remembered in advertising circles as the year the *Daily Mail* made its sensational attack on the patent preparation 'Yadil'. Full-page advertisements of this product, which was not without value in the treatment of certain minor conditions, had been appearing in a number of newspapers and 'Yadil' was already a household name. On 22 July 1924, out of a clear sky, the *Daily Mail* published a long article entitled 'YADIL: An exposure by Sir William J. Pope K.B.E., F.R.S., M.A., D.SC., LL.D., Professor of Chemistry in the University of Cambridge.' Sir William said he would set out to show that 'Yadil' was not 'trimethenal allylic carbide' as it professed to be, but a dilute solution of a well-known substance; that it was sold at a price some sixty times the actual cost of the materials used; and that no valid evidence had been produced to show that it had any efficacy in curing the maladies listed in its advertisements – namely, consumption, cancer, bronchitis, pleurisy, pneumonia, malaria, scarlet fever, measles, diphtheria, pernicious anaemia, and others. To the layman, the evidence in Sir William Pope's article seemed disturbing enough. The proprietors of 'Yadil' flew to court in an effort to restrain publication of further attacks; they were unsuccessful. Sir William Pope's article was followed by a broadside from Professor W. E. Dixon, Reader in Pharmacology at Cambridge. The *Daily Mail* also printed names of directors of the firm and of its associated printing company, many of them men of distinction. Within a very brief period, the preparation which had been hailed as 'the antiseptic sought by Lister' was off the market, rejected by the chemists.

To say that the 'Yadil' case fluttered the advertising world would be like saying that Pearl Harbor fluttered America. If one firm of such eminence could be put out of business as easily and swiftly, what of the others? Some advertising agents were worried by a sentence in Sir William Pope's exposure. He had said:

That the selling price is sixty times the actual cost of the materials should cause no surprise when it is remembered that the product is sold largely through the agency of full-page advertisements in the daily press.

Had it not been proclaimed for years that advertising reduced the cost to the consumer, that the cost of it was more than offset by the reduction in overheads? There were cautious attempts to point out that the economics of 'Yadil' were exceptional.

The 'Yadil' exposure, which would have cost the *Daily Mail* a vast sum if the charges had been contested and disproved, turned out to be a solitary incident. The man in the street may have suspected that other widely-advertised commodities were no less vulnerable than 'Yadil', but if they were, it appeared that no other newspaper was prepared to take the risk, or court the honour, of destroying them. According to H. G. Wells in *The Work, Wealth, and Happiness of Mankind*, 'No newspaper . . . has any interest in the exposure of fraudulent or adulterated commodities, unless such an exposure will frighten or flatter the owners of competing articles, to its profit.'

The man in the street soon forgot about 'Yadil'. It was a day when the public mind was easily distracted; the day of jazz and cocktails, of face-lifting, of long-distance flights (in themselves an elaborate form of advertising), of Ethel M. Dell, of '£1,000 Must Be Won'. It was also a day of self-conscious sex-appeal, and much of this controversial commodity was now finding its way into the advertising columns. Instead of the drapers' dreary sketches of unsexed matrons in their camisoles, there appeared large photographs of long-legged young women in the ever-scantier rayon underwear. As an eye-stopper, the pretty model was a fashion which once started was not to be halted. But advertisers had much to learn; for a girl who was supposed to be drawing attention to a brassière might be admired by women for her hair style and by men for her legs, and a bathing belle deputed to draw attention to a chest of tools performed no such function. During this period the trade of photographic model received a powerful stimulus and has never looked back. Even a girl with no other asset than a good pair of breasts could find remunerative employment.

The 'never never' system was making rapid headway, but it was not yet wholly respectable. Unless it could be made to appear so, the outflow from the factories – particularly the furniture factories – would be arrested. The man who did much to break down the prejudice was the benevolent Mr Drage, whose immaculate courtesies bestowed on Mr and Mrs Everyman were inescapable in the newspapers of the late twenties. His rivals were, or should have been, grateful to him. Here he is in 1926:

Mr Everyman: Your new Drage Way of furnishing appeals to self-respecting people.

Mr Drage: I am glad to hear it. They are the very folk I aim at – independent-minded men who want fair treatment without patronage, and to furnish out of income with absolute security. . . .

Mr Everyman: Well, my wife's chosen £90 worth of your furniture.

Mrs Everyman: I should like to have chosen a lot more, for your furniture is so beautiful, Mr Drage.

Mr Drage: There is nothing to prevent you choosing more, Mrs Everyman, only we make it a rule never to press our subscribers to buy.

Mr Everyman: I should like to pay £8 now and 45s. a month on our £90 order.

If Mr Everyman nervously suggested producing references, Mr Drage would say, 'I am offered references fifty times a day, and I always decline even to look at them. The Drage Way would cease to be confidential if we asked our customers' friends or employers about them.'

A rival to Mr Drage in the field of bespectacled benevolence was Mr Barratt, who was always ready to listen to any suburban housewife limping into his shoe shop with a 'George loves walking, Mr Barratt – but I don't'. Among those hard-pushed to defend advertising it has been argued that advertisements like those of Mr Drage and Mr Barratt set a public example of courtesy which cannot fail to have a good effect on the firms' employees, inspiring them to unusual civility and solicitude; a pleasing thought.

The year 1926 saw the founding of the Empire Marketing Board, authorized to spend £1,000,000 a year on persuading the housewife to put British goods in her larder. For the work he threw into the early stages of this well-mounted campaign, in which Sir Stephen Tallents and Frank Pick played a big part, William Crawford received his knighthood. The Board harangued the housewife in terms like these:

This Can't be You!

There is a woman who finds shopping dull – just a weary round of small change and parcels, day in, day out.

And yet – every food shop is a little living map of the world brought into her street. All the Empire fruits just tumbling off the shelves in their eagerness to tell their story of good quality and good fellowship.

But *she* can't hear.

Every shop window invites her to ask where it all comes from, to remember she is British – to *think*.

And she won't.

But of course she is not you?

Even if this appeal did not inspire women shoppers to pace the streets bright-eyed, eager, and inquisitive, there is no gainsaying that the seven years' propaganda of the Empire Marketing Board did much to quicken interest in Empire produce.

Many people today, if asked to name the advertising campaign which most took their fancy in the twenties, would give their vote to the Mustard Club. This was a lively, knockabout series run by Colman's. Leading members of the Club, which all were invited to join, were the Baron de Beef and Miss Di Gester (from whom a lapel badge of membership might be obtained). A typical Mustard Club advertisement showed the Baron de Beef, attired as a barrister, lying in an empty bath in a court of law. 'What is a Bath? Baron de Beef appeals to the House of Lords,' ran the heading. The Baron's case was that the bath was not big enough to wallow in, and for a mustard bath it was essential to wallow.

'Now the value of a Mustard bath is complete and comfortable submersion. In that way you get a feeling of absolute rest and peace, and the mustard and water flowing all over the body opens the pores of the skin and enables one to sweat colds and influenza out of the system. A lively tingling sensation comes over you, all your muscles grow supple –'

'That's enough,' said his Lordship. 'We don't want any advertising.'

By such painless methods the public was persuaded to use mustard at breakfast as well as at dinner, to throw away the unused mustard at the end of every day, and to pour mustard in its bath. The usual influenza epidemic arrived opportunely to give the promoters of the Mustard Club new scope.

So far the standard of copywriting, with a few exceptions, was indifferent to poor. There was little sign of any fulfilment of the prophecy made in 1923 at Atlantic City by H. Dennis Bradley: 'The copy of tomorrow will be written by men of genius – representatives of literature, and with the help of great painters there will be born a new great public garden of art.' It was the American copywriters assaulting the British market who penned the more imaginative prose. In 1926 the firm of Pears, once the *enfant terrible* of advertising, in announcing a new soap, merely discoursed on the qualities, not the possibilities, of that soap. By contrast, the American firm of Palmolive ('Keep that Schoolgirl Complexion') had a full front page, simply and forcefully laid out, showing a girl with a dreamy love-light in her eyes speaking on the telephone, with the query in big letters: 'Will his eyes confirm what his lips are saying?' The copy which followed began: 'The kindly candles of last night, the tell-tale revealments of noon! Do you fear the contrast they may offer?'

Although the First World War had shown the effectiveness of the psychological attack, many British advertisers, many agents too, were still nervous about employing it. Was it, they asked themselves, the decent thing to do? Might not a policy of appealing to greed, fear, and snobbishness rebound eventually on the advertiser? The American public, notoriously, were conditioned to crudities. Besides, their mass-production machine was geared to such a tremendous output that drastic measures had to be employed to keep it going. The British public was different. . . .

It was a painfully long time before copywriters rose above pedestrian exposition or hackneyed superlatives. But the *avant garde* were already dabbling in what later came to be known derisively as 'word magic'. Some of it was deft and nimble enough, cunningly poised between poetry and bathos. The peril of fine writing in advertising is that the higher-flown the imagery and language, the more abysmal the anticlimax when the product comes to be mentioned.

One copywriter, T. C. Steel, thought so highly of the style of some of his contemporaries that he published a diverting anthology – probably the first of its kind – in 1931, called *Prose of Persuasion*. Among lyricists quoted were the copywriters for the Buoyant mattress – 'adds to sleep the bloom which is the very bloom of the grape'; and for Johnson's Baby Powder – 'Happy is the baby born in a world made beneficial and bland by the soft caressing touch of —'.

But the most fascinating period specimens enshrined in *Prose of Persuasion* are those of the Jaeger copywriter Marchant Smith, written in the language of the Bright Young People.

My lovelies, with Paris and Berlin doing the most *angular* things with concrete, glass, and metal – *so* stimulating – one does heave the old bosom just once to find mahoganized, diluvian London shedding the mildew at last. I mean, on the new floor at Jaeger's positively *all* the fungus has died in the night.

My dears, they've gone *completely* chromium! Tubey chairs, vulcanite tables, glass walls, plus-ultra pictures, and *wholly* immediate carpets. A simply *gladdening* spot, darlings. Utterly 1930 and corpse-reviving! The cerebral background, of course, for the *stupefying* smartness of the new Jaeger clothes.

After praising the 'slenderizing' quality of the clothes – 'cut with lethal precision but touched with the *coyest* inconsequence' – the writer ended: 'And so, my quinces, to see the pride of the Place Vendôme look *perfectly* paleolithic, one canters round to Jaeger's.' A variant of this was: 'If you want to see Paris look like a suburb of Gath . . .'

Jaeger's clothes were only 'for the most *compatible* people', or 'the most congenial and *lucid* people'; in other words, the cocktail, sports car, bridge, and point-to-point set. One advertisement discoursed on how consoling it was, after losing on the racecourse all the money one had won at cards, to 'drift along and *petrify* the paddock with some Elysian *ensemble*, don't you *utterly* concur?' Life had no more to offer than the 'trim festooning of the old carcase' with '*eupeptic* frocks' which were 'the wildest thrill since the zip-fastener'. Of one garment it was said: 'Bundle it into the dickey, treat it with the most *secular* indifference – it will still emerge trim and uncreased, still fall into *sculptured* lines with simply *monastic* good humour.'

There was sporadic debate then, as there is today, about what constitutes a good slogan. Those which were in vogue between the wars were not necessarily the wittiest nor the most original– 'That Kruschen Feeling', 'Friday Night is Amami Night', 'Great Stuff This Bass', ' *Daily Mail* Million Sale' (though the latter was admired for its scansion). The wiseacres said a slogan was no use unless, like those just cited, it mentioned the product. A motorcar firm advertised 'Safety Fast' – but which firm? A whisky firm boasted 'Equal to a Fine Liqueur' – but again, which? True, everyone knew the products referred to in the slogans 'Worth a Guinea a Box' and 'Born 1820 – Still Going Strong', but that was only because of the enormous sums unremittingly spent on popularizing these slogans over generations. The lesson seemed to be that the wittiest slogan was no use unless the firm was prepared to use it constantly, year in, year out. By sheer weight of expenditure and repetition, even an indifferent slogan could be made a household phrase.

As in America, the depression of the early thirties tended to strengthen the advertiser's appeal to the emotions. Goods *must* be sold, otherwise unemployment would grow steadily worse and worse. Some advertisers who had long been crying 'Buy British!' grew tired of appealing to the public's better nature. On 27 March 1930 the motor trade addressed this sharp reproof, in heavy black type, to readers of *The Times*:

> Do You Know That
> nearly £10,000,000 was spent last year
> by our own people in these Islands for
> FOREIGN MOTOR PRODUCTS?
> A colossal loss to British trade and British workers.
> No Government can cure unemployment
> if this sort of thing goes on.
> Do you realize this? You should.

Other industries tried the appeal to patriotism, with varying results. The shipping industry contrived to save much from the wreck by popularizing the notion of cruises. In the mournful winter of 1931, an advertising agency suggested to the newspapers that a little less gloom might stimulate Christmas trade; not perhaps a very grave attempt to interfere with the liberty of the Press.

How the manufacturers of a tonic wine met the challenge of the depression was described with unusual candour to the *Advertiser's Weekly* by a representative of the firm in January 1931:

Rising unemployment figures, it seemed, were inevitably reducing our market; yet we refused to be intimidated by this. Consideration of the matter showed that even those who drew unemployment benefit represented a potential market and one likely to be productive enough if approached in the right way. So instead of neglecting the unemployed we visualized them as a prospective market of 2,500,000 people.

As a result of this visionary change of policy sales of the wine increased spectacularly.

Even before the depression the drink trade had been spending £2,000,000 a year on advertising. Licensing policy was to satisfy not to create demand for intoxicants; but advertising gave the 'Trade' a chance 'to capture the younger generation growing up' (in the words of the *Brewers' Journal*). Disapproval of these tactics was expressed by the Royal Commission on Licensing 1929–1931:

We are unable to accept the contention that the effect [of liquor advertising] is merely to transfer demand from unadvertised to advertised beverages. That admittedly is one of the results, but all advertising experience establishes that the advertisement of goods of any particular brand tends to swell the total demand for all goods of that kind. Support for this view may be found in the strong advocacy by leading 'Trade' journals of bulk advertisement of intoxicants.

The Commission also complained that many liquor advertisements contained palpable scientific untruths, and deplored the use made of anonymous medical testimonials. It thought the flow of advertisements was 'almost a public nuisance', but could think of no way of limitation which would not be open to substantial objection.

With the depression came an outbreak of aggressive 'gift wars' among the big advertisers, notably the tobacco companies and the Press barons. Apologists of the 'premium' offer argued that it was an ideal tonic in times of slump, for a manufacturer gingered up not only his own trade but the one whose goods he 'gave' away. Also, they said, it was a hallowed way of hacking into a monopoly market. As the battles intensified, not only pots and pans but shirts, pairs of shoes, and trousers were distributed by the half million and then the million. The most ruthless competition was that between the newspapers, jostling for the elusive two-million circulation. Some 50,000 canvassers tramped the streets, persuading housewives who already took in more than one paper to take another, even if only for the duration of the latest free offer. Some households changed their allegiance as the needs of the kitchen varied. On top of all this there were 'mammoth' contests, calling for the minimum of skill, in which 'pension prizes' of up to £10 a week for life were offered.

By 1931 the pace had become too hot even for Fleet Street. Besides, advertisers were growing angry. Although newspapers were at last revealing their audited net sales (the Audit Bureau of Circulations was established in 1931), it was obvious that circulations built on bribery were useless; the public did not read half the newspapers it took in. An armistice of sorts was declared in 1932. Just over a year later, on 6 March 1933, the *Daily Herald* invited its readers to turn to page four of the next day's issue in order to read of 'A Stupendous Attraction'. Those who did so had their expectations dashed when they found a small paragraph reading: 'Owing to unforeseen circumstances, the announcement of the Stupendous Attraction referred to yesterday is postponed.' Six days later, however, the unforeseen circumstances had evidently been mastered, and the 'Stupendous Attraction' had become a 'Stupendous Sensation'. In a full-page announcement the *Daily Herald* said that it had decided to present its readers with 'a wonderful souvenir to celebrate the Third Birthday under its new management and also its unparalleled progress towards the two million'. The souvenir was a sixteen-volume set of the works of Charles Dickens, of 'a rare, exquisite beauty', bound in 'lustrous silk-grained cloth, tooled and decorated in real 22-carat gold', each volume protected by 'glassine'. Any comparable set bought elsewhere would cost at least £4 4s., yet *Herald* readers could obtain this set for 11s. Production was costing £100,000 and was giving employment to thousands of British workpeople. 'A complete set of Dickens is the rightful heritage of every English home,' said the announcement; and in an afterthought: 'Needless to say, no advertising matter of any kind appears in any volume in the set.'

After twelve giftless months it seemed too good an offer to miss, and the public rose to the bait. Intense exasperation was created in the camps of the *Daily Mail*, the *Daily Express*, and the *News Chronicle*, which quickly warned their readers that if they were contemplating changing their allegiance to a certain other newspaper, 'it has been ascertained that the cost of production and delivery of the books in question is *less than the* 11*s. they are being asked to pay*'. ('A Dickens of a Bargain' was the *News Chronicle*'s heading.) At last, dog had rounded on dog.

Nor was that all. After the lapse of only a very few days, the *Daily Mail*, the *Daily Express*, and the *News Chronicle* all offered sets of Dickens's works for ten shillings – at an undoubted loss. The *Mail*, though it had belittled the *Herald*'s offer, was not prepared to belittle Dickens. 'No one can turn to this library in vain,' it said, 'It offers the delights of unrivalled comedy, the stimulus of the drama, the inspiration of many emotions.' Soon the country was in danger of foundering beneath a deadweight of Dickens; millions of sets were distributed. For the most part unread, they still ornament the shelves of countless homes up and down Britain. Both the *Daily Herald* and *Daily Express* achieved their two-million circulation. Lord Beaverbrook was candid enough to admit that during the later stages of the gift wars he was buying 'readers' by the hundred thousand at a cost of 8s. 3d. each.

The presentation of free gifts, whether by newspapers or tobacco firms, was often represented as a social service, an act of dedication to the common weal. On 7 March 1933 the *Daily Herald* carried this advertisement, under a bold heading:

AN OPEN LETTER TO THE RIGHT HON. GEORGE LANSBURY, PC MP
Sir, you have always given prime consideration to developments that will improve the social life of the people. This prompts us to call your attention to a plan directed towards a similar aim – the Kensitas Greater Service Plan.
We, along with other cigarette manufacturers, have given cards and inserts in the packets which were of little or no value. But today we give instead FIVE CERTIFICATES in EVERY PACKET of 20 CIGARETTES – certificates of real definite worth, exchangeable for articles of finest craftsmanship. . . .

These advertisements were sharply criticized in Parliament by supporters of the Gift Coupons Bill introduced in 1933 by Lt-Col. J. T. C. Moore-Brabazon (Lord Brabazon). Its object was 'to make unlawful the issue and redemption of gift coupons', but not to ban cash discounts. 'We say it is intolerable that if I buy cigarettes I can eventually, by the saving of coupons, get a watch or some other commodity and deprive the jeweller of the opportunity of selling me that watch,' said Lt-Col. Moore-Brabazon. 'No retailer today knows where he is, because at any moment a commodity which he normally stocks may become a gift for coupons.' There was a traffic in coupons in journals like *Exchange and Mart*. A man wanting a guinea razor could get it by buying ten shillings' worth of coupons, without ever having eaten, smoked, or worn the product which the razor was supposed to advertise.

Opponents of the Bill argued, in or out of Parliament, that to offer premiums was a legitimate form of advertising; that a man who handed on to the customer a share of his profit, while helping himself to a bigger share of the market, was committing no crime; that the premium advertiser offered a finer gradation of price than the man who simply added or subtracted halfpence; and that a discount in kind was no less ethical than the co-operative societies' discount in cash. The Bill was withdrawn, and the battles continued.

There were two kinds of unemployment, 'normal' and seasonal. In 1933 a one-man drive was started with the object of reducing the latter kind. A larger-than-usual heading read: 'I dare not write home to Madge and tell her I've lost my job!' Something about the layout suggested that this was not just another cry from an errant young husband who had been sacked for not slicking back his hair with the correct dressing. It was in fact an advertisement by the pipe-smoking Mr Murphy, who made radio sets. The advertisement went on:

I did not make that up. It is from a letter one of our 'hands' wrote when he got a week's notice recently. He was a good man. Why was he discharged? Why? Because you don't need wireless sets in the summer. Because you'd rather wait for the autumn. And that is why hundreds of good men from every radio factory in the country get the sack during the spring and summer.

Who says you don't want wireless sets in the summer? Do you know anyone with a wireless set who shuts it off from April to September?

Why do you wait for the Exhibition? Are you expecting some marvellous new inventions? Well, you've seen some of them in the last few years. This 'marvellous invention' business is claptrap – and nobody knows it better than the wireless manufacturer.

Mr Murphy kept up the attack throughout the summer. 'We are going to spend thousands of pounds on advertising, at the time when it produces the least results. If anyone says this is a stunt to sell Murphy sets, then he is an ass.' Half of his readers, Murphy pointed out, paid for their sets all the year round, so they might as well take delivery of them all the year round. In this way they would get better and cheaper sets, and give work-people permanent employment.

The public had often been reminded that if they did not buy British they would put their fellow Britons out of work. Murphy put a specific, concrete case to them. His campaign was successful; and it affords a useful and meritorious example of advertising being used to spread a seasonal demand.

The advertisers whose ascendancy began in the depression were the manufacturers of patent foods and medicines, vitamin pills, and nerve tonics. On them is to be blamed the frenetic, frightened look of so much of the newspaper advertising in the middle thirties. Some of these products were useful and filled a need; it was the method by which they were publicized that called for condemnation. Fierceness of competition no doubt led firms into making claims they would rather not have made. It is important to remember that there were sensible, intelligent, stimulating advertisements of worth-while goods in this decade, but they had to struggle hard for attention.

One half of the world, it appeared, was undernourished, and the other half was trying to slim. The most improbable commodities were advertised as being ideal for building up tissue; beer, for instance. Equally improbable commodities were proclaimed as ideal for stripping off 'ugly fat'. A cartoonist could have drawn (and possibly did) a picture of a board of directors watching a coin-tossing ceremony: 'Heads we say it puts on weight, tails we say it takes off fat.' Everywhere were ugly pictures of fat women in one-piece bathing costumes; only slim, pretty women were portrayed in two-piece suits.

The world was further divided into those who were trying to grow hair and those who were trying to remove it. No other decade can have produced so many 'amazing hair discoveries' as this. No less depressing than the pictures of fat women in bathing costumes were those of completely bald women who were said to have grown luxuriant hair after a lapse of anything up to twenty years.

Many a page had a grim completeness of its own. At the top, news headlines told of Hitler and Mussolini, of Armageddon round the corner. At the bottom and sides were offers of aspirin and nerve tonics and vitamin pills, illustrated often by pictures of women with vibrating heads and suicidal looks in their eyes ('she didn't care whether she lived or not'). Not only were daughters implored to buy tonics for their depressed mothers, and mothers to coax yeast into their ailing daughters, but all classes were ordered to push pills down the throats of their dogs and cats and thereafter give them the 'vitaminized' foods without which they could not hope to survive in this strident century.

In 'the golden morning of the world', according to one advertiser, it had all been very different. People had been vital, buoyant, carefree. (Sceptics wanted to know how the firm knew this.) Now the world was full of men and women tired out at thirty, suffering not only from the old primal diseases but from Incomplete Elimination, Summer Sluggishness, Enlarged Pores, Middle-Aged Spread, Cosmetic Skin, Body Odour, Iron Starvation, Tell-Tale Tongue, Smoker's Fur, Itching Scalp, and a score of other afflictions.

According to the makers of tonic wines, Britain was a nation of nagging homes. One firm recommended its wine 'to put an end to those bickerings when your eyes get moist and your husband doesn't notice . . . those evenings when there seems to be nothing to do but turn on the radio . . . to make your lips red without lipstick and your eyes bright without tears and you and your husband lovers again'. A rival wine had a similar promise under a screaming headline: 'I'm fed up with your eternal nag, nag, nag!'

One advertiser – Horlick's – had discovered that what people were suffering from was Night Starvation: 'Right through the night you've been burning up reserves of energy, without food to replace it. Breathing alone takes twenty thousand muscular efforts every night.' It was a daunting thought; few had supposed that sleeping could be so strenuous a pastime. Other advertisers were blaming the malaise of civilization on uric acid, showing magnified pictures of bits of shrapnel in fantastic shapes which were said to be 'acid daggers' in the human veins.

So it went on. . . . 'Ted just sits and reads the paper.' 'Bill says it's just too hot to dance.' . . . 'He stopped holding hands, and it was her fault.' . . . 'George says he'll be late – it's that blonde again, I'm sure.' . . . 'It's not only active people who get B.O.' . . . 'My feet are cold and wet and I'm all shivery. . . . My feet are wet too, but it makes no difference, because I'm wearing Iodine Socks.' . . .

Even the Postmaster-General joined in the nerve war. 'Fears and doubts thrive well in the home where the telephone is not,' he said, below a picture of a husband worrying because his wife had not returned home from visiting friends. One of the Post Office advertisements was harshly criticized in 1936 in Parliament, and probably also at teachers' conferences of that year. It suggested that the telephone could be used by anxious parents to ring up school to inquire whether their children were on the way home or had been kept in. One use of the telephone which the Postmaster-General did not advocate was as a medium of advertising. Insurance agents, among others, hit on the idea of ringing up prospective customers and delivering a brisk, cheery sales talk. *The Times* warned on 10 March 1927 that any extension of the idea would make the telephone service unpopular; but the practice still survives.

Occasionally, even the least curious member of the public must have wondered what evidence an advertiser could produce, if challenged, to support the claims which began 'Scientific tests prove . . .' No doubt it was true, as one advertisement said, that 'the acid in your stomach would burn a hole in the carpet'. It was not the sort of experiment of which the average man would seek personal proof. But what about the advertiser who said: 'Tests show . . . users have ONE-THIRD EXTRA energy at their command.' How were these tests conducted? How was human energy measured? Were a hundred men and women segregated from their fellows, half of them given the appropriate night food and the others not, and then the whole lot set to work in separate treadmills, while 'scientists' took observations? Other advertisements quoted doctors as saying that a certain soap gave one in three women lovelier skins over a given period. How did the doctors contrive a laboratory test for assessing loveliness? A face powder manufacturer cried: 'Women, Here's a Contract! . . . Try this new mystifying complexion secret. Be popular with men tonight or your money refunded. This powder has been thoroughly tested by scientists and guaranteed to be definitely lectro-static.' How many women took up this challenge? How many scientists could have defined 'lectro-static'?

Yet perhaps this way of selling cosmetics was no worse than that recorded by Robert Sinclair in *Metropolitan Man*: 'Manufacturers of cosmetics have now taken to advertising their wares by claiming that they were successfully used by harlots to seduce diseased Bourbon princes.'

Occasionally, but very occasionally, an advertiser tripped up, as the manufacturers of the Carbolic Smoke Ball had tripped up. In 1932 a firm manufacturing 'Letrik' electric combs found itself taken to court. Its advertisements had run:

What is your trouble?
Is it grey hair? In ten days not a grey hair left. £500 Guarantee.
Is it a bald patch? Covered with new hair in 72 hours. £500 Guarantee.
Is it straight and lifeless? Permanent wave starts the first day. Becomes full and natural colour in 48 hours. £500 Guarantee.
Is it falling out? Roots are strengthened and falling out stops in 18 hours. £500 Guarantee.
Is it dandruff? Definitely stopped same day. Scalp clear in three days. £500 Guarantee.

It was explained that electricity flowed from the battery in the comb 'down the hair stems and through the roots – waking them up, bringing them to life, like pouring life-giving water on parched soil'.

The plaintiff, who was a director of an advertising company, paid 3s. 6d. for a comb, used it for ten days as directed and found that his hair was still grey. He said the only result was that the comb 'scratched his head and made him very uncomfortable'. He therefore claimed £500.

The case inspired a certain amount of judicial humour, Mr Justice Rowlatt being anxious to know whether the comb would turn his ermine black. The plaintiff was asked:

Which would you rather have – your hair black again or £500? – My hair black.

A director of the defending company said that a million of the combs had been sold, and only four claims made. The guarantee of £500 was 'a mere flourish'. Mr Justice Rowlatt awarded £500 against the company – 'rather a windfall for the plaintiff'. He had said earlier that he was not in favour of this kind of action; leaving it to be presumed that he was not in favour of this type of advertisement.

Sex appeal was now used to sell other things besides rayon. One of Mr Drage's rivals had a curious advertisement of this kind in the *Daily Herald*, and doubtless elsewhere, in November 1933. An attractive lady in undress, sitting at her dressing-table, hears a knock and calls out 'Who's that? You can't come in yet!' The caller is insistent, so without bothering to put on a dressing-gown, the lady half-opens the door of her bedroom, and exclaims: 'Good heavens, Rob! What's bitten you? You look all washed up!' It emerges in due course that Rob is the lady's brother, and that she is a married woman, though it does not emerge how he gained admission into the house. While she stands with a shapely leg displayed in the doorway, her brother tells his story:

I'm back again in circulation! Carol's given me the air – says I'm wasting her life – Ought to have a home for her by now – that I'm a flat tyre – AND SOME! You know I can't afford to sink all my savings on furniture.

M'm. That's so. But it's 'Easier to Pay —'s Four-Year Way'. Wouldn't a home like this suit you both?

Gosh, that's an idea. Carol says this place always looks simply swagger. I'd forgotten you went to —'s.

Carol's right – you need gingering up. Why keep her waiting, with —'s ready to do the waiting for you?

The conversation goes on in this vein, while the reader waits apprehensively for Rob's brother-in-law to return suddenly. But Rob eventually goes away to order some furniture on credit, and his sister goes away to put on some clothes.

Social historians of the future must make what they can of advertisements like that; and also of dialogues like this:

ELEANOR: Who ever is that handsome young man who has just come into the room? I have never seen him before. He has all the room looking at him: How bronzed and healthy he looks!

HER FRIEND: Oh, that's Jack Mordaunt. He is just home from the East. He's been excavating, and you call him a young man, why, he is older than I am, and I'm 48. While he was in the East he put on his dinner jacket every night. He let the Arabs know that he was civilized and he swears by — Cream. . . . Many a time he has shaved without water. You have often to do those things in the East, as water is so scarce.

ELEANOR: How interesting! I want to be the first girl to be introduced.

In 1935 the drink trade survived an attempt in the House of Lords to curb its methods of advertising. Lord Arnold quoted some of the brewers' slogans of the day, which included 'For an A1 Nation Beer is Best' and 'Rich Nourishment in Every Glass'. There was as much nourishment in a glass of beer, he said, as in three fifths of an ounce of bread, and for the same outlay a man could buy twenty-two times as much nourishment in the form of milk. 'I see but little difference between some of these advertisements and getting money by false pretences,' said Lord Arnold. The indoctrination of the young generation had now reached the stage at which schoolchildren were wearing lapel badges in praise of stout.

The 'Trade' did not lack defenders in the House. This excerpt from *Hansard* of 28 March speaks for itself:

Lord Rhayader: I see advertisements all over the place 'Guinness is good for you' –
The Earl of Iveagh: It is true.
Lord Rhayader: It is a matter of opinion, perhaps.
The Earl of Iveagh: My word is as good as yours.
Lord Rhayader: I am told that if I put up 'Guinness is bad for you' –
The Earl of Iveagh: It would be untrue.

The Earl of Rhayader was trying to say that if he did as he said, he would presumably be sued for libel. Collective propaganda on the lines of 'Beer is best' could be challenged less expensively. Temperance propagandists answered that particular boast with 'Beer is best left alone' – a reminder that the ideal slogan is one which cannot readily be perverted by the hostile or the humorous.

Probably few of the public resorted to beer for the sake of its rich nourishment; they drank it for stimulation. In their daring moments the copywriters claimed that beer would 'set you up' or 'put heart in you', but usually – when not offering rich nourishment – they enthused about the product's cleanness, sparkle, honesty, purity, flavour, and golden glow. They invited drinkers to admire the bubbles rising and the lacy pattern made by the froth. In short they wrote of beer as if it were a teetotal beverage. Even more restrained were the copywriters who praised spirits; an innocent might have supposed that the biggest kick one could get out of whisky was to hold it up to the light and admire its magical colour. The makers of tonic wines, as we have seen, had fewer inhibitions; theirs was a product to recreate wedded bliss.

Most newspapers and magazines maintained their own black lists of advertisers, their own lists of banned phrases. In the former category came firms who ignored customers' complaints or who had not the distributive machinery to fulfil their promises; manufacturers of nostrums known to contain actively dangerous drugs; firms engaging in 'snowball' enterprises; firms peddling land overseas; firms with directors of proved or strongly suspected dishonesty; companies with too-boastful prospectuses. Some newspapers refused to take moneylenders' advertisements or adoption appeals. Most of them 'vetted' with great care the advertisements of massage establishments, private dancing classes, and French teachers.

The Advertising Association, having failed to bring about a general agreement among newspapers and advertisers to clean up medicinal advertising, began to press for legislation. In 1936 a Bill which had been four years in the framing, and which was approved by the Pharmaceutical Society and even by some of the proprietary medicine firms, was presented to Parliament. It proposed to ban the advertising of cures for cancer, tuberculosis, and the other intractable illnesses which had been listed by the Select Committee of 1914. Unfortunately the Bill came up in the House of Commons on a day when the minds of all right-thinking Englishmen were focused on a point more than two hundred miles from Westminster: at Aintree. Nevertheless the initial attendance in the Commons on 27 March 1936 was such as to inspire one speaker to congratulate the Bill's chief pilot on 'such a good house on this *grand national* occasion'. Mr A. Duckworth, who moved the second reading, went to perhaps unnecessary pains to point out that the Bill attempted to do much less than had been recommended by the Select Committee in 1914. Even if passed, 'it would still leave open an enormous field for the swindler and the cheapjack'. Also it was milder in its provisions than legislation which had been passed in the Dominions. These were not the most cogent arguments in the Bill's favour, and its critics – notably Sir Arnold Wilson – attacked it on the grounds that it did not go far enough. Why did it not also ban the advertising of cures for asthma, rheumatism, the common cold, and even baldness?

Others thought that the Bill was more likely to safeguard the interests of the doctors than of the public. There had been a great deal of lobbying by those whose activities stood to be curtailed; one Member had received 1,350 letters on behalf of a single advertiser. Much eloquence was expended for and against the Bill, but at sixteen minutes after one o'clock it was found that there were not forty members present, and the House was counted out. That year £2,500,000 was spent on Press advertising of proprietary medicines.

Next year the Government was inspired to run its own slogan 'Use Your Health Services', but the amount spent on this campaign was only what a private manufacturer would have spent on a single laxative. In its *Report on the British Health Service*, published in 1937, P.E.P. (Political and Economic Planning) said:

It is particularly disturbing to observe how official and scientific pronouncements and advice on health matters are promptly seized by the commercial interests to make capital for products the consumption of which is often irrelevant to, and may even be directly opposed to, the straightforward following of the advice quoted.

P.E.P. also deplored that the spreading of distorted notions by the makers of proprietary medicines had made it necessary to mount costly campaigns on behalf of elementary products such as milk and basic services which ought to be widely known. Besides the Drink More Milk campaign of the Milk Marketing Board, there was an Eat More Bread campaign by the Millers Mutual Association, a Herrings For Health campaign by the Herring Industry Board and an Eat More Bananas campaign by the firm of Fyffe.

That Drink More Milk campaign led to a keen controversy in January 1938, when the British Medical Association asked newspapers to insert an advertisement headed 'Is ALL MILK Safe to Drink?' (the contention being that milk ought to be tested for tuberculosis). Leading newspapers turned down this advertisement, on the grounds that it 'knocked' the Drink More Milk campaign and furthermore was a 'scare' advertisement. As the newspapers were already full of scare advertisements, this sudden solicitude puzzled many. However, the British Medical Association modified its copy to read 'Drink Safe Milk', and most of the newspapers published it. The *Daily Express* still declined, arguing that the effect of the advertisement was to persuade the public that only pasteurized milk was safe.

Lord Horder was the next to enter the lists against the medicine firms. Vexed that these interests had been excluded from the provisions of the Food and Drugs Act, he rose in the Lords on 26 July 1938 to call for a curtailment of their operations. Each year, he said, they bled the country of between £25,000,000 and £30,000,000, which was nearly equal to the total budget of the hospitals. In the long run, doctors had more patients, not fewer, through the activities of the proprietary medicine trade: 'ultimately the undertaker benefits sooner and oftener than he might'. The Government had launched a campaign to improve the national physique, but the makers of medicines and foods waged another campaign, 'led by very subtle and skilled generals bent on maintaining national ill-health, moral and physical, in order to have a ready market for their goods'. For every £100 that the Government spent on making people health-conscious, quack medicine mongers spent £1,000 in making them disease-conscious.[1] The Government derived £1,000,000 out of the sorry business, which was less than it could have derived if it had plugged some of the tax loopholes. As it was, cough mixtures and pills for backache were taxed, but chest mixtures and kidney pills were not.

Lord Horder criticized the way medicine vendors preyed on human fears. 'Much of this trade is in fact a huge form of blackmail. . . . The wretched man who does not take a laxative begins to wonder if he can possibly be well without it.' It was an eloquent indictment, but no Parliamentary action resulted. The country had to wait until it was neck-high in another world war before the appropriate Act was passed.

The 'debunking' of advertising which was so popular in America in the early thirties (*see* next chapter) had its echoes in Britain. In 1933 Dorothy Sayers, who had worked in an advertising agency, let out some of the secrets in her detective story *Murder Must Advertise*. The novice in this story had to learn 'that the word "pure" was dangerous, because, if lightly used, it laid the client open to prosecution by Government inspectors,

1. In 1937 the heaviest expenditure on advertising was by manufacturers of proprietary medicines; then followed toilet goods, cigarettes, drink, soap.

whereas the words "highest quality", "finest ingredients", "packed under the best conditions" had no legal meaning and were therefore safe ... that the *Morning Star* would not accept any advertisements containing the word "cure", though there was no objection to such expressions as "relieve" or "ameliorate" ... that if, by the most far-fetched stretch of ingenuity, an indecent meaning could be read into a headline, that was the meaning that the great British Public would infallibly read into it. ...'[1]

Miss Sayers discoursed further on the subject of advertisers' double-talk in an article in the *Spectator* of 19 November 1937. 'Plain lies are dangerous,' she said. 'The only weapons left [to the copywriter] are the *suggestio falsi* and the *suppressio veri*, and his use even of these would be very much more circumscribed if one person in ten had ever been taught how to read.' Her conclusion was that 'we have the kind of advertising we deserve', and that 'those who prefer their English sloppy have only themselves to thank if the advertising writer uses his mastery of vocabulary and syntax to mislead their minds'. This pleased neither advertisers nor their critics. Surely, it was argued, the ill-educated were entitled to some protection? Surely the reading of an advertisement need not be a battle of wits?

Advertisers were sometimes accused of trying to influence editorial policy, but little serious evidence was ever produced. One or two attempts recoiled on those who made them. In 1933 Sir Edgar Sanders, of the Brewers Society, launching a £130,000 publicity drive, said:

If we begin advertising in the Press we shall see that the continuation of our advertising is contingent upon the fact that we get editorial support as well in the same newspapers. In that way it is wonderful how you can educate public opinion, and generally without making it too obvious that there is a publicity campaign behind it.

These rash words brought a smart rebuff from the newspaper proprietors, and also from the Archbishop of Canterbury.

The P.E.P. Report on the Press, published in 1938, said:

There is undoubtedly a tendency to tone down or suppress minor items of news or features if they seem likely to annoy advertisers or

1. Both the British and American publics are also adept at detecting the omission of wedding rings in pictures of mothers.

potential advertisers, and an even more serious tendency to prevent problems, emphasis on which would be inconvenient to advertisers, from securing widespread discussion, if possible. Nevertheless if a big issue burst into prominence no newspaper would dare to jeopardize its circulation by suppressing it or even making too little of it to please its advertisers.

The Report considered that 'if the advertisement manager [of a newspaper] wants a policy toned down in case advertisers should be offended, it is more likely to be done than if the advertisers themselves actively complained'.

A famous editor went so far as to tell the Empire Press Union that newspapers ought to avoid the 'needless folly' of placing reports of traffic accidents next to motor-car advertisements. He might have added 'or of putting paragraphs about drunken drivers next to advertisements of beers which claimed to "stimulate the faculties" '.

America:
8 Giving 'Ginks' a Goal

In 1916, before America entered the First World War, the publisher of the *New York Times*, Adolph S. Ochs, addressed the Associated Advertising Clubs of the World, who five years earlier had pledged themselves to a policy of 'Truth in Advertising'. He said:

It may startle you if I say that I doubt if there is any business in the world in which there is so much waste of time, money, and energy as in advertising and its correlative instrumentalities. It may be rank heresy for me to say this, yet I affirm that more than fifty per cent of money spent on advertising is squandered and is a sheer waste of printer's ink, because little thought and less intelligence are applied, and ordinary common sense is entirely lacking; too frequently the dishonesty stamped on its face is about all the intelligent reader discerns.

These were harsh words, but the advertising men bore them bravely. Ochs had always been quick to find fault with the advertising offered him, and he had rejected millions of dollars' worth – a policy which had paid handsomely. Now his paper was offering 100 dollars for information leading to the conviction of anyone inserting a false or misleading advertisement in the newspaper. Other papers were cleaning up their advertising columns too, and claiming great virtue thereby, even boasting how much their honesty was costing them.

All too soon the American advertising men were to have an opportunity, like their opposite numbers in England, of proving their skill, high-mindedness, and patriotism by promoting fervent campaigns on behalf of the Red Cross and Liberty Bonds. Against all their professional instincts, they appealed to the public *not* to spend money. One Boston paper, presumably under pressure of the big stores, declined to print an advertisement urging the public to buy only necessities and had to pay 500 dollars for breach of contract. Despite such difficulties, the Liberty Bonds campaign was triumphantly successful. For every dollar spent on advertising, some 1,500 dollars were coaxed into savings.

With the end of the war, all shackles on output were snapped. Now came the rush to capture the new fields of commerce. War profits which the tax collector might otherwise have garnered were thrown into vast advertising campaigns. Among those climbing over each other on the hill of riches, few listened to the Government recruiting advertisements of 1919, offering 'the chance of a lifetime to see the battlefields of France and the Rhine . . . You go to shows, dances, movies, you meet agreeable people in the hostess houses, you get acquainted with nice girls, in fact you have a better time than most civilians.'

Soon the factories were pouring out a stream of highly covetable but expensive commodities which somehow had to be absorbed into the American way of life – cars by the hundred thousand, vastly more reliable, and cheaper; newfangled radio sets (the great boom began in 1922); ice-boxes and refrigerators, automatic furnaces, washing machines, pastel-hued water-closets, plushier coffins. On his bathroom alone a man was expected to spend six months' salary in order to bring it up to Hollywood standards. 'From a mere utility, the modern bathroom has developed into a spacious shrine of cleanliness and health,' said an advertisement of the house of Crane in 1925, and the shrine in the picture was of an arrogant magnificence. It contained, among other things, a 'dental lavatory of vitreous china, twice fired'.

People had to be taught to want these things, to feel ashamed of not having them. The volume of production grew terrifyingly. Soon it was not enough for a man merely to buy a new car, a new radio, a new washing machine. He must buy the latest model every year, and discard the old one, whether it functioned efficiently or not. Otherwise factories would close from the Atlantic to the Pacific and the golden century would come down in ruins. It was an American's patriotic duty to 'buy till it hurts'. To plead lack of money was no excuse, when he could gain almost anything he wanted by making a down payment. The man who was contented with his lot was a traitor to the community, un-American.

The twin pillars of this civilization were the copywriter and the salesman (though there were some who called them caterpillars). In *Only Yesterday*, Frederick Lewis Allen wrote:

The public generally speaking could be relied upon to regard with complacence the most flagrant assaults upon its credulity by the advertiser and the most outrageous invasions of its privacy by the salesman; for the public was in a mood to forgive every sin committed in the holy name of business.

The torch-bearers, the trail-blazers of advertising gathered at Atlantic City[1] in 1923, and delivered themselves of such aphorisms as: 'Appeal to reason in your advertising, and you appeal to about four per cent of the human race'. They noted with pleasure that 'thanks to modern education, teaching today includes matters of practical use and swings the gateway to the child mind wide open for the entrance of the advertising message' – and then went on to discuss how best to break down the sales resistance of Boy Scouts. One speaker who was applauded as much for his enterprise as his sense of humour was J. H. Mowbray, vice-president of a Pennsylvania firm. He opened his speech as follows:

Our ultimate consumer never reorders, yet we manufacture 500 articles, and are in first place by so wide a margin that we have no near competitors. We never get a second shot at our man. This may seem strange, but there are a million and a third deaths in the United States each year, and our principal product is embalming fluid.

Some of the methods by which the American nation was cozened and coerced into embalming its dead will be familiar to those who have read Cedric Belfrage's scarifying *Abide With Me*. To the average person in Britain, content that his body should rot 'to flowers and fruit with Adam and all mankind', the advertisements of the American casket and vault manufacturers, with their promises of bodily immortality, were oddly shocking. Here are excerpts from an announcement which appeared in a family magazine, the *Saturday Evening Post*, on 12 February 1927:

How often we find cause only for regret in our memories of the manner in which we disposed of the remains of our loved ones!

1. Their deliberations are recorded in *Advertising and Selling*, edited by Noble T. Praigg.

We were thoughtless, perhaps. It might have been that at the time we didn't know. It would have been so easy to provide adequate protection against the elements.

However, it is idle to dwell on things past. Let us look into the future calmly and follow the example of thousands of families who rely upon the Clark Grave Vault to defeat Nature's destructive forces.

For never yet has this vault failed to protect its precious contents from the hurtful elements of the earth. . . .

On a cruder level, as Belfrage describes, the manufacturers of preposterous caskets instructed funeral directors how to bully the bereaved. 'This is the last tribute you will ever be able to pay to your dear mother (father, wife, sister, husband, etc.). *How can anything be too good?*' So the worst racket of all was built up: the embalming or 'preparing' of the 'loved one', the painting with cosmetics, the replacing of damaged ears and noses by 'new', the dressing up in expensive new clothes; the lying in state in dim tapestried pavilions, traversed by theatrical shafts of light; the perpetual organ music, the paintings, the statues; the final reluctant interment in Gardens of Rest, Vales of Sleep. Death was a cunning and greedy advertiser. He even demanded silver and gold plated coffins for his elect. And on their last resting-places he stipulated a Greek-pillared mausoleum of immemorial granite, or at the least a perdurable headstone styled by the Rock of Ages Corporation (see almost any issue of the *National Geographic Magazine* in the middle twenties). Who, with the power to invest in such funerary splendours, would lend an ear to the cry of the low-price mortician, with his 'Repose-Room Free, and Use of Twenty Palms'?

The delegates to that convention of 1923 talked at some length about church advertising. Joseph A. Richards, president of a New York advertising agency, said that if he were consulted by a group of churchmen, he would first ensure that their church was a worthwhile, going concern. He would say to them:

It may be that you have the reputation of having stale goods; maybe you are foolishly stressing the sidelines. It may be the first assistant sales manager, the pastor, is out of harmony with the Sales Manager, the Holy Spirit, and therefore all the salesmen, the members, are demoralized and don't know what they are selling, or have quit their job and are just hanging around, blaming the preacher and their fellow members for the fact that the church does not 'go'.

Once assured that the church had 'something to sell worth having', however, the agency would throw all its efforts into the campaign. 'I would make my church advertising prayed-over advertising', the speaker promised. 'I would no more expect to put out an announcement of any kind which had not been individually submitted to the Sales Manager in prayer than I would expect to preach a sermon or lead a prayer meeting without so doing.'

The integration of the Holy Trinity with the advertising business was carried a stage further by Bruce Barton, author of the best-seller *The Man Nobody Knows* (1925). From this it appeared that Jesus 'would be a national advertiser today ... as he was the great advertiser of his own day'. He had always been 'the most popular dinner guest in Jerusalem'. Of his enterprise, sufficient to say that 'he picked up twelve men from the bottom ranks of business and forged them into an organization that conquered the world'. Jesus, according to Barton, 'recognized the basic principle that all good advertising is news'. And as a copy-writer he was without equal. 'Take any one of the parables, no matter which – you will find that it exemplifies all the principles on which advertising textbooks are written. Always a picture in the first sentence; crisp, graphic language and a message so clear that even the dullest cannot escape it.'

It was inspirational stuff this, for the copywriter who had begun to doubt the dignity of his calling, who had been sulking because Thorstein Veblen had described his job as the administering of 'shock effects, tropismatic reactions, animal orientations, forced movements, fixation of ideas, verbal intoxication ... a trading on the range of human infirmities which blossom in devout observances and bear fruit in the psychopathic wards'.[1]

Half-way through the twenties there was a campaign to adver-tise advertising. Examples are to be found in the pages of *Life* in 1925. One full-page announcement shows a meek, hard-driven husband wincing as his wife looks up from a magazine to say: 'Andy, I want one of these electric washing machines.' Andy begins to blow off steam; he is even allowed to say: 'Sometimes I get mighty mad at advertising.' But everybody knows, including Andy, that this is a foolish attitude. When Andy cools off a little,

1. *Absentee Ownership.*

he admits that though it was quite a strain working to pay off that furnace, the results are wonderfully worth while. And Andy goes on:

I begin to see that it's advertising that makes America hum. It gives ginks like me a goal. Makes us want something. And the world is so much the better for our heaving a little harder.

Looking at the advertisements makes me think I've GOT to succeed. Every advertisement is an advertisement for success.

I guess one reason there is so much success in America is because there is so much advertising – of things to want – things to work for.

Another time the little man, whose full name is Andy Consumer, expounds the advertiser's favourite theory of economics:

If you are a manufacturer, don't come round to me with a tape measure and say that you would like to measure me for soup or soap. First go get one million other guys like me, and then I'll listen.

My reason for being so inexclusive is this. I figure that if you get one million other customers, your soup or soap is bound to be good. You can afford to take pains with it. You can hire a lot of experts to experiment their heads off. You can put in the best soup or soap machinery in the world. Your soup will be SOME soup. Your soap will WASH DIRT.

If I placed my order with you PERSONALLY for one can of soup or cake of soap, you might fuss round with it, and it might be good or it might NOT. And if I didn't like it and kicked, you should worry!

But with one million other birds to please, you will please or perish. I should worry!

The only way I know for you to get one million other buyers is for you to advertise. I should worry!

Jollied along by Andy Consumer, dazzled by the flow of glittering goods, the American male began to extend the mortgage on his future. It was no longer enough to buy a new car every year; a man must be taught to buy two cars. He owed it not only to himself and to his family, but to the nation. He must instal not one bathroom but two. He must have a radio not only in his living-room but in every other room. Why should he be allowed to spend the whole day wearing the same pair of spectacles? As early as 1921 the American Association of Wholesale Opticians had begun a campaign to urge people to wear one kind of spectacles for work, another for leisure, another for sport and so on. Mr Boldero, the advertising man in Aldous Huxley's *Antic Hay*

(1923), refers to this campaign, with its insistence on the need for attaining 'incisive poise', and says: 'Since there are few who would not rather be taken in adultery than in provincialism, they rush out to buy four new pairs of spectacles'.

There were limitations to the game of doubling or quadrupling every need. A woman could hardly be expected to wear two wedding rings; but a singularly successful campaign was run to belittle in woman's eyes a plain gold ring and make her demand a platinum one, preferably encrusted with diamonds. Think how many more craftsmen (sound American craftsmen) she was providing with employment!

Many and importunate were the efforts to widen seasonal trade. The Greeting Card Association of America showed much ingenuity in devising cards for other occasions than Christmas and birthdays – get-well cards, sorry-I-forgot-your-anniversary cards and, in due course, sorry-you've-been-run-over cards. The country had to be made more and more anniversary conscious, if necessary by creating and fostering new anniversaries. There had to be new pretexts for gallantries. For a long time the florists had been pointing the path – those same florists who at one time had persuaded certain newspapers to ban the regrettable phrase 'No flowers, by request' in death notices. They had now hit on the highly successful slogan 'Say It With Flowers' – a slogan capable of almost infinite elaboration, humorous or sentimental. Between them, the florists, the greeting-card makers, the candy manufacturers, and the cable companies fostered one of the most successful sales stimulants in Mother's Day, which was worked up from a sentimental idea to a national racket (Father's Day has never enjoyed the same prestige). In a Mom-dominated land, no son dared *not* to send flowers on Mother's Day, and the florists raised the price of flowers steeply when the Day came. It was almost impossible (in the writer's experience) to buy a box of chocolates which was not inscribed with a tribute like 'For you, Mother o' Mine'. And the cables were choked with messages, many of them suggested by the companies themselves, like 'I send a blessing for every thread of silver on my mother's head'. Much of this was achieved by moral pressure on the lines of 'Nothing is too good for your loved ones' – the same tactics which had quadrupled the price of a funeral.

There were other pools into which the American advertiser boldly plunged while Britain – for reasons of nervousness, inhibition, or even good taste – teetered on the brink. One of them was the pool of Culture. Sinclair Lewis's *Babbitt* had assured an audience of realtors that culture – in reasonable doses – was manly and American, even though in other countries art and literature were left to 'a lot of shabby bums living in attics and feeding on booze and spaghetti'. Knowledge, Vocabulary, Conversation, Languages, Etiquette, Poise – these were not only worth acquiring, but *must* be acquired. Of particular interest were the reasons now offered why people should learn French. Nearly a hundred years earlier an English publisher had commended his teach-yourself-French book by saying that it enabled a man to learn the language without exposing himself to the corrupting influence of Paris. Now Americans were urged to make themselves worthy of Paris. The risks of social discomfiture were stressed. One advertisement showed a dinner-jacketed young man humiliated by his inability to explain the menu to his girl. 'A French phrase deftly turned is a devastating weapon', cried another advertiser. 'You can gain a quick mastery of smart French repartee'. An accompanying picture showed one female sophisticate being catty to another; the victim vowed; 'Next time I'll get even with that Mrs B.!'

Other advertisers, instead of needling the reader for being unable to speak French, sought to throw him off his stroke by suggesting that he did not know how to speak English. The boss at his big shiny desk was seen turning down a man for promotion, not because his heels were worn but because he was guilty of saying 'can't hardly'. Whispering women told each other how sorry they were for Mary, married to a man who said 'you was'. How foolish, when nine tenths of everyday mistakes consisted of a mere twenty-five simple-to-correct errors! Another advertiser said: 'You may be using the right words, but are you sure you are *pronouncing* them properly?' Most to be pitied was the man who had no words at all. His fur-laden wife would nag him on the way home from an evening out, and he would accept it abjectly.

'I was never so embarrassed! Just when I wanted to be proud of you, you sat there all evening without saying a single word!'

'Aren't you a bit harsh?'

'Not in the least. Couldn't you think of *anything* to say?'

'No, I couldn't. How was I to get in on that kind of conversation?'

'What did you expect them to talk about – your business?'

'Really Ja –'

'Oh, I'm so ashamed! I wanted to be proud of you, Ted. You are cleverer and more successful than any man at that dinner tonight – but you acted as though you were afraid to open your mouth.'

'I was, dear. What do I know about that philosopher they were talking about – what was his name? Nietzsche. I couldn't even follow their conversation half the time.'

'You should read more. It's pitiful! Why, you didn't even contribute one idea or opinion all evening!'

'I'd like to read more, but you know how much time I have! . . . You made up for both of us, Jane! You were wonderful! How did you ever find out so many things to talk about?'

'I found all that information in Elbert Hubbard's Scrap Book. Now don't tell me you don't know who Elbert Hubbard was! One of America's most versatile men – a writer, craftsman, orator, business man – a many-sided genius. Well, when he was quite young he started reading the greatest thoughts of all the greatest men of all ages. He marked the passages which inspired him most – the *highlights* of literature, the greatest thoughts of the last 2,500 years. He did all your reading for you. . . . It will make you so well-informed – you'll never need to feel embarrassed or uncomfortable in company again.'

Another advertisement showed a man who had swallowed somebody's pocket university holding an audience spellbound with tales of Cleopatra and Diogenes. Such a man, it might be thought, was as likely to be nagged on the way home for hogging the conversation as for failing to enter into it.

Still another short cut to culture was the *Daily Reading Guide*. A picture showed a harassed young man entering an editor's office and saying:

'I can't read worth-while literature! For the past two weeks I've tried daily to read the works of Carlyle, yet I –'

'Stop,' exclaimed the editor. 'Have you ever tried to eat roast beef three times a day seven days a week? That is what is the matter with your reading. You need variety, *daily variety*! Then you will find the reading of immortal literature one of the most engrossing pursuits of your life. Yes, and the most profitable.'

The *Guide* was designed to give twenty minutes' reading a day.

'It is for busy men and women. One year's reading brings you broad culture.'

'He who runs may read' was adopted as a slogan by the publishers of the *Golden Book*. They claimed, moreover, that their volume was just the thing to counteract the jazz fever of the day:

Cocktails, dance halls, freak dress, petting parties are simply defence reactions to the present age. To offer the young people something just as daring, just as exciting, just as amusing – but something that leaves a finely stimulated memory, is the job of the editor of the *Golden Book*.

The editor of this volume was only one of a great band of advertisers with a touching faith in the power of their products to lure the younger generation from dubious ways. Later, stay-out-late daughters were shown coming home early, and bringing their boy friends with them, because Mum was using the only permissible sandwich spread.

Though there was no lack of publishers to predigest, or even to rewrite, the classics, there were still determined attempts to market the classics 'neat'. Plato's *Dialogues* were represented as being topical, challenging, and smart. A copywriter adopted the Hollywood technique in lauding a new edition of the works of Shakespeare – 'every word he ever wrote' – and said: 'Be fascinated by sensuous Cleopatra! Shudder at murderous Macbeth! Chuckle with Falstaff! Thrill with lovesick Romeo!'

Affectionately remembered by many is the advertisement of the U.S. School of Music:

THEY LAUGHED WHEN I SAT DOWN
AT THE PIANO
BUT WHEN I STARTED TO PLAY –!

Arthur had just played 'The Rosary'. The room rang with applause. I decided that this would be a dramatic moment for me to make my debut. To the amazement of all my friends, I strode confidently over to the piano and sat down.

'Jack is up to his old tricks,' somebody chuckled. The crowd laughed. They were all certain that I couldn't play a single note. . . .

Then Jack staggered them all by playing, effortlessly, Beethoven's *Moonlight Sonata*, coyly admitting afterwards that he had learned to play by mail.

Yet there were other things besides culture that the well-rounded citizen must absorb, and the advertiser had them all ready. Babbitt's son had been attracted by the type of advertisement which read:

CAN YOU PLAY A MAN'S PART?

If you are walking with your mother, sister, or best girl, and someone passes a slighting remark or uses improper language, won't you be ashamed if you can't take her part? Well, can you?

We teach boxing and self-defence by mail. . . .

Varied and often improbable were the skills which could be learned by correspondence. In the early years of the century Professor Jesse Beery, of Ohio, had taught horse-riding in this way, imparting (as he said) much information never before disclosed. The secrets of the Samurai were available for a modest subscription, and were as effective for countering gunmen as for relieving constipation. Steadily over the years the field had extended to take in anything from taxidermy ('Mount trophies for sportsmen!') to the making of dental plates. 'Be a Detective!' cried one advertiser. 'Make Secret Investigations. Earn big money. Work home or travel. Fascinating work. Experience unnecessary.' Fascinating it might be, but why waste time in study when one could earn $146 in the first week by operating an electric pants presser?

In a more sober field – and it is important to remember that there *was* a sober field – America's leading insurance company was pioneering a form of advertising for which there could be little but praise. Its purpose was to improve the nation's health, confounding those who obstinately believed that insurance companies were interested only in encouraging sudden death. As well as preaching health in the Press, the Metropolitan Life Insurance Company conducted clean-up campaigns in many big cities, organized health exhibitions, distributed millions of pieces of literature. It tried to persuade parents to take their children to the doctor when they were fit and well. This was a revolutionary policy, at a time when many a British insurance firm's notion of advertising was to print the names of the directors and a balance sheet underneath. The Metropolitan claimed that its strategy was richly successful. 'Measured in dollars and cents it meant the payment in 1922 of $11,828,000 less in death claims than would have been paid if the death rate of 1911 had prevailed in 1922.'

At one stage, the Metropolitan, divining that America's beset-ting ailment was constipation, but deploring the way in which the public was being urged to take daily laxatives, decided to take dignified action. 'One in three suffers from Dyskinesia,' it said, a phrase which no doubt halted readers in their tracks. By the time they found that it meant constipation, they were perhaps ready to send for a free booklet explaining how diet and exercise could remove the complaint.

The Metropolitan's concern to save America from its follies went far beyond illness and constipation. Under a bold heading 'The Toll of Water' in the *National Geographic Magazine* of July 1925, the company told how six thousand persons a year were drowned in America, and urged bathers against showing off and taking risks which jeopardized others. Also it urged the public at large to learn the rules of artificial respiration. 'In July 1924,' said the advertisement, 'the number of deaths from drown-ing among Metropolitan policy-holders was about twice as many as from typhoid fever and diphtheria together.' Three years later the Metropolitan was urging every American to take a sun bath daily.

Not all insurance companies were concerned with fostering health. It was a tempting field for scare methods like 'What will *they* do if you are knocked down?' or 'Would you want *your* wife to go out and work?' Once again it was implied that no sacrifice was too great for the 'loved ones'. Fire-insurance firms sought to shake a man's nerve by showing his house roaring up in flames. Under the heading 'Stick 'Em Up, Santa Claus!' appeared the warning: 'It will be a good plan to apply for insurance . . . the very day you receive your Christmas jewels.' And the Prudential sounded a new alarm, pointing out that the chances of the Stork bringing twins were 'greater than you may think. One in eighty-nine, in fact.'

American bankers also began to burst the fetters of conserva-tism in which they had been self-confined. They adopted the man-to-man approach. A bank manager was painted as a likeable fellow only too anxious to help a client. More and more, public utilities began to advertise their services, as much perhaps to impress their own employees as the public. Big business tried to appear human, friendly, tolerant, sympathetic. When strikes broke out, a corporation sometimes took advertising space to put its own case; so also, if it could raise the funds, did the opposition. Startling to the British eye was another type of advertisement which sometimes appeared at times of industrial unrest: 'We Break Strikes'.

The rawest advertising of the twenties – the advertising which inspired organized protest – was that of the film companies. It was the time when screen actresses were being built up into *femmes fatales*, whose passion destroyed, whose love was death. The 'wickedest' of them all was Theda Bara (anagram of Arab Death). Of Pola Negri, Paramount said in 1925: 'Her magnetism is the divine logic of art, as potent as the perfume of the tuberose which sways the senses. People who saw her first picture *Passion* left the theatre feeling that they had experienced an electric storm.'

One Hollywood copywriter helped himself liberally to a stanza from Byron's *Don Juan*:

HER HUSBAND DREW THE GIRL TO HIM AND – A long, long kiss, a kiss of love and youth and beauty, all concentrating like rays into one focus, kindled from above; such kisses as belong to early days, where heart, soul, and sense in concert move, and the blood is lava, and the pulse is ablaze.

Under pressure from the churches, the women's clubs, and the leagues of decency, Hollywood undertook from time to time to restrain its advertising exuberances. 'Good taste shall be the guiding rule of motion picture advertising,' said a code drawn up in 1930. But still today bosoms burst indefatigably from their containers and half naked lovers are shown in a clinch with lines like 'Emotion swept them like a tidal wave', and the words 'Shame!' 'Lust!' 'Violence!' 'Vengeance!' stab out as freely as they did in the dawn of motion pictures. Quite recently they have been joined by 'Rape!'

No industry did more to destroy the meaning of words. The follies are too familiar to need labouring here – how the story of a couple of cowboys quarrelling over a girl became an epic, the tale of a small-time 'hoofer' a deathless saga. Colossal, terrific, titanic, stupendous – these words became the small change of film advertising. A reservation was put on a whole series of other adjectives, like throbbing, rending, tingling, pulsating, pounding, sizzling, scorching and searing. No story was ever taken from life – it was ripped or torn from the mighty canvas of humanity. When a better-than-ordinary film came along, there were no words left to describe it. 'The greatest love story since the world began' meant in fact 'the greatest love story since last week'. No film maker dared return to a use of modest words, for fear the public should suspect him of lack of confidence in his production. A *Punch* cartoon summed the whole thing up: outside a cinema blazoned with superlatives one citizen was saying to another: 'I wonder if it's worth seeing?'

Cinema managers on both sides of the Atlantic were deluged with 'campaign sheets' full of brash ideas for engineering local publicity and 'tie-ups'. Any manager who carried out one tenth of these suggestions was well on the way to becoming the most unpopular man in his community. He was urged to suborn local clergymen, Army officers and heads of stores to help publicize his attractions; he was told to invite senior pupils from schools to see films about adultery; he was prodded to promote kissing contests and leg competitions, to hire hunchbacks. In a bad week, his instructions might begin: 'Get hold of a couple of camels. . . .' If a safety-first drive was in progress, he would be expected to put out posters saying 'DRIVE SLOWLY to see —'. If a salvage campaign, to say: 'DON'T WASTE a moment: see —'. He was told in starkest terms how to make the most capital out of an 'Adults Only' film.

In cigarette advertising, one of the most aggressive campaigns was that waged on behalf of Lucky Strike, which made its first appearance in 1917 with the slogan 'It's Toasted'. When its rumbustious manufacturer, George Washington Hill, teamed up with Albert Lasker and declared war on Camels, America was smoking some thirty billion cigarettes a year; in his lifetime that total was to be multiplied by ten. Women were the main target. To break down their resistance, Chesterfield showed a girl sitting on a couch with a male smoker, saying: 'Blow some my way.' Hill is credited, if that is the right word, with doing more than any other man to turn women into tobacco slaves. From time to time there were clashes with the Federal Trade Commission, notably over the slogan 'Reach for a Lucky instead of a Sweet', later amended to 'Reach for a Lucky instead'. When Hill died in 1946 he had spent $250,000,000 advertising Lucky Strike.

In December 1927 came an advertising campaign which roused America to near-hysteria: the proclamation and unveiling of the Model 'A' Ford. For eighteen years the famous Model 'T' – the car which was incapable of improvement – had clattered its way round the world. With deep reluctance, and at fabulous cost, Henry Ford had decided to retool his factories in order to produce a new model which could hold its own with the flashy multicoloured Chevrolets and Chryslers which were making the Model 'T' look like a survival from Covered Wagon days. A wildly successful policy of secrecy made the new Ford the nation's main talking-point. Newspaper photographers haunted the roads near Detroit in the hope of catching the new model out on test; they photographed many cars, but not the right one. On 2 December, the day of the unveiling, a million people in New York tried to view the Model 'A', which by late afternoon had to be removed from its showroom and installed in Madison Square Garden. In two thousand newspapers, at a cost of $1,300,000, Ford ran a five-day series of full-page advertisements, revealing all that had hitherto been a matter for speculation. The manufacturer who had sneered at fancy colours and styling now admitted that his new model had 'a bit of the European touch in its coachwork'. Henceforth a customer could buy a Ford in any colour so long as it was Arabian Sand, Niagara Blue, Dawn Grey, or Gun-Metal Blue.

Ford had triumphed again. And he was active now in another dimension. The copy for his aircraft advertisements of 1928 was rich and visionary:

When forest fires or tornadoes strew the paths of civilization with wreckage and suffering . . . when levees melt away before uncontrollable floods, and entire countrysides are inundated . . . when blizzards smother city and country under paralysing burdens of snow and sleet, *where does man look first for help from his fellow men*?

Upward! For across the fenceless sky first aid will come!

It was a daunting thought that the air might soon be swarming with Model 'T's.

The depression which began in 1929 gave a swift quietus to hundreds of advertising campaigns. In vain advertising agents quoted precedents to show that a depression was just the time to advertise, and that in the past those who had greatly dared had greatly won. Most manufacturers were content to draw in their horns. The Gadarene race was over. Others decided that desperate measures alone could shift the contents of their gorged warehouses; and there were agents ready enough to undertake desperate campaigns rather than go under.

So, with the depression, began a period of strenuous vulgarity in advertising. Most of the offenders were those concerned with products for personal hygiene, a field which left plentiful scope for crudities. 'The comic strip technique was adopted with a vengeance', writes Professor R. M. Hower, historian of the Ayer Agency. 'The use of testimonials of all kinds increased, while premiums were recklessly offered and prize contests swept the country as swiftly as the craze for jigsaw puzzles. The shrieking headlines, gross exaggeration, and even downright deceit which appeared had no parallel except the patent medicine advertising of the nineteenth century, while the use of pseudo-scientific arguments and appeals to emotion and appetite surpassed all previous efforts and violated the previously accepted standards of decency.'

Preoccupation with bodily hygiene and functions had grown steadily during the postwar years. From itching scalp to fungus-ridden toes, no part of the body escaped the accusing arrows and revealing lenses of the advertiser. 'His heart quickened at the soft fragrance of her cheeks, BUT HER SHOES HID A SORRY CASE OF ATHLETE'S FOOT'. A wife obviously near breaking-point appealed to her husband 'Please do something about this!' 'This' was 'white coat-collar'. 'Four out of five are pyorrhoea's victims', cried a tooth-paste firm. There were pictures of men purporting to be steel tycoons and movie producers who yet knew so little of the facts of life that they accepted 'pink toothbrush' as inevitable. Sufferers from indigestion 'burped' in the reader's face. Every other page would have a close-up of a woman's armpit, miraculously cleared of unsightly hair ('His quick eye saw the soft white beauty of her underarm . . . intriguingly beautiful it showed . . . into his eyes there sprang a quick look of tenderness . . .'). Intimate details of female hygiene, previously obtainable only by sending to Nurse So-and-So for a discreet booklet, now found their way into bold print. It may be that in this latter field the advertisers did a bold and necessary job of education which could have been achieved in no other way. 'Nothing in Lasker's career ever satisfied him more than his success with Kotex,' says John Gunther.[1] Is it ungenerous, then, to complain that in the process 'protection' and 'confidence' joined the long list of words debased by the advertiser?

There was another physical shortcoming which even the ancients had recognized. 'A noisome breath with citron cure' urged Ovid in his *Art of Love*. It was necessary first to find a scientific-sounding name for this complaint, and the choice fell on halitosis, a word still spurned by many dictionaries. Halitosis was the spectre which Listerine conjured up, gigantic and menacing, until it shadowed the continent. Old-time medicine men had been content to call halitosis bad breath, without dilating on its social handicaps; though usually they were too busy 'curing' cancer and tuberculosis even to mention it. Until halitosis was discovered, an antiseptic had been something for rubbing on a schoolboy's knee.

For sheer fertility in creating situations in which halitosis could spell business ruin and the wreck of romance, Listerine must not be grudged a grain of admiration. There was the straight sentimental approach, with a colour picture of a lovely woman in distress, exclaiming: 'HER Honeymoon – and It Should Have Been MINE!' There was a picture strip which showed stages in the rise to success of a young fashion artist. His works were approved by the firm's chief client, a fastidious fashion editress. All seemed rosy for the young artist. Then one day the editress rounded on him suddenly and snarled: 'You are a very ill-mannered young man. The sooner you leave the better.' Mystified, he returned to his office, to find that the boss had already received a telephone call from the fashion editress demanding that he be discharged.

'I don't entirely blame her', said the boss. 'Halitosis has no place in business, so take that hint. Use a little Listerine once in a while, and come back in two weeks and I will hire you over again.'

This advertisement at least ended on a note of hope. Less cheerful was one which showed a young man eagerly offering his card to a prospective employer. Alas, it contained the words

1. *Taken At The Flood.*

'formerly with' above the name of his last firm. Any employer seeing those words – 'the phrase that wrecks a million men' – could see instantly that here was a fugitive from Listerine on the downward slide.

Another young man, an insurance salesman, found himself a guest at a millionaire's house party. By ill luck the others were playing 'nose-to-nose, Society's new game', the rules of which were explained by Jean, the millionaire's pretty daughter. 'You place a piece of tissue paper to your nose and the person next to you must take if from you by breathing through his or her nose. Each one who misses must pay a forfeit. It's barrels of fun and develops your lungs.' It seemed only fair that the girl who roped in her guests to play Society's new game should herself be drawn against the young salesman. . . .

Halitosis was such a money-spinner that many other firms, notably makers of dentifrices, 'angled' their copy accordingly. There was another social unpleasantness, hitherto talked about only in the most tactful terms, namely, Body Odour. Ovid had called it 'the goat below the arm'. It was left to Lifebuoy to inflate this rival spectre, which it did with much ingenuity, and with the help of numerous imitators. Again it has to be conceded that, though these anti-effluvia campaigns were often in dubious taste, the cumulative effect was undoubtedly to make the population look to its pores and its breath, to the benefit of a congested civilization. Because one individual dared not whisper a word to another, it was necessary to shout the word in the ears of millions.

Inevitably, the advertising of perfume also underwent a change. Until the First World War it was being offered as something which lent the virtuous woman an aura of innocent 'freshness'. In the thirties it was beginning to be sold with a wink and a leer; it was now a man trap, a weapon for stealing the other girl's boy. A shampoo, which had been a means of ridding the scalp of dandruff, was now a weapon by which the typist ensnared her boss. And so it went on. There was hardly a product which could not be sold on raw 'psychological' lines. Razor blades? The Gillette advertising had travelled a long way. 'Keep an eye on your wife!' cried a 1930 advertisement, which contained a picture of a wife looking distrait. The text ran:

Possibly she's not as happy as she seems. Sometimes you may catch her when she's off guard, and surprise a little wistful look on her face. Is she worrying about you? After all, most wives are loyal and proud, and rather reluctant to speak up. This may be far from the fact – but there is a chance she's distressed because you aren't as careful about shaving as you were in times past. . . .

For an advertiser to admit that 'this may be far from the fact' was unusual. Most copywriters swept the victim swiftly and irresistibly into the snare of their own setting. Their plausible humbugs of doctors in the picture strips diagnosed the complaint before the victim had entered the room. Spectacled and white-overalled, they spouted pseudo-science and bogus statistics, and sent the victim hot-foot round the corner to buy the magic product. Gone were the days when it was necessary to pretend that the secret of an ointment had been whispered to a titled traveller by a dying hermit in a cave at Petra. Now every specific was the result of years of testing in laboratories. Science had found the way 'to destroy millions of germs that swarm into your mouth with every breath and attack teeth and gums'. Science had ascertained that only nine men in a hundred need be bald.

Some time in the twenties it was discovered – doubtless in some scientifically conducted poll – that twenty million Americans fell so far short of the ideal of 'gracious living' that they did not buy toilet paper. Here was a challenge to the unfastidious copywriter. How could the shameless twenty million be saved? One advertiser decided to put them all on parade; he set an artist to draw a picture of a shambling, hangdog multitude stretching away into a doomed infinity, each with the mark of infamy on his brow.

While the manufacturers strove for the custom of the twenty millions who did not buy toilet paper, they also fought vigorously for the custom of the 100,000,000 who did. A full-page advertisement in the *Saturday Evening Post* showed a masked surgeon conducting an unseen, but, as the text revealed, an intimate operation. The heading ran: 'And The Trouble Began With Harsh Toilet Tissue'. Another advertiser, taking advantage of the convention that outrageous statements may safely be put into the mouth of a 'cute' child, drew up a full-page advertisement showing a little girl whispering into her mother's ear: 'Mummy, they have a lovely house, *but their bathroom paper hurts*!' Robert Waithman in his *Report on America* tells the story of Joan Foster. In Picture One her job hangs in the balance. She is rebuked (Picture Two) because her department has been slipping lately. She goes to see her doctor (Picture Three) who tells her that harsh toilet paper is making her 'condition' worse. She buys the right kind (Pictures Four and Five). In Joan's next appearance (Picture Six) she is back at her job, thinking to herself: 'The work is going smoothly again – thanks to Soft-Weave Waldorf!'

If the inventor of the zip fastener had guessed how his innocent device was to be exploited in advertisements of men's trousers he might have paused before giving the world the benefit of his genius. One full-page magazine advertisement showed a young man, alert and self-confident, posing in sleekly fitting 'gap-free' trousers fastened by a zipper. Beside him, in a negligent attitude, was a young man whose trousers were fastened in the same way that his father's and grandfather's trousers had been fastened. A savage arrow pointed to the offending irregularities, and a black headline cried INEXCUSABLE! Every device was tried to sap the self-confidence of young men walking about in trousers with the old-time closure. They were left to discover for themselves the embarrassment caused by zippers which failed to close.

About this time great emphasis began to be placed on the importance of svelte-fitting undergarments for men, and the reader's eyes were focused increasingly on the male crotch. The men who had conquered the West had done so without the benefit of 'support', but an effete new generation evidently stood in constant need of it. 'Support' had to be achieved without causing the wearer discomfort. Mr Cecil Beaton is one of many who have come to the conclusion that 'American men must be crotch-bound'.

A few of the more reckless advertisers of the lean years fell foul of the Federal Trade Commission. In January 1930 the *New York Times* was able to report that 'an unnamed cigarette firm' had promised to abstain from claiming that 'women retain slender figures' through smoking their cigarettes and to give up using phrases like 'overweight banished'. The Federal Trade Commission had been invited to take action not only by envious competitors but by observant citizens who had noticed that non-smoking celebrities were being represented as owing their slender figures to smoking the cigarettes in question. The *New York Times* thought that the Commission's intervention had given national good taste a push forward. Now the cigarette firms would have to fall back upon 'the doubtless excellent intrinsic merits of the cigarettes as smoking material only'.

The cigarette firms did nothing of the sort. Instead they 'proved' that cigarettes aided digestion, increased alkalinity, and saved people from such neurotic dissipations as doodling, pencil-chewing, and key-juggling. 'How are your nerves? asked one firm, and invited its male readers to try a simple test. This consisted of unbuttoning the waistcoat with one hand, starting at the top, and then rebuttoning it with the same hand, also starting at the top. Bogey for this operation was twelve seconds. If anyone failed, it was a sign his nerves were bad and that he needed to start smoking. Or perhaps that his waistcoat buttons were stiff.

The war between the Federal Trade Commission and the American cigarette manufacturers went on year after year, and is still in progress. One by one, firms found themselves debarred from saying that their cigarettes contained less nicotine, aided digestion, relieved fatigue, were recommended by nose and throat specialists, or were preferred by tobacco experts.

Occasionally the chewing-gum firms were not far behind the cigarette manufacturers in the fancifulness of their claims. One announcement of this product, headed 'A Tip to Motorists', said: 'Time passes faster – your wits are keener and your nerves are steadier, with —'s help'. Gum-chewing also cured ill-temper in traffic cops and saved marriages from dissolution. The knowledgeable housewife laid sticks of gum beside her guests' dinner plates, so that they need not suffer from 'logginess' after meals.

The absurdity and growing effrontery of many advertisements had long been irking an articulate minority, but advertisers were not interested in minorities. An advertising man, H. A. Batten, testified in the *Atlantic Monthly* in July 1932 that 'even a brief excursion through the average newspaper and magazine is, for the advertising man who respects his calling, a disheartening experience'. He noted how some advertisers were reluctantly being forced into sensational advertising because of unscrupulous competition by their rivals, and said regretfully: 'My own feeling is that there are few of us here on earth with enough moral courage to sacrifice our bread and butter for the sake of an abstract ideal'. The only way to put an end to advertising which was 'a stench in the nostrils of the civilized world' was for individuals to refuse to buy the products thus advertised, and to tell as many as possible why.

There was perhaps another way – to deflate advertising by ridicule. In the early thirties was published a strangely successful magazine called *Ballyhoo*, which thumbed its nose at the world of publicity. It introduced a character called Elmer Zilch, who propounded such heresies as 'if you can build a lousy mousetrap and spend $10,000,000 advertising it, the world will beat a path to your door'. His associate, Harvey K. Poop the Second, was introduced as 'the man who first proved statistically that four out of five have pyorrhoea and that nine out of ten believe it'. *Ballyhoo* published a 'Ten Commandments of Advertising', number three being 'Honour thy Father's Day and thy Mother's Day' and number ten 'Thou *shalt* covet thy neighbour's car and his radio and his silverware and his refrigerator and everything that is his'. It gave a glossary of advertising terms, which included:

Delicate membrane	– any part of the body.
Lubricate the skin texture	– put on grease.
Pore-deep cleansing	– washing the face.
Harsh irritants	– all the ingredients of a competitor's product.
Great scientist	– anyone who will sign an endorsement.
Lifetime	– until the new model comes out.
Exclusive	– expensive.

Readers of *Ballyhoo* were invited to send in samples of folly in advertising and they responded briskly. The magazine carried a small number of genuine advertisements and a large number of bogus ones, also a few indeterminate ones. There was much speculation about a full-page announcement reading:

Be a man and wear a Tarzan chest wig.
Are you bald-chested?
Are you afraid to expose your bare chest? Be a real he-man by wearing a Tarzan chest wig!

Blond chest wig $3.50	Brunette chest wig $3.49.
Tarzan Chest Wig Co.	Chester, Arkansas.

Whether or not there was a chest-wig factory at Chester, Arkansas, chest wigs have undoubtedly appeared on the market.

The popularity of *Ballyhoo* inspired many rivals, of varying degrees of wit and irreverence. *Ballyhoo* itself, perhaps under pressure of competition, gradually lapsed from its high purpose and became a journal mainly of leg jokes, interspersed by rather perfunctory tilts at advertising. It was easier perhaps to ring the changes on the oldest joke in the world than on the newest.

The disillusioned view of advertising was intensified by a number of books which 'took the lid off' the business and exposed the chicanery beneath. All this satire and 'muckraking' undoubtedly helped to promote a wariness of outlook in some of the public and eventually to create a climate in which such measures as the Food, Drugs, and Cosmetics Act of 1938 could be passed.

By about 1933 the worst of the depression was over. In that year came the repeal of Prohibition, a godsend to advertising agencies and the Press alike. It was a blow, perhaps, to the soft drink firms, whose advertisements were intoxicating even if their wares were not. A ginger ale company had been running a large advertisement headed:

O MAGIC NIGHTS BENEATH THE MOON
Where Eye Meets Eye Beneath The Southern Cross

There was a great deal more in the same heady strain, revealing finally that the grand catalyst of romance was the 'champagne of ginger ales', with its 'exhilaration and unusual zest'.

Overnight, drinking of intoxicants ceased to be a hole-in-the-corner hobby and became a mark of good breeding. In a two-page advertisement, addressed 'To The 73 Per Cent Who Said Yes', in *Life* for January 1934, the Schenley Distillers Corporation touched on a point which must have puzzled many:

After these fourteen years of barred distillery doors, of rusting vats and stills, of grapes rotting on neglected vines, and empty warehouses, in which fine old whisky should have been rightly mellowing – after these fourteen years of such discouraging inactivity, you must be inclined to wonder how really fine wine and spirits may now be produced or bought. ...

Some liquor firms, the announcement went on to say, had grown tired of waiting for Repeal and had gone into other business; but 'there were a few who never lost faith in the ultimate decision of America's millions', firms which went on 'building earnestly, soundly, confidently, through those fourteen years of shadow in preparation for the dawn'. What all this boiled down to was that Schenleys had spent their time obtaining control of many old-established American liquor firms and more recently had renewed relations with British breweries and French vineyards. Another firm explained its preparedness by saying that 'even during Prohibition the Company continued to operate, under one of the seven medicinal licences granted by the Government'.

Other staples of the advertising pages of the thirties were refrigerators, self-changing radiograms, home movies, frosted foods, silk stockings, and the new-style brassières ('lift, mould, restrain, hold'). While makers of brushless shaving creams were still crying 'Shaving Brush and Soapy Ear Went Out of Style With Hoops, My Dear', the electric razor came on the market and once more man was nagged to 'revolutionize' his method of shaving. (Astonishingly, after generations of razor advertising, it was discovered in 1950 that only one man in seven in America shaved daily.)

Airlines produced some impressive advertisements, the prize going to the one which advertised *noiseless* typewriters in its flagship. Shipping firms offered more and more sybaritic cruises. One of them ran, year in, year out, a line which seemed to have escaped from a poem: 'Dining-rooms with roll-back domes that open to the sky'.

As the thirties progressed, American copywriters also dabbled in 'word magic'. Much of it came from the hothouses of fashion, in whose service toiled a new, precious, rather inbred race of feminine wordsmiths. What the inarticulate layman might dismiss as a tight skirt was described by these adepts as a stem-slim classic of lethal grace ... panther-sleek and fabulously disciplined. There was lace like a wicked whisper; there were shadowed sunbursts of tulle; there were moonstruck rayons which flashed a frankly flirtatious glitter of jet, or parody-pearls trilling with pride; there were mischievous triple-rilled *derrières*; and there were necklines which sported daringly on the slopes of decorum but never lost their innocence.

The motor-car industry devised for itself a complete new vocabulary. It offered a levelized ride in a unisteel body, with sound-sorbers, powered by a micropoised engine with an eezee-drain sump. There were flashway signals fore 'n aft, the steering was permi-firm or safe-t-flex, and fresh air came in through rear-opening ventipanes, or ventiports.

More excruciating was the line of baby talk developed to accompany polychromatic pictures showing foods of an un-earthly succulence. Breakfast cereals of the 'snap, crackle, pop' variety had long had a nursery nomenclature of their own. Now makers of other foods began to boost their specialities as 'yummy', 'tangy', 'zippy', 'chewy', 'crispy' (or 'krispy'), 'crunchy' (or 'krunchy'), all just the thing for 'oomph 'n energy'. The ex-asperating device 'n had been popularized, no doubt, by 'Amos 'n Andy'; it became the scourge of magazine copy. So did the process of hyphening up, as in jiffy-quick, sun-sweet, and oven-hot. Stretch became s-t-r-e-t-c-h, cool became c-o-o-l. Coy apostrophes crept in everywhere – 'specially for you. Bafflingly, the word 'eating' became an adjective – 'a wonderful eating cheese'; then followed 'eatingest' – the 'eatingest corn that ever tossed a golden tassel'. Another school of copywriters used a highly charged prose better suited to the Song of Solomon to describe everyday phenomena – 'picked when the tender kernels are welling with milkiness'. Perhaps 'welling with milkiness' is as good a description of this style as any.

'Word magic' was frowned on by the inventor of a much-discussed system for assessing 'readability': Dr Rudolph Flesch.[1] This pundit out of Austria held that most advertising copy of the late thirties was being written to please the seller rather than the buyer; indeed, he might have said that it was being written to impress fellow copywriters. It fell to Dr Flesch to make the dis-covery that sentences of up to eight words were very easy to read; up to 11 words, easy; up to 17, standard; up to 23, difficult; up to 29 and over, very difficult. There was a little more to it than that, however. Dr Flesch counted the number of affixes in any given 100 words; 54 or more put the writing into the 'very difficult' class. Counting affixes was skilled labour, for it was necessary to count the am- in ambiguous, the apo- in apostasy, the dys- in

1. *The Art of Plain Talk.*

dysentery, the -ade in lemonade. The doctor also took into account the number of personal references per 100 words – words like you, me, I, wife, husband, dame, pal, and so on. Nineteen or more of these put the writing into the very easy class, fewer than two into the very difficult class.

In the early thirties the foundations were laid of the sprawling and laborious shrine of market research, in which the lamp of advertising (its acolytes said) could not fail to burn with a purer, cleaner flame. John Wanamaker, among others, has been credited with saying that he knew half his advertising appropriation was wasted – the problem was 'Which half?' It was a fair question, and market researchers now undertook to answer it. For several decades there had been spasmodic investigations into the pulling power of newspapers and magazines. In 1922 Daniel Starch (of 'Starch ratings' fame) conducted surveys into the readership of advertisements. George Gallup earned his doctorate of philosophy in 1928 with a thesis entitled *A New Technique For Objective Methods For Measuring Readers' Interest in Newspapers*. In 1932, on behalf of the Young and Rubicam agency, he carried out studies in magazine readership. But media research was only one branch of the burgeoning science: the investigators were now concentrating on the consumer himself – his tastes, habits, prejudices, ambitions, and social background. Old-time advertising men were sceptical of this trend, preferring to rely on inspiration and their own flair for discovering a 'newsworthy' selling angle. The less successful of them had wasted millions of other people's money by backing uninspired hunches, and they did not relish the rise of a science which claimed to show what people really said and thought about their advertisements. The more sober practitioners in market research had to fight not only this enmity but the disillusion of a world already sated with 'statistics' showing that nine persons out of ten had piles or dandruff. They knew that their research could be little more than a rough guide to the copywriter, who would still need all the flair he could muster.

Another field of research involved a critical, even clinical, appraisal of the product before it was launched. If careful investigation could prevent a manufacturer from putting out an imperfect commodity, or an ill-packaged one, or an ill-named one, or one for which there was no measurable demand, or one which could not be manufactured quickly enough, then obviously research was serving a useful function. If it showed there was scope for a product, then 'test runs' of advertisements in a carefully chosen locality, under controlled conditions, would show which selling angles were likely to be most successful. (A favourite device was the newspaper 'split run': half the copies would contain one version of an advertisement, the rest would carry an alternative version.)

What it all added up to was that hit-and-miss methods were gradually being abandoned in favour of a grand marketing strategy. Advertising worked hand-in-glove with a new religion whose missionaries, in the form of interviewers and canvassers, began to descend in swarms on the housewives of America, many of whom were by no means reluctant to answer questions or to keep diaries. Indeed, it was smart to be a member of a 'consumer jury' or a guinea-pig in a 'copy laboratory'.

One method of copy-testing involved submitting differently 'angled' versions of the same advertisement to a large number of women, and inviting them to pick out the presentations most likely, and least likely, to spur them to go out and buy the product. Sometimes the jury agreed that a certain presentation was outstandingly good; at other times they disagreed hopelessly. It was not long before someone hit on the happy idea of submitting to consumer juries advertisements which had already proved their worth, as judged by the number of keyed replies received. The juries frequently picked out for praise the least effective advertisements. The same test was then applied to highly paid advertising executives, many of whom also confidently chose the worst-pulling advertisements. The most that could honestly be said for the 'consumer jury' system was that it might in certain circumstances be better than nothing. It was important, pleaded the defence, that those questioned should be people with a 'consumer interest'. That is, it was no use asking non-smokers to criticize tobacco advertisements, or low-paid workers to consider exhortations to visit Italy. Again, it was essential that a member of the jury should be intelligent, equable, normal, and above any temptation to flatter the advertiser. Where was this prodigy to be found? All too soon researchers found, by trick questioning, that even intelligent, equable, and normal people were often plain liars, in that they professed to use products or read magazines which they felt would raise their social status in the interviewer's eyes.

Another method of copy-testing was for the interviewer to sit down cosily with an 'average' housewife and go page by page through a magazine which she claimed to have read, and noting which advertisements had impressed her eye and her memory, which ones seemed credible, and how far she had read them before turning over. Many readers, it was suspected, read the eye-stopping headlines and little more. In an attempt to discover how far down certain advertisements were read, the 'hidden offer' idea was tried out. In modest type, near the end of the advertisement, a free gift would be offered; there would be no prominent head-line crying 'Sensational Free Offer!' Then the number of applica-tions received would be carefully analysed. The system known as 'unaided recall' involved asking readers questions like 'Which razor blade manufacturer urges "Banish five o'clock shadow"?' Or perhaps the guinea-pig would be asked to lie down on the equivalent of the psycho-analyst's confessional couch, and would there be subjected to a list of words like 'toothpaste' and 'beer', to which he would respond with those proprietary names which first sprang to mind. Or he might be asked for his instinctive reactions to a list of proposed brand names.

But more sensational (in the literal sense) methods of pre-testing copy were being developed. From time to time news-papers had carried reports of an 'intimate' device used to measure the impact of sex-charged film stars on young men and women. This was the galvanometer (alias psychogalvanometer, alias lie detector), to which humanity supposedly betrayed its secret emotions. The adventurers of market research saw in it a potent instrument for their purpose. They seated their guinea-pig in a comfortable chair, with no distractions other than electrodes attached to his arms. When he felt at peace with the world, he began to study advertisements set before him, and as he did so instruments in an adjoining room charted his interest or apathy as the case might be. The dubious theory behind this device was that a person whose emotions were aroused was likely to go out and buy the product; no allowance would appear to have been made for the individual whose actions were not entirely governed by his emotions. Another difficulty was that pleasure and dislike both agitated the needle equally. A variation of this device involved the guinea-pigs pressing buttons inscribed 'like' or 'dislike' (this method was often used in testing radio programmes – see Chapter 12).

One additional test of copy would seem to be to have the copy-writer recite it when coupled up to a lie detector; though for all the writer knows this may already have been done.

9 Sobering Down

During the Second World War advertisements in the British press followed a predictable pattern. Boot-polish firms brought out the comic sergeant major to commend their wares; girls balanced military hats, not always at military angles, on their shampooed locks. Soon the cry was 'Go easy with —', 'Please use — sparingly'. Firms boasted how they had given up making saucepans to make steel helmets. Economy was an easy wagon on which to ride; by using such-and-such razor blades, which lasted longer, a man could help conserve the nation's supplies of steel. Proprietary medicine firms had magnificent new opportunities ('Worry floods the stomach with acid'). There were 'blackout nerves' to be conquered. Tonic wines were more than ever necessary for 'heroines of the home'. Trying to strike a bright convivial note, one firm advertised 'the cider for the shelter'. And on top of it all the Government nagged everyone to be brave and cheerful.

Much advertising space was 'presented to the nation' by private firms; only the churlish reader reflected that this was as good a way of spending taxable money as any. By the war's end some of the public had grown exasperated at the constant reminders of goods which were not in the shops. They grew still more exasperated when in the years of peace they found that these elusive goods were being shipped overseas. 'Yes, you want a — sweater. So do thousands of American women. Only about twenty per cent of American women who want — get —'. The British housewife found it difficult to shed tears over the deprivations of the American housewife.

The 'battle of the bulge' became a corsetier's problem. An electronic, jet-engined, sudsy, nyloned, chlorophyll-cleaned age was at hand, offering splendid new opportunities to the advertising men to raise the standards of gracious living and at the same time to stimulate the nation's debilitated export trade.

The introduction of a National Health Service, the optimists believed, would lessen the British passion for self-medication; but they were quickly disillusioned. For the more reckless cure-mongers, however, the opportunities had shrunk. In 1939 the Cancer Act had banned the advertising of cures for cancer, and the Pharmacy and Medicines Act of 1941 at last made illegal the advertising of cures for Bright's disease, cataract, diabetes, epilepsy, fits, glaucoma, locomotor ataxy, paralysis, and tuberculosis. With 1950 came a new British Code of Standards on medicines and treatments, consolidating and extending earlier codes. It was approved by the Advertising Association, the Newspaper Proprietors Association, the Newspaper Society, the Periodical Proprietors Association, the Institute of Incorporated Practitioners in Advertising, the Incorporated Society of British Advertisers, and other bodies; and it was drawn up in conjunction with the Proprietary Association of Great Britain. The Code forbade any claim to cure any ailment or symptom of ill-health; any misleading or exaggerated claim 'as to composition, character, or action of the medicine or treatment'; the disparaging of other products or of the medical profession; the use of words like clinic, college, and laboratory, unless such establishments existed; the use of the terms 'Doctor' or 'Dr' in the name of a product, unless it was on the market before 1 January 1944; the use in advertisements of medicines or treatments for women of any phrases implying that the product could be effective in inducing miscarriage – for instance 'Female Pills', 'Not to be used in cases of pregnancy', and 'Never known to fail'; the use of words like magical and miraculous; the inclusion of references suggesting that the product or treatment had some special property 'which is in fact unknown or unrecognized'; and the use of phrases suggesting that a product could promote sexual virility.

A long list of diseases, illnesses, and conditions for which medical treatments, products or appliances might not be advertised included anaemia (pernicious), arthritis, baldness, blood pressure, heart troubles, gallstones, indigestion (chronic or persistent), insomnia (chronic or persistent), leg troubles, pyorrhoea, rheumatism (chronic or persistent), and varicose veins. Asthma might be mentioned only if it was made clear that the product was merely for the alleviation of an attack, and if the advertisement recommended sufferers to seek medical advice.

As for slimming, 'no reference may be made in any advertisement to weight reduction or limitation, slimming or figure control', though this did not apply to offers of exercise courses or articles used for physical exercise.

The Code was not without its loopholes. It did not wholly frustrate anyone determined to invent a new 'disease'. There are many useful and hard-worked near-synonyms for 'cure'. Some critics wanted to see the spirit of the Code extended to cover the advertising of certain foods and drinks, and other commodities to which powerful virtues are ascribed. But in the field of medicines the Code did mark a big – and a voluntary – step forward.

Soon after this Code was agreed, a poster censor, with a bundle of strips of paper and a paste brush, toured the bright catacombs of the London Underground. He pasted over a slogan reading 'Keeps you healthy, slim and attractive' with another one which said 'Keeps you healthy, vital, and attractive'. On another poster the phrase 'acts like a charm' was blotted out, and excisions were made in the lists of afflictions for which solace was offered. The inquisitive public, who peeled off these stickers to see what was underneath, were puzzled and disappointed. Perhaps they thought: why delete a trivial flourish like 'acts like a charm', when so many much more extravagant claims, as on drink posters, went uncensored?

Besides critically examining claims made on behalf of new medicines and treatments, the Advertising Association during the postwar years continued to tackle abuses in other spheres – bogus home work schemes, the offering of worthless diplomas, and so on. It was instrumental in prosecuting offenders or running them out of business. The Retail Trading Standards Association also harried advertisers who too lightly employed words like 'wool' and 'linen'.

Those who had looked for a brave new world in which advertising would be found serving the fundamental needs of the community, as distinct from the profit makers in that community, were still not satisfied. In and out of office, the socialists complained of the 'waste' and 'irresponsibility' of big-scale campaigns. A Labour Party discussion pamphlet issued on the eve of the General Election of 1951 attacked advertising for its continued part in sustaining monopolies:

Vast sums of money are spent in attempts to convince the consumer that the particular advertised goods are unique – even when they differ from their rivals only in the colour of the label or the shape of the bottle. A monopoly is created in so far as advertising convinces the customer that no substitute exists.

The forces of free enterprise fought back, and in the summer of 1951 they used the picture-strip technique. At first glance this advertisement looked like just another in the series showing how foreign correspondents and continuity girls on the edge of failure were saved by drinking the right nightcap and thus ensuring a night's sleep which would reach down into their subconscious. The first picture, entitled 'Jim took his chance', portrayed a distressed young husband being consoled by his pretty wife. 'Don't carry on so, Jim,' she said, with tears in her eyes. 'I believe in you. I will stand by you if you want to take a chance and have a go at another job.' Reflecting, 'Well, it's a free country,' Jim gave his firm 'the push'. Two months later he was shown receiving promotion at another factory. And that night he told his wife: 'Betty, darling, I've got a better job and more money already, and it was you who gave me the confidence to take a chance.'

Underneath, to clinch the whole thing, ran the slogan:

FREE ENTERPRISE GIVES EVERYONE A CHANCE

The fall of the Socialist Government was given as the reason for discontinuing this campaign. It is conceivable that not all employers relished the idea of encouraging ambitious young men to give their firms 'the push'. While this campaign was running, a suggestion was made that a national advertising scheme should be launched to promote chastity in Britain, to make young people 'feel that illicit relations are unworthy of them'.[1] It is interesting to speculate how this subject might have been tackled on the lines of the 'private enterprise' campaign.

1. In the book *English Life and Leisure* by B. Seebohm Rowntree and Commander G. R. Lavers.

The most pervasive and tedious advertising of the postwar years was that of the soap powder and detergent manufacturers, who – as in the soap wars earlier this century – spent prodigious sums trying to shift the demand curve away from each other. 'Whiter than white' became a national joke. In the soap men's eyes, there was no greater love than that of the mother who, watching her sons at play, solemnly resolved to give them the finest conceivable advantage in life – a really white shirt in which to go to school. To weary consumers, these campaigns had all the ruinous characteristics of an armaments race, but the answer to the question 'Why not cut the advertising and lower the price?' was usually: 'The man who stops advertising goes to the wall.' And of course there was no lack of precedents to prove this. Then the petrol companies joined in the race. To the motorist all petrols were the same, but the companies spent enormous sums arguing that they were different.

The brewers for a while dabbled in a form of 'word magic' which could be described, a shade unkindly, as 'brewers' patriotic'. A sample:

LIKE SOME BELOVED and familiar face that we do hardly note till fear or danger bring it sharp before our eyes, so does This England bloom again in every heart. (Ill indeed is the wind that bloweth no man good.) For we are not aggressive patriots, with insistent symbols and official cries; there is no need. We love England for itself, not for the name; an England whose history is alive in beauty. . . .

Beer, this copywriter asserted, was an integral part of England's courageous, lusty past. He did not say that beer had given England her courage; but another brewer was heading his advertisement 'If you want to feel brave – ' and following up with: 'After a — you feel a bit more able to deal with difficult situations.'

Cigarette advertising began to attract heavy criticism, chiefly on the ground that it was anti-social to spread a habit which, on strong evidence, was a contributory cause of lung cancer. In 1962 the Royal College of Physicians, which three centuries earlier had tried to goad the Government to take action against 'plague cure' quacks, urged a ban or restriction on cigarette advertising. The tobacco firms had greatly increased their advertising budgets, and the total had reached £11,000,000 a year, while local authorities were spending on anti-smoking propaganda a sum which would not have bought a Rolls-Royce. Among other criticisms were these: that smoking was being associated with manliness ('If you're a REAL smoker . . .'); that the lighting of a cigarette was shown as the first imperative necessity whenever boy met girl, the implication being that it was the sparking-plug of romance; and that smoking was being represented as a cure for loneliness ('You are never alone with a Strand'). After some controversy the he-man and romantic angles were played down and the companies fell back on stressing flavour, roundness, quality, and prestige. They also resumed coupon warfare, one company offering vouchers which could be used for a flutter on the football pools.

The Press had its own good reasons for not wanting to see a curb on the big advertisers. Television had drained away much of its revenue, and many popular magazines had gone to the wall. More and more, newspapers resorted to putting out advertising supplements, in which specially solicited advertisements were supported by editorial copy. Sometimes these supplements had a legitimate news value, but often they had not. Journalists debated whether they were prostituting themselves in writing such copy but the answer seemed to be that newspapers must clutch at every source of revenue to stay alive. Advertising men, who had always boasted that they paid the journalists' salaries, smiled grimly. The public, noting that even *The Times* was prepared to put out an eight-page supplement about George Wimpey and Company or a twelve-page one about the J. Walter Thompson Company, often tossed the supplements away unread (no doubt researchers could say how often).

What of the status of the advertising man? Addressing an international advertising conference in London in 1951, Mr J. B. Nicholas, an advertising agent, said that 'in comparison with other professions – the Church, Education, the Law, the higher levels of journalism, and the BBC – I am afraid that it must be admitted that advertising sits rather below the salt. A chair of advertising should be established without delay in our leading universities, not to deal with technical aspects . . . but to study and examine particularly its social implications and its service to human relations.' There is still no chair of advertising in Britain, but in 1957 Mr Walter Taplin was appointed a Senior

Research Fellow in Advertising and Promotional Activity at the London School of Economics (London University). Soon afterwards he published *Advertising: A New Approach*, in the pages of which the advertising man may find fuel to rekindle his faith.

At that same international conference Mr Cyrus Ducker, director of the London Press Exchange, said the trouble with advertising was the Fifth Column of cynics within its gates. He thought that when the next census was taken very few would be found to have given their occupation as 'advertising'. The advertising man had been portrayed on film, stage, and radio as a cold-eyed, hard-faced, back-stabbing desperado who would cheerfully sell his best friend down the river and cheat his own mother for the sake of a good laugh. But the advertising man of today, at the top level, was

... generally a kindly and respectable-looking man of rather more than middle age, who lives in the best suburb, belongs to the best clubs in Town, avoids publicity like the plague, seldom goes to the pictures, always reads *The Times*, and never goes to the dogs.

To make the picture complete, Mr Ducker might have added that this dweller in the 'best suburb' could be relied upon to fight to the death any proposal to put up posters near his house.

In the postwar years, controversy over advertising methods resulted in the passing of several Acts of Parliament imposing tighter controls; notably on aerial advertising (Chapter 11), poster sites, and the wording of hire-purchase advertisements. From 1957 onwards two consumer bodies began to look critically at advertisers' claims and the products on which they were based. One of them was the Consumers' Association, publishers of *Which?*, and the other was the Consumers' Council of the British Standards Institution, publishers of *Shoppers' Guide* (this journal later broke away from its parent body). There was also an Advertising Enquiry Council, a non-political consumers' organization, which kept an eye open for abuses. Fleet Street had always said that anyone who criticized commercial products would be wiped out by libel suits; but Fleet Street soon began to quote extensively the often hostile judgements of journals like *Which?*

In 1962 the Advertising Association and twelve other bodies drew up a new British Code of Advertising Practices. This consolidated many other codes, laid down that all advertisements must be legal, clean, honest, and truthful; that they must not be of a kind to bring advertising in contempt; that there must be no exploitation of superstition and fear; that statistics with limited validity must not be used so as to suggest that they are universally true; that there must be no exploiting of the credulity of children; and that there must be no 'switch selling', namely advertising one article at a cheap price in the hope of persuading the customer to switch to a more expensive one.

As yet another earnest of good faith the advertising industry set up in the same year an Advertising Standards Authority to investigate and weigh complaints from the public. Its spokesmen claimed that this was the first time an industry in Britain had invited laymen to join a body sitting in authority over it – an example later followed by the Press Council.

AMERICA: OUT OF THE DEPTHS

In America the empire of the advertising men had become increasingly concentrated on Madison Avenue, New York, known flippantly as 'Ad Alley' and 'Ulcer Gulch'. Postwar recovery was swift; within two or three years the leading agencies were 'billing' upwards of one hundred million dollars a year[1] (that is, they were spending one hundred million of clients' money). Not only did they hire and fire the nation's radio entertainers (see Chapter 12) but they now employed cooks and dieticians, doctors, economists, tabulators, sociologists, psychologists, and psychiatrists. The more research-minded had their coast-to-coast consumer panels, their testing theatres, their computers to process the results of 'nose-counting' forays. No information, it seemed, was unavailable. How many housewives in Dubuque looked at advertisements on left-hand pages of magazines? How many households kept their *Saturday Evening Post* in the bathroom? How often did clerks in the Bronx change their shirts? The answer was there, somewhere, in somebody's file. Yet much

1. In 1961 the J. Walter Thompson Company, with forty-two offices throughout the world, had a billing of $380 million.

of this information was known to be based on polite falsehoods, and half the population did not know their own minds for two days running. Well aware of this, the *avant garde* were now dabbling in what they called motivational research, seeking by the methods of clinical psychiatry to uncover the secret impulses which made men and women buy this and reject that. Their questioners conducted long painstaking 'depth interviews' deliberately angled so as to lead the subject to suppose that the researcher was seeking a line of information other than that which he really sought. Soon the depth men were dragging up dark and often ludicrous debris from the Freudian well. Inter-office memoranda began to talk of phallic symbolism, castration complexes, and the rage for oral gratification. Christmas candles were said to outsell other lines because candles, like cigars, were virility symbols. One researcher came up with the theory that people liked soup because they associated its warm beneficence with the amniotic fluid which protectively surrounded them in the womb. Another said that men chewed gum because they were frustrated breast-feeders. Another argued that when a woman bakes a cake she is symbolically presenting her family with a new baby. Many of these 'discoveries' – as somewhat unsceptically described by Vance Packard in *The Hidden Persuaders* – were good for a coarse if expensive laugh. Even if the theories were correct, there was nothing much to be done with the information. Clients began to suspect that if they hired twelve psychiatrists they would get twelve different theories and enjoy twelve different laughs (Packard tells of a soap-maker who hired two experts, one of whom said that people wanted to get rid of their body odours, the other that they secretly wanted to retain them). There was also the tiresome complication that even if persons sometimes did things for the reason the depth men said, they often did them for sensible or economic reasons. Yet out of this flatulent nonsense sometimes came an idea or a suggestion which was worth following up; and to a layman it was usually the sort of notion which could just as well have emerged from intelligent straightforward questioning as from a trick confessional. However, in their anxiety not to miss any potentially useful idea, those agencies which could afford to do so continued to pay huge sums to their 'head-shrinkers' and the 'head-shrinkers' continued to operate their hidden cameras and their ink-blot tests and to seek in the menstrual cycle of women the secret of selling cake-mixes.

Much controversy went on between the advocates of the 'hard sell' and the 'soft sell'. Rosser Reeves, of the former school, argued in his *Reality in Advertising* (1961) that the only course was to find a Unique Selling Proposition (which was roughly the Lasker technique) and hammer away at it in plain words, tested for impact in a copy laboratory. He mocked the awarding of prizes for advertisements with pretentious artwork and text but demonstrably lacking in intelligibility and pull. 'The true role of advertising,' he said, 'is exactly that of the first salesman ever hired by the first manufacturer – to get business away from his competitors. Or, as the economists phrase it, "to shift the demand curve between products".' Rarely was the function of advertising defined as nakedly as this; and there were many on Madison Avenue who thought such definitions rash in the extreme.

The less strident technique was to build up esteem for a product by indirect methods, and one way to do this was to project a carefully calculated 'brand image' – an image which would associate the product with well-being, elegance, youth, social success, cheerfulness, masculinity, or romance; some quality which would help to distinguish it in the public mind from other products which were fundamentally identical. Where 'product parity' existed, a successful brand image, however basically unreal or silly, could spell the difference between triumph and collapse. Besides creating images, the experts were called upon to wipe out faded images and replace them with new; thus Marlboro cigarettes, which had become known as 'a woman's smoke', extended their male market when they were shown being smoked by tattooed he-men. It was not, of course, a new technique (though the jargon was); before the Second World War the tea industry in America had campaigned vigorously and not unsuccessfully to change the popular notion of tea from a 'sissy' foreign drink to a delectable American beverage.

The brand image was a favourite philosophy of David Ogilvy, an invader from Scotland who was behind many much-discussed postwar campaigns, from the selling of bubbly drinks to the popularizing of Puerto Rico. Ogilvy's images were supported by a generous ration of old-fashioned 'reason why'. He also had a touch of Barnumesque inspiration, badly needed when so much copy was beginning to smell of the laboratory. To sell expensive shirts, he sought out a male model of unusual presence in Baron George Wrangel, whom he persuaded – as an extra touch of distinction – to wear a black eye-patch of a type similar to that then worn by Mr Lewis Douglas, American Ambassador to Britain. As a curiosity-rouser and a money-spinner the idea was brilliantly successful, even though some criticized it as being in bad taste. Soon eye-patches were seen in other advertisements, notably on a female model in a girdle.

Madison Avenue worried a good deal about its own image. A severe critic was Professor J. K. Galbraith, whose advice as an economist was sought by Mr John F. Kennedy during his Presidential election campaign. As noted earlier, Professor Galbraith charged the advertising men with using their best talents to spread addictions which met no real human need. They had the normal human wish to be wanted, but they strove anti-socially to sell more and more tobacco, liquor, fast cars, and deodorants 'in a land which is already suffering from nicotine poisoning and alcoholism, which is nutritionally gorged with sugar, which is filling its hospitals and cemeteries with those who have been maimed or murdered on its highways, and which is dangerously neurotic about normal body odours'.[1] Other critics complained bitterly of the part played by Madison Avenue, which they now dubbed Medicine Avenue, in making America drug-addicted; not so much by direct advertising to the public as by a ceaseless and infinitely expensive bombardment of doctors with literature on behalf of 'ethical' drugs. Of these there were between 300 and 400 new formulations every year, but very few of them offered anything really new. The bizarre aspect was that while only doctors could prescribe these drugs to laymen, it was laymen who were telling the doctors what to prescribe; laymen who threw full-colour 'spreads' at them, played ducks and drakes with scientific findings, minimized or omitted any inconvenient facts, and all too often talked to the heirs of Aesculapius as if they were trying to sell glamour toothpaste to teenagers. With all this cajolery went a lavish distribution of gifts. It was not America's

1. Prof. J. K. Galbraith, *American Capitalism*.

problem alone; in Britain also doctors were under heavy pressure from the drug houses.

There was no lack of other criticisms. Advertising men were blamed for the policy of 'built-in obsolescence' supposedly incorporated in expendables; they were accused of bullying the public in its subconscious; they were suspected of rigging quiz games on the radio. And year after year best-selling novels, usually written from the inside, continued to portray them as power-crazed adulterers. Martin Mayer, author of that most knowledgeable book *Madison Avenue U.S.A.*, says: 'It is the disgruntled advertising copywriter rather than the malign intellectual critic who has given the industry the unfortunate part of its reputation.'

The Federal Trade Commission continued to cast a critical eye on the output of Madison Avenue, and especially on cigarette advertising. Tobacco firms were ordered to stop using phrases like 'not harmful', 'not irritating', and 'less irritating'. Obstinately, the Commission took the old-fashioned view that the chief irritant in tobacco was tobacco. One of the Commission's showdowns was preceded by an astonishing series of 'scientific' tests. The firm defending its honour bubbled smoke from various cigarettes through water and dripped the solutions on the eyes of rabbits; only the solutions of rival brands, it claimed, caused irritation. Embattled and embittered competitors devised their own smoking machines to blow smoke against rabbits' eyelids. All smokes, they reported, had an identical effect. Another test, later disallowed by the Federal authorities, involved cutting off the rabbits' upper eyelids, weighing the membraneous linings, drying them in an oven and weighing them again. The firm under attack then cut holes in the air passages of the rabbits and pumped smoke into their lungs (presumably because the rabbits were reluctant to inhale). Five of the animals died, but, argued the experimenters, they were all smoking rival brands. It was a haunting glimpse into the mad laboratories of advertising.

The war for hygiene continued unabated: AN HOUR UNDER THE MISTLETOE AND NOTHING HAPPENS ... HOW DO YOU GET TO BE AN OLD MAID, AUNTIE? ... A MAN CAN CHANGE, JUST LIKE THAT ... ME, JOHN, ME? UNRESPONSIVE? COLD? Suddenly came the sweet green age of chlorophyll, offering new hope for wallflowers and old maids. At least two hundred different articles containing chlorophyll were marketed – including chewing gum, toothpaste, soap, mouthwashes, cigarettes, shampoos, room sweeteners, shirts, insoles, and dog foods ('some breeds of dogs, though loveable, are pretty gamy'). Not before time, scepticism set in and chlorophyll was forgotten.

In the toothpaste field an admired entry was the picture-strip advertisement telling the story of Tommy, who had come home from school with a black eye. Questioned by his lovely young mother, he said that the boys had been taunting him because his father had begun to go out with other women. Tommy had lashed out in defence of his mother's sex appeal, but had been unlucky enough to receive a black eye. Mortified, his mother ran out to buy the only talisman which could bring back her husband's love – and began to rub it on her teeth. Next morning, radiant in panties and brassière, she whispered to Tommy: 'It works.' A later picture showed the children looking round the corner into the living-room, where Dad was waltzing Mom to radio music. 'Gee, looks like he's going to haul her off and kiss her,' said one of them. 'Yes,' replied Tommy, 'you can't say my Dad hangs around with other girls now.' [1]

All that needs to be said about Tommy is that he is right up in the same class as Jane Porter and her Soft-Weave Waldorf.

In the main, the American public was still prepared to countenance all kinds of wayward practices in the name of advertising, right down to the attaching of advertisements to girls' legs (the theory was that this was where everyone looked). Yet on one issue the public rebelled, or was induced to rebel. That was when it found itself being bombarded by loud-speaker advertisements in New York's Grand Central station. The campaign of protest was led by Harold Ross, then editor of the *New Yorker*. As a result, the nuisance was stopped. Ross then turned his attention to the loud-speaker advertising which had been started in public service vehicles in Washington. The *New Yorker* said:

> The role of the advertising man in this modern drama is unique, for he not only dreamed up the technique of catching the consumer when he was helpless but made the fatal blunder of calling his victims by their exact name, 'captive audience'. This phrase, coined in a

1. Quoted by Herbert Marshall McLuhan in *Horizon*, October 1947.

moment of triumph, turned and bit the advertising man, and it will live to bite him again. There is just something in the American temperament that doesn't like captivity – even the mild captivity of a streetcar ride with a radio that cannot be turned off.

On another occasion the *New Yorker* said:

The issue of the captive audience is simply the issue of the life contemplative; whether or not there is any obligation to preserve the individual's mental quietude, whether a citizen has a right to twirl his thoughts round as he pleases, or whether his thoughts may be twirled round at the pleasure (and profit) of a transit company. ... Free government cannot thrive without Contemplative Man.

And a spokesman of the American Civil Liberties Union was quoted as saying 'The Bill of Rights can keep up with anything that an advertising man can think of' – a heartening assurance.

10   Hoardings in Retreat

When the twentieth century came in, many a hoarding in Britain was still a sorry hodge-podge. Big posters and small were pasted side by side, above and below each other according to the whim of the man with the brush. A hoarding of this type might run housetop-high for the length of a street. There was some excuse for artists of repute refusing to design posters when they knew their works would inevitably be jostled by highly coloured crudities. Some improvement was to be seen, however, in 1904, when one contractor began to erect 'solus' sites, that is sites exclusive to one advertiser.

In 1905 Parliament was invited to pass an Advertisement Regulation Bill which would consolidate some of the ideas contained in the protective Acts secured by Dover and Edinburgh. The sponsors of this measure recognized that it was no use appealing any further to the good sense and good taste of the outdoor advertiser: competition was far too intense. The Bill reached the Statute Book in 1907. It empowered local authorities to 'regulate and control' hoardings over twelve feet in height and to 'regulate, restrict, or prevent' advertisements overlooking pleasure parks and promenades or disfiguring 'the natural beauty of the landscape'. This Act inspired many edifying but inconclusive arguments in court on such questions as 'What is natural beauty?' and 'What is a landscape?' For instance, was the bare sweep of the Sussex Downs a landscape within the meaning of the Act? There was nothing there, as Kipling had testified, except

> . . . our close-bit thyme that smells
> Like dawn in Paradise.

Surely, it was argued, a landscape needed trees, a river, a church spire, or a stately home? How could beauty dwell in emptiness?

In spite of these uncertainties, a number of local authorities did pass protective by-laws, and the bill-posting interests were soon complaining loudly of the conflicting rules which confronted them up and down the country. Sensing the drift of public opinion, a few firms, notably Michelin, began to take down their railside signs.

In towns, a flagrant new eyesore was the cinema poster, as crude and unregenerate as it often is today. Harry Furniss had this to say about cinema advertising in *Our Lady Cinema* (1914):

> Any ordinary theatrical venture would be ruined instanter by the exhibition of posters such as these. They are fifty per cent worse than the most atrocious poster advertising the most plebeian play in the vilest and most poverty-stricken purlieus frequented by the veriest riff-raff of the amusement-going public. Decent people are instantly shocked and repelled by their flaunting hideousness, and that the less educated section of the community is in any way attracted to them is open to considerable doubt.

John Hassall's view of cinema posters was shorter but just as crushing: 'Artistically too bad for words.'

When the National Council of Public Morals issued the report of its inquiry into the cinema in 1917, it said that censorship of posters was 'in some respects even more necessary than of films'. Although the bill-posting trade had power to exclude objectionable posters from the hoardings, it could not touch the posters on the cinemas themselves.

The First World War gave a violent impetus to the poster industry. It has been computed that two and a half million posters, by more than a hundred artists, were pasted up before conscription came in. Alfred Leete's Kitchener poster – 'Your Country needs YOU!' – was the most famous and inescapable. 'Women of Britain say "Go!"' was the title to a picture of a woman looking down, grave but fearful, from an open window. John Bull, wearing a Union Jack for waistcoat, joined in the finger-stabbing, crying, 'Who's Absent? Is it you?' A spirited picture of the *Lusitania* sinking was headed 'IRISHMEN! Avenge the *Lusitania*! Join an Irish Regiment today!' Not all these rousing pictures were sponsored by the Government. One, entitled 'The Vow of Vengeance', showed a soldier looking up from a woman's corpse to shake his fist at a German airship. Underneath was the reminder: ' *Daily Chronicle* readers are covered against the risks of bombardment by Zeppelin or aeroplane.'

Some of these wartime posters were crude in execution. A few were magnificent. The most illustrious artists now recognized that painting posters was their patriotic duty; there could be no question of the hoardings being beneath them. Yet in 1917, when Whistler's 'Mother' was set to work on behalf of War Bonds, there were still many who protested that art was being wantonly degraded.

When the war ended, the public were in danger of being poster-weary. London was seedy-looking under the remains of the recruiting appeals, partly over-pasted by the pill-men. The bill-posting industry began to clean up its heritage and to design new standard hoardings on the American pattern, with frames protecting the sheets from wind and rain.

Hundreds of railside hoardings were now falling to pieces; hundreds more had been voluntarily removed. A pill company is said to have defended its field signs on the grounds that they were made of tastefully enamelled iron and were therefore unexceptionable. Such concessions as were made were more than offset by the rush to build hoardings along the highways. Motoring was at last becoming a popular pastime (the Austin Seven emerged in 1922), and there was a real danger that thousands of people might remove themselves beyond the reach of the advertiser every week-end. Along every highway the boards began to multiply. Though a motorist was expected to be able to see a pedestrian at fifty yards in pitch blackness, he was assumed to be incapable of spotting a petrol pump by day unless it was prefaced by a series of overbearing announcements. In some places green English hedgerows which had stood for generations were pulled up and replaced by hoardings. If a tree hampered the traveller's view of a giant sauce bottle, it was cut down. Metal railway bridges, often eyesores in themselves, were made quadruply more offensive by the posting of announcements on the sides, underneath the arch and along the adjacent embankments.

Almost every year from 1920 onwards, Bills were brought forward in an effort to check these excesses. Some of them wilted under the sneers of Lord Birkenhead, the Lord Chancellor, in whom outdoor advertising inspired a curiously warm-hearted tolerance. On railway journeys, said the Lord Chancellor in 1921, it was common to see a large bottle appearing at frequent intervals by the rail side:

I will confess that I am so unaesthetic and so unexacting in this matter that if the bottle gives me the information how many miles we have passed since London was left, how many miles remain before London is reached, I withdraw all my aesthetic objections, because I consider that the bottle has played its part. The bottle very soon disappears. . . .

Sponsoring an unsuccessful Bill in 1922, Lord Newton said that if the Lord Chancellor had to live permanently in the neighbourhood of a bottle or a sausage he would probably regard such sights with different feelings.

Vested interests were not necessarily hostile to Lord Newton's Bill. Lord Riddell had let it be known that he wanted to see out-door advertising suppressed, an avowal which (said Lord Newton) must have caused him 'many pangs', in view of the open-handed way in which his newspaper was advertised. The Bill was described by Lord Birkenhead as 'futile and unnecessary'. Local authorities, he said, did not want it, and would not even use the powers they already had.

Readers of *The Times* held much debate about the extravagances of outdoor advertising in the early twenties, and the newspaper itself sought the views of many authorities. A Mr W. H. Atkinson, of Ealing, voiced the view of 'those with the misfortune to live in a street where their view is limited to the distance from their windows to the hoarding on the opposite side of the street'. He said:

Many of the manufacturers of goods so publicly eulogized are titled gentlemen and perhaps collect works of art. I wonder what they would think if they looked out of their windows one morning to find their beautiful trees and Japanese gardens hidden by a hoarding displaying pictures of oil engines and coal scuttles.

It was fair comment then and it remains fair comment now. A generation before, Thomas Holloway had retired to a spot where he was unlikely to be vexed by the sight of his own name. The merchant princes of the twentieth century lived in districts which jealously defended their amenities. Only advertising could bring worldly success, and only worldly success could bring relief from advertising. Model towns like Port Sunlight and Bournville escaped the attention of bill-posters, yet a few miles away less privileged communities would be plastered with posters for 'Sunlight Soap' and 'Cadbury's Chocolate'.

The Times noted that there was a general agreement on electric signs, which were 'all for the increasing of public happiness. They are an unfailing source of wonder to visitors from the country; they reassure the crumbling belief in magic of the youngest revellers, and they provide a field of considerable dimensions for the exercise of ingenuity.'

The poster firms were by now inured to unfriendly criticism, yet sometimes praise fell from unexpected quarters. At the Royal Academy banquet of 1923 the Prince of Wales (now Duke of Windsor) described hoardings as 'the art galleries of the great public . . . their refinement has advanced by leaps and bounds'. But only two days after it reported this speech, *The Times* lost its temper with outdoor advertisers: 'The motorist and the bicyclist, the pedestrian, the excursionist, and the native are alike disgusted at the insolent vulgarities which so constantly thrust themselves upon the eyes of every user of the roads.' There was a 'system of anarchical assault on the eyes' by 'ugly and lying puffs', and by-laws were frequently defied. The occasion for this tirade was the introduction of still another Advertisements Regulation Bill. The Government had failed to support any of the previous measures, complained *The Times*. Lord Newton's new Bill was intended to protect historic buildings – 'it will no longer be legally possible to prevent anyone from seeing Tintern Abbey, Magdalen Tower, or Kenilworth Castle without also seeing an advertisement of somebody's boots or soap'.

That same year the Minister of Transport noted with displeasure the way in which hoardings were being erected along London's new arterial roads even before they were opened. He issued a circular to road authorities reminding them of their powers and urging them to take action. But the most encouraging development of the year was the lead given by the big petrol companies in removing, at heavy expense, the most obtrusive of their rural signs. The great retreat began when the Isle of Wight Chamber of Commerce suggested to the Shell-Mex, British Petroleum, and Anglo-American companies that they should remove their boards from the island. They did; and Anglo-American offered to withdraw its field sites throughout the rest of the country if the others would follow suit. Shell-Mex, not to be outdone in public spirit, started pulling up its signs without more ado. Soon the three companies were joined by National Benzole, United Petroleum Products, Dunlop, and others. It was 'a triumph on the heroic scale', said Richardson Evans, of SCAPA, and nobody grudged the oil companies the virtue in which they basked. On town sites and filling stations the same firms still retained their advertisements.

Ironically it was the railways, drawing an impressive revenue from the eyesores on their bridges and embankments, which conspicuously improved the level of poster art after the First World War. The movement had begun just before the war, when Frank Pick began to commission distinguished artists to paint posters for the London Underground. Pick has been described as the nearest approach to Lorenzo the Magnificent that a modern democracy could achieve. After the war the big railway companies also began to give a free hand to leading Academicians. Some of the railway directors were unhappy about the pictures that were painted; so, for that matter, were some of the public. What (the directors may well have thought) would King George V say when he saw Clive Gardiner's poster of Windsor Castle, unrecognizable as such? The artist Oleg Zinger, after viewing (presumably) all the glories of Hampton Court, had elected to paint a single water lily. It was a very good water lily, but it was still only a water lily. There were some who preferred the more intelligible John Hassall Underground poster showing an old lady at the entrance to a Tube station – 'No need to ask a p'liceman' – or Alfred Leete's night watchman, with the comment: 'The roads are never up on the Underground.'

Not all Royal Academicians produced posters of distinction. There was no comfort for the failures in the view expressed by E. McKnight Kauffer that bad painters designed bad posters and that good painters always designed good posters. McKnight Kauffer, who himself excelled at expressing the bold essence of an idea in arresting colours, published his poster 'Bible' in 1924: *The Art of the Poster*. The reproductions consisted mainly of travel themes. There was one solitary film poster – by Will

Dyson, advertising *Moriarty*, a Goldwyn picture. And there was one of a lavatory cleaner. 'The appearance of a really good poster for an everyday commodity is still something of an event,' said Kauffer.

The new poster names were now those of Norman Wilkinson, Laura Knight, Edmund Dulac, G. Spencer Pryse, Maurice Greiffenhagen, C. R. W. Nevinson, E. J. Sullivan, Graham Sutherland, and C. Lovat Fraser. These artists had the advantage that they were able to draw on the wealth of Britain's scenery and historic places for their subjects. In due course they and others were called upon by the Empire Marketing Board, which in its heyday had twenty thousand hoardings of its own design. Seaside towns and inland spas were also crying for scenic posters (the Health Resorts and Watering Places Act of 1921 had empowered them to advertise out of the rates). Many of the resorts ordered pictures of bathing belles, which did not please the more conservative ratepayers. One of the best-remembered seaside posters was John Hassall's ebullient fisherman, who spread the fame of Skegness.

The improved Advertisement Regulation Act for which *The Times* had been calling was eventually passed in 1925. It gave local authorities power to restrain advertisements which would spoil a view of rural scenery from highway or railway or from any public place or water, or destroy the amenities of a village or historic place or monument, or of any place frequented by the public because of its beauty or historic interest. Model by-laws were prepared by the Home Office. The problem now was to induce local authorities to use their powers, and to see that they were not openly defied.

A *cause célèbre* of 1925 followed an act of defilement on the much-abused South Downs. Hove County Council prosecuted several defendants for erecting unsightly and intrusive hoardings, one of them 170 feet long, near Patcham. The owner of the land had himself put up a large poster which read:

> Watch and pray.
> The time is short and man brings about his own destruction.
> The air battle will be the end of the world.

As the new Act was not yet effective, it was necessary to prove that the scenery affected was a landscape. A representative of the

Brighton Arts Club testified that in his opinion it was, and that the hoardings ruined it even when the viewer was a mile away. For the defence, it was argued that the adjurement to 'Watch and pray' was not an advertisement. Surely the Court would not rule that a man of strong religious convictions was barred from putting up a text on his own ground? The Court decided that texts ought not to be propagated in such a way as to exasperate the public.[1]

Though the Act of 1925 was a step forward, it still allowed the flouting of urban and near-urban amenities. To take one example at random, a contractor set up in Southborough, Kent, a hoarding 12 feet high by 120 feet long. More than seven hundred signatures were collected in protest, but no action could be taken because Southborough was not a village and the hoarding did not obstruct the view of rural scenery. Industrial towns suffered renewed indignities. Here the bill-posters' argument was the old familiar one that there were no amenities to destroy. The streets were so drab, they said, that the plastering of bridges and gable ends could only serve to brighten them. To some observers it seemed that these mean streets might recover a little of their lost dignity if they were stripped of the advertisers' motley. It was a strange arrogance on the part of a soap-maker or a pill-seller that he should presume to decide which streets stood in need of 'brightening'.

In 1930 a Countryside Conference and Exhibition was held at Leicester. It had the effect of inducing more roadside advertisers to withdraw their signs, as the petrol companies had done. There was now quite a long list of firms which had voluntarily abstained from highway placarding, and there was little doubt that many other firms were advertising only because their rivals had forced them into it. Certain counties, notably Kent and Surrey, were more active in invoking their powers than others. Many hoardings were removed after amicable negotiations. Old quarry faces continued to exercise an inextinguishable fascination for some advertisers. In 1930 there were several outbreaks of advertising by turf cutting; on Cissbury Down, near Worthing, an advertisement 200 yards long, visible for miles, was hacked in the chalk slopes to advertise a building estate. Each letter was forty-five feet long.

1. Some of the most obtrusive 'advertisements' in rural areas have always been religious texts and exhortations, notably 'Prepare To Meet Thy God'.

The vulgarization of the highways could not be blamed exclusively on the poster firms. Crude signs erected by café owners, painted walls, whitewashed slogans on corrugated iron roofs, flyposted bills on backs of farm buildings, enamelled plaques on village shops, bills in house windows – these often were more repellent than the hoardings themselves. There was always someone ready to ruin a neighbour's view for the sake of an occasional pair of theatre tickets or a subscription to a magazine.

There had been a time when the cloak of night had concealed the worst of the roadside importunities. Now, however, reflecting signs sprang into dazzling life at every bend in the road, and neon signs were spreading out from the cities to the smallest villages. Few novelties created more controversy in the thirties than the 'red rash' of neon. It imposed its fiery outline on the bulls and griffins of inn signs; it glimmered under the thatch of tea shoppes. In his *Second Essays on Advertising* Mr J. Murray Allison said:

Some electric light signs are very beautiful – the neon light, for instance. In my opinion it beautifies every position it occupies. The *Daily Mail* in neon on the south side of the Thames near Blackfriars Bridge is a most glorious thing, and the light it sheds upon that portion of the river is just as beautiful, I believe, as the light that Whistler saw at Battersea.

So convinced were some advertisers of the glory of neon that they introduced the neon boat at seaside resorts. Hardly had the sunset died before a garish craft would be towed across the bay, covered with brilliant illuminated signs.

One objection levelled against extravagances like these was: 'How should we celebrate a great victory, a royal jubilee, when we make every night a carnival night?' A more weighty objection, perhaps, was that the multiplicity of signs was a danger to life. Often a motorist entering a strange town at night had difficulty in distinguishing the modest red and green of traffic lights against the effulgence of light on almost every façade. Advocates of safety first on the highways did not fail to stress this danger.

Between the world wars, the efforts of SCAPA had been heavily reinforced by the Council for the Preservation of Rural England, which carried out surveys of the number of advertisements per mile on popular highways. Some progress was being made towards further legislation, when the Second World War broke out and once again the hoardings of Britain were monopolized by Government exhortations – Dig for Victory, Careless Talk Costs Lives, Arm Him, Help Them Finish The Job, Let Us Go Forward Together, Bravo British Shipyards, and a hundred others. After the war the Government retained its grip on the hoardings, even while the Minister of Town and Country Planning was seeking to prevent amenities being ruined by posters – including Government posters.

In 1946 the Council for the Preservation of Rural England conducted a survey of the London–Hastings road. It listed 1,075 separate advertisements, of which more than 400 were on gable ends of buildings. Of the grand total, no fewer than 744 were encountered on the ten miles between London Bridge and Bromley. In some stretches of Sussex there were only one or two advertisements to the mile. Clearly it was now the urban areas which stood in need of protection.

Mr Lewis (later Baron) Silkin's Town and Country Planning Bill 1947, which came into force on 1 August 1948, laid down a code for the complete control of outdoor advertisements in England and Wales. Local authorities were now empowered, though not compelled, to nominate rural districts as 'areas of special control' and to limit advertisements therein as stringently as they wished. Control of posters was to be considered from the dual points of view of amenity and public safety. When reviewing an advertisement, a planning authority could consider the general characteristics of a neighbourhood, without reference to any existing posters. From 1 August 1948 no new advertisements were to be set up without consent of the planning authority; and from 1 August 1951 existing advertisements could be challenged by the planning authority, if it felt impelled to take action.

The poster firms showed a certain nervousness as 1 August 1951 approached, but there was no immediate rush of challenges. This was partly because the Minister had urged local authorities to settle disputes amicably, partly because local councils were overworked, and partly because the ordinary citizen was not yet aware of his new privileges. One of the first battlegrounds was Trafalgar Square, where the Westminster City Council was unsuccessful in its efforts to rid the south side of all electric signs.

From time to time *Advertiser's Weekly* reproduced photographs of advertisement sites banned by the Minister after contractors had appealed. The Minister did not take the trade view that the existence of a number of posters was sufficient excuse for adding another. He apparently disliked gable-end signs. And he disapproved of many advertisements on the sides of railway arches; these, he ruled, were likely to distract drivers.

Some poster firms accepted that they would be expected to give better value than hitherto. Any new site would have to incorporate a garden or ornamental plot, perhaps a shelter or a rustic seat. Many of these embellished sites now began to appear. Sometimes the posters behind them were a happy choice; as often as not they showed soap packets and sauce bottles. Sir Hugh Casson, the architect, stigmatized the garden site as 'the ultimate hypocrisy' and Mr Stephen Bone likened it to 'a gorilla with lipstick'.

In their own trade advertisements, bill-posting firms delighted to show 'before' and 'after' pictures of outdoor sites which they claimed to have dignified. A typical example featured the side wall of a house in an unpretentious city street. The 'before' picture showed the wall covered with tatters of paper, the remains of haphazardly posted bills: an undisputed eyesore. The 'after' picture showed the wall cleaned and painted white, and bearing a single large advertisement, not less than fifteen feet in height, reading 'Nestlé's Milk – Richest in Cream.' The legend said: 'This photograph of a — Solus Site shows how a derelict wall can be cleaned up and re-modelled to become an attractive strong-selling poster position – and at the same time greatly improve the local amenities.' The average man of goodwill will probably find the greatest difficulty in understanding how a sign of these dimensions – bearing a bold boast, and nothing else – can 'greatly improve the local amenities'. At that point he recognizes that he and the professional advertiser inhabit different worlds.

In the last few years the advertising industry has made a big effort to clean up 'clutter' on shop fronts, notably in rural areas. For far too long, the outstanding disgrace of the English village had been the all-purpose shop, covered with posters, plaques, shields, stickers, and bannerettes, and sometimes with a forecourt crowded with advertising stands. The postwar rage for luminous inks served to heighten the crudity of it all. To vulgarize the scene still further, tobacco manufacturers and others began to flood the country with sponsored fascia boards, on which the name of the shopkeeper appeared, if at all, in much more modest letters than those of the product. Easily the worst offender was the firm of Player's, whose ubiquitous pale blue, cheap-looking, graceless fascias were a sad reflection on a company of its standing. In 1962 Mr W. F. Deedes M.P. introduced into Parliament a Protection of Amenity Bill, the object of which was to prevent the obliteration of the identity of shops by advertisements of the branded products they sold. Planning officers, complained Mr Deedes, were fighting a losing battle against the fascia-mongers. The Government view was that the problem should be tackled voluntarily by the advertising industry, if possible. 'We are determined,' said the Parliamentary Secretary of the Ministry of Housing, 'to see that all forms of objectionable clutter on business premises, including sponsored fascia board advertising, will be removed.' Mr Deedes withdrew his Bill. Even as the industry was cleaning up the villages, the new supermarkets in the towns were disfiguring the High Streets by using the insides of their main windows as bill-posting stations, sometimes with sixty or eighty bills, banners, stars, and sunbursts, all in the most violent of luminous inks. Since bad manners are catching, neighbouring shopkeepers who had always regarded glass as something to look through also began to turn their windows into hoardings. It was clear that the clean-up brigade had a long and hard task in front of them.

In new towns and newly planned shopping precincts, outdoor advertisers resorted to the use of specially built kiosks and 'public information panels'. The attractiveness of the latter (the panels may be set out zigzag or at right angles) varies, inevitably, with the type of poster put on them. This, no doubt, is the form that outdoor advertising will take in the future. In a seemly town, with no bomb damage to be hidden and no building operations to be screened, there would seem to be little or no scope for the traditional hoarding.

AMERICA: BILLBOARD BLUES

In America, the passion for daubing slogans on rock faces had begun to abate by the time the twentieth century dawned. The tendency now was to erect hoardings in front of the beauty spots. 'The distinction is a fine one, but it means some gain,' wrote Charles Milford Robinson, a leader in the struggle against disfigurement, in the *Atlantic Monthly* of March 1904. As in Britain, field signs had sprung up in thousands beside railway lines, a practice which, to their credit, many of the railways actively resented. One company planted quick-growing trees to conceal the signs; another put pressure on landowners to reject poster advertisements. There was an attempt to foster the idea that a farmer who filled his fields with signs was thereby proclaiming his own poverty and ill-success.

Urban hoardings followed the British pattern, and the sky sign had now come to stay. 'The glory of the sunset silhouettes against the sky the title of a breakfast food; and the windows of the defenceless home look out on circus girls, corsets, and malt whisky,' complained Charles Milford Robinson. A widespread infliction was the setting up of large hoardings overlooking parks. Chicago and many other cities took special measures to frustrate such enterprise. Two of the New England States passed laws to prohibit advertising on trees. All over the continent there were moves to limit the size of posters. Of their own accord, contractors began to standardize hoardings and to keep them in better repair. The 'solus' hoarding was devised earlier than in England, and some advertisers found it worth while to lease, but not to use, adjacent advertising rights in order to ensure better display. In 1914 the Poster Advertising Association drew up a uniform specification for poster sites, and began voluntary censorship.

Between the wars, the advertiser flagged and flogged the motorist to an extent unmatched anywhere in the world. Inescapable was the word 'Eat', used as an imperative and as a noun with equal impartiality. 'Eat Here.' 'Joe's Eat.' 'Billy's Eat.' 'Good Eats.' And just plain: 'Eat.' The other ubiquitous three-letter word was 'Gas'. Crude and often home-made signs reading 'Orange Drink', 'Auto Camp', and 'Comfort Station' did probably more to vulgarize the highways than giant hoardings.

Aggressive, too, were the thousands of bright red Coca-Cola signs – the same red signs that today spread like a measles rash over scores of countries, notably in the Middle East.

One coast-to-coast advertiser hit on the idea of running four-line verses, one line to a board, with the boards mounted in series, so that the message could be assimilated at speed. Thus the first board would read 'TO GET AWAY'; the next a few yards further on, 'FROM HAIRY APES'; the third 'LADIES JUMP' and the fourth 'FROM FIRE ESCAPES', with the name of the advertiser bringing up the rear, 'Burma Shave'. If a verse could be serialized in this fashion, why not (said the wags) a short story – or even 'Gone With The Wind' for transcontinental reading?

Harsher critics said serial signs were dangerous; but some advertisers argued that there was so little to occupy the motorist's mind on these endless fast highways that their messages were doing a public service in keeping him awake and entertained. Over a dull route in Indiana, the writer encountered a series of recreational signs, bearing no sponsor's name, which carried the kind of statements once popular as 'fillers' in magazines: 'The vocabulary of the average man is 3,500 words'; 'The voyage of Columbus cost only 7,000 dollars'; and so on. After a while the anonymous advertiser began to conduct a quiz. 'Who said don't shoot till you see the whites of their eyes?' and 'What three coins make 76 cents?' The answer would be given after a suitable interval. When this palled, there came a series of French lessons, then algebra problems and other brain-teasers. No clue was given as to the purpose of the signs; no doubt it was some contractor's idea of creating goodwill, or drawing attention to his business. He desisted only when the approach of a big town offered the motorist a more generous ration of reading matter: 'Big Hop To-Nite', 'Burlesk', 'We Buy Pawn Tickets', and all the rest of it.

At any time between the wars, a battle was going on in half a dozen States between 'billboard' interests and local ratepayers' associations, women's clubs, chambers of commerce, safety-first associations, and architects' institutes. Legislation was piecemeal, and varied from State to State. Advertisers were persistent and ingenious; sometimes an exasperated local authority would set up screens in front of offensive hoardings. In Ohio poison ivy was grown on a long embankment to deter advertisers.

Outdoor advertising, like all other forms of publicity, had been put on as 'scientific' a basis as possible. Statisticians in the Traffic Audit Bureau could quote, or at least estimate, the 'circulation' of any advertisement, that is the number of persons likely to pass the point of exhibition daily. A big sign in Times Square, New York, was said to attract more than a million pairs of eyes every twenty-four hours. Cities were meticulously mapped to show all the available advertising sites and the numbers of persons whose attention could be challenged over a given period.

In the field of 'electric spectaculars' the big American cities – though they got away to a slow start – had little serious competition. There were many claims to have erected the 'biggest sign in the world' – but how was bigness to be measured? By area covered (there have been signs 380 feet long)? By number of bulbs (the Citroën sign erected in 1925 on the Eiffel Tower had 250,000)? Or by distance at which the sign was legible (the Citroën sign glowed for twenty-four miles)? Then there were claims to have built the most costly sign, or the sign with the longest run (Citroën's showed for eleven years). A historic 'spectacular' erected about 1910 over Herald Square, New York, showing a Roman chariot race, ran for four years and lured uncounted thousands of sightseers to New York. A Wrigley's sign of vast brilliance and complexity installed during the First World War ran for eight years. Millions who had never visited New York knew through the cinema or through illustrated magazines that Times Square was dominated by Wrigley and Chevrolet signs; an unseen audience which no Traffic Audit Bureau could count.

Though Times Square, New York, may well be the most ruthlessly exploited area in the world, it is impossible not to be awed by the wild exuberance of light, by the blinding multi-coloured cliffs soaring skywards, dripping with fire. 'Magnificent – if only one could not read!' is said to have been G. K. Chesterton's comment. It is a sad thought that a savage's dream of beauty should resolve itself in the mind of literate man into a boast by the Supreme Pants Company.

If the electric sign advertisers ever decided to call off this free entertainment, it would probably pay the city of New York to run the signs on its own account. The situation seems unlikely to arise. Both the advertisers and the city authorities are proud that on a clear night the red glow in the sky above Broadway is visible some fifty miles out to sea.

11   The Sky's the Limit

The idea of advertising on the sky had been a popular joke for generations. Between the world wars, like many popular jokes, it became a reality.

In 1886 *Punch* had published a cartoon showing a plain blunt business man and his wife gazing at the night sky. The wife was rhapsodizing over the beauty of the full moon, but the husband was sighing for lost opportunities. If only the moon had 'Blokey's Pickles' printed across it . . .

Also in the eighties, Villiers de L'Isle Adam wrote an extravaganza entitled 'L'Affichage Céleste', in his *Contes Cruels*. In this story the night sky became a hoarding, on which the Great Bear was embarrassed to find between her paws the legend, 'Faut-il des corsets, oui ou non?' and on the cluster of Virgo an angel appeared holding a flask and saying, 'Dieu, que c'est bon!' On seeing these mirific visions in the sky, the brawling citizens of Lyons and Bordeaux were so impressed that they forgot even the bitterest family feuds and sat down amiably together to study the new wonders of the firmament.

Villiers de L'Isle Adam may well have been inspired to this fantasy by a news item of the day, for inventors were already busy with monstrous lanterns. In 1893 a cloud projector was set up on the roof of the Manufactures Building at the Chicago Exhibition; it was used to announce how many people had visited the Fair during the day. At the close of the Exhibition it was installed on the roof of the Pulitzer building in New York. When there were no clouds it was necessary to make them – with the aid of high-exploding rockets. Inventors continued to experiment along these lines, but little more was heard of sky advertising until the period between the world wars. Then four main types of sky publicity were to be distinguished: smoke-writing, cloud projection, sky-shouting, and banner-towing.

THE
PICTURE
MAGAZINE

Cloud projection over New York in the nineties
From a contemporary magazine

When the First World War ended, Britain had hundreds of unwanted military aircraft, thousands of unwanted pilots. It was not long before units of this disintegrated air force began to fly on less heroic missions. As early as 1919 the Air Ministry was appealing to the public to report all instances of pilots dropping leaflets and other advertising matter. The Ministry also sought to prevent pilots from covering their registration marks with advertisements pasted or painted over wings and fuselage. Some pilots did not even pause to remove the military markings from their machines before taking wing in the service of commerce. But painting slogans on aircraft was too primitive a method of advertising; moreover, aircraft had to be flown dangerously low for the messages to be read. And the public gradually tired of the novelty of scrambling for coloured leaflets fluttering from the skies.

Smoke-writing was the first effective form of aerial advertising. In Britain it was taken up with eagerness and much self-congratulation by the *Daily Mail*, and was used with startling effect above the heads of the Derby crowds in 1922. Delightedly, the *Daily Mail* next day devoted its leading columns to a description of its own enterprise. Readers were told that the invention, full details of which could not be divulged, was that of Major J. C. Savage, late Royal Flying Corps, who had been experimenting since 1913. He and his pilot, Captain Cyril Turner, had spent more than three months 'learning to write and think backwards', for the technique was not the same as for ordinary writing. The machine used was a Sweep racing aircraft, and the total length of the letters traced was ten miles. Writing the words took two minutes and the effect lasted for five. As soon as the multitude saw the letters 'Dail —', according to the report, they burst into a chorus of 'Daily Mail!' From no other daily newspaper was such enterprise to be expected. The spectacle was said to have caused wide satisfaction over eighty square miles.

Next day the feat was repeated over London, the trace being seen by 3,000,000 people over an area of a hundred square miles (how this was calculated was not made clear). A number of children in a north London school wrote to the *Daily Mail* expressing gratitude for this handsome entertainment, and a schoolmaster quoted one of his young pupils as saying 'Is it an angel writing in the sky?' The public were eagerly debating how the trick was performed. In answer to inquiries, the *Daily Mail* explained that the pilot did not loop the loop. The writing was all done on a horizontal plane, except for an occasional deviation to avoid smudging part of a letter already written. Captain Turner disclosed that writing a large 'D' was child's play; the really difficult letter was the small 'y'.

Although the skies of Britain rarely offer a suitable background for skywriting, the *Daily Mail* and Major Savage persevered. In the summer of 1924 the familiar advertisement was being written over nearly a score of seaside towns. That same year readers of the newspaper were invited to admire a photograph of St Paul's with 'Daily Mail' proudly scrawled above the dome. The *Daily Mail* also published a large photograph taken in the grounds of the Danish Embassy in London, showing the King of Denmark excitedly pointing out the smoke-writing aircraft to his guests. The inscription which so captured the royal interest was executed in 'huge flame-coloured letters'.

Little public controversy seems to have been roused at this stage by smoke-writing, which indeed inspired in most people only an ungrudged admiration for the skill of the pilot. The eyesore, if eyesore it was, was quickly dissipated on the breeze. In support of the practice it could be – and was – argued that skilled pilots were kept in training at no cost to the State. It was also hinted that the Air Ministry was keenly interested in the signalling and smoke-laying possibilities of the invention.

A less friendly reception – in some quarters, at least – was accorded to the practice of cloud projection, in which notable technical advances were made soon after 1930. One method involved inserting a stencil into a beam of light, another employed an elaborate system of mirrors. Early in 1931 there were reports that Alfred Ganthier of New York was working out the final details of a 91,000,000 candle-power projector capable of projecting an advertisement fifty miles. Clouds were unnecessary; the message appeared as if fixed in the beam at a predetermined range. One experimental message was projected over Brooklyn Bridge and a larger one over New Jersey. A rumour gained currency among the watching crowds that bootleggers had discovered a new method of signalling to ships.

That same year strange signs began to appear in the night sky of England, and once again it turned out that Major J. C. Savage was the brains behind the venture. On the first day of 1932 *The Times* printed an enthusiastic article by its aviation correspondent describing Major Savage's methods. Messages flung on the clouds were clearly legible six or seven miles away, 'and in one case where the operator followed the last retreating cloud towards the eastern horizon the legend cast upon it was read fifteen miles away'. The aviation correspondent thought that there could be little criticism on the grounds of amenities, as the message occupied 'comparatively little space'. He pointed out, almost in the same breath, that there was nothing to stop projectors being mounted in tandem. 'The best conditions,' he said, 'are given by high solid clouds with a clean regular base.'

This New Year message of cheer was sourly received by readers of *The Times*. Indeed, one of the first to condemn such enterprise was *The Times*'s own leader writer. The best he could say for the invention was that it might be of some use in time of war, by throwing a grid of light over a raiding aircraft, to help anti-aircraft gunners. Otherwise, the idea was intolerable. 'If it is sentimental to object to the use of the sky as a bill-posting station, let us be sentimental and proud of it. . . . Best of all would be a Government declaration that this was an indecent form of advertisement to which no civilized nation ought to be subjected and that it was therefore unconditionally forbidden.' Mr Lionel Curtis wrote protesting against 'the most comprehensive vulgarization of Nature that the wit of man can devise'. Professor G. M. Trevelyan thought that a project of this kind would 'brutalize life', and urged a Government inquiry. Then the legal issue was raised. Miss A. Mure Mackenzie wrote: 'The law forbids anyone to hang up in my garden an advertisement of, say, pills. Will it permit anyone to hang it above my head on a surface which belongs to me in common with the rest of the nation?' The answer from Lord Dunedin was not encouraging: 'He who owns a plot of the soil owns all that is above and below it; a tapering wedge towards the centre of the earth, an expanding wedge towards the heavens.' Unfortunately, he said, it was not possible to plot accurately the individual's portion of sky infringed by an advertiser.

Not all who joined in the correspondence were hostile to the new invention. Sir A. Verdon-Roe said that 'if the unimaginative are to have their way and crush the activities of the progressive, we are finished as a nation. England owes her present position to the enterprise of men like Major Savage. This hysterical outburst reminds me of the outcry raised against railways when they were first suggested.'

Major Savage was soon to have an opportunity to defend his brainchild, for the agitation in *The Times* resulted in the appointment that year of a Select Committee on Skywriting. His arguments appear to have greatly impressed the committee. What was the difference in principle, he asked, between smoke-writing and cloud writing, that one should incur such odium? 'The younger generation regard the sky as a thing of utility.'

Major Savage said that he had inserted advertisements in English newspapers inviting the public to say what they thought of cloud projection. With one exception, the replies were favourable. He produced a box containing 1,600 letters, of which specimen tributes were 'I saw the most wonderful writing in the sky' and 'I have never seen such a beautiful advertisement'. When asked whether he thought that a very large number of the population would welcome a message on the clouds 'Buy Baxter's Pills and Cure Constipation', the inventor said: 'I often wonder why it is that when approaching this question my opponents always think of the most beastly kind of slogan.'

The committee went to some pains to elicit from Major Savage exactly what type of image he could throw on to the sky. 'A beautiful glass of beer, for example?' suggested one member. The Major replied that he could project only a very simple silhouette. But another witness, Major C. F. Davey M.C. of Sky Publicity Ltd, said he could transmit coloured images; and as an illustration of his firm's virtuosity he added: 'We can put a clock in the sky with the hands keeping time.' From this, the least imaginative could begin to visualize moving pictures in the sky.

One witness who unreservedly opposed sky projection was the Dean of Westminster. Asked whether he would object to the clouds on a dull day being 'fretted with golden fire', he said he would not mind so long as the fire was Nature's own – 'the clouds are no less beautiful than the rest of the sky'. A suggestion was made that prayers or texts might be projected in the sky. To this the Dean's comment was that such a development would be the one thing needed to give Christianity its quietus in Britain. As for the charge that he was condemning something he had never seen, the Dean answered that he did not need to see a drunk man to know that he ought not to be drunk.

Major Savage then reappeared before the committee to point out that the Dean seemed to forget the enormous service once rendered to Christianity by a sign in the heavens. In AD 300 had not Constantine seen a flaming cross in the sky inscribed 'In This Sign Conquer', and thereafter become a convert to Christianity? Then Major Savage played his trump card; he had been invited to project texts in the night sky over Dublin, for the benefit of the Eucharistic Congress, and though a Nonconformist he was prepared to accept the contract. It was a dark hour for the Dean of Westminster.

The committee, announcing their findings, declared that they were 'not much impressed by the evidence of persons as to the hideousness of a sight which they had never witnessed.' Their view was that sky projection

... forms a relief to the squalor of the poorest streets and to the dull monotony of many others. It is open to question whether the leaden gloom of heavy clouds will be seriously desecrated by the loom of an unseen light. It is not necessary, unless one wishes to do so, to follow the beam to its termination. In fact this form of advertising may be less obtrusive and therefore less offensive than brilliantly lit signs or buildings at such a level that the eye cannot avoid seeing them without being lowered to the ground.

The only restrictions proposed were that advertisements should not be projected in rural areas, or in the vicinity of famous buildings, or on Sundays. It was a victory for the 'progressive' over the 'unimaginative'. Cloud projection continued on a modest scale, and created no more furores.

The committee's terms of reference had included an inquiry into sky-shouting, an art which had been practised in America, Sweden, and Italy, but not yet in Britain. After some difficulty, a witness was found who had experienced this form of attack from the receiving end. 'Suddenly you will hear a voice from heaven shouting "Smoke Old Gold", and then you will hear a bit of music. It is very discouraging to any mental application,' the witness said. This time the committee were ready to condemn what they had not experienced. Sky-shouting, they said, would be 'an unnecessary and intolerable imposition', and they were pleased to note that it appeared to have met with little commercial success.

Sky-shouting did not always meet with 'consumer resistance'. When readers of the *New York Times*, in the summer of 1933, were debating the practice, a Brooklyn resident told how he and his wife had been so impressed by a sales talk from a low-flying aircraft that his wife had gone out and bought the article advertised. 'I would rather listen for a moment to such a message and have it over with, instead of tuning in on my radio and being compelled to listen to many minutes of blah about Ajax Dog Blubber in order to hear a good dance orchestra.'

Meanwhile, a new method of sky advertising was being pioneered – banner-towing. One of the first demonstrations, perhaps the first, was held at Hanworth Air Park in July 1930 (in the same month that a dirigible inscribed 'Advertise by airship' flew over London). Royal Air Force aircraft had been towing gunnery sleeves for some years; now, with the devising of a paravane, it had been found possible to tow a long advertising banner steadily and safely. Flown at 3,000 feet, the message could be read, or so it was optimistically claimed, eight miles away. The cost was £100 an hour; minimum charter, five hours. Banner-towing aircraft were not widely used, however, until four or five years later. At first the public response was the usual one of admiration for man's ingenuity, rather than regret at his talent for importunity. Then, as the novelty began to wear off, there were many complaints that pilots flew too low over cities and too intrusively over public gatherings. It was even suggested that the aircraft companies deliberately put old and noisy aircraft on to this service, in order to be sure of competing successfully with urban din. Derby Day seems to have encouraged pilots to audacities. They were cautioned against flying low over the London Zoo, lest they should stampede animals carrying children. One pilot was carpeted for flying in the vicinity of a Buckingham Palace garden party; he was dismissed with a caution. Not so lucky was the pilot who towed a banner over Manchester during the two minutes silence on 11 November 1937; he was fined £3.

In his autobiography *The Mad Major*, Major Christopher Draper D. S. C. tells how, armed with a defective time-table, he flew a banner advertising cream crackers over Merseyside in 1934 as King George V was opening the Mersey Tunnel. There was an outcry, and the manufacturers paid £5,000 to charities.

One man who clamoured for action against low-flying advertising aircraft was Mr (later Sir) Alan Herbert. *Hansard* for 11 July 1938 contains this *cri de cœur*:

Mr A. P. Herbert: I was unable to hear your last ruling but five, Mr Speaker, owing to an advertising aeroplane passing across the sky. Can you give orders that our proceedings shall not be disturbed in this manner?

No reply was given. That year Mr Herbert introduced a private Bill to abolish aerial advertising, but it was lost in the press of Parliamentary business.

In 1938 the practice of banner-towing came up for review by an Air Ministry Committee set up under Lord Gorell to consider the control of flying. According to the committee, the reports of disturbance were somewhat exaggerated, but the members agreed that there were many people who thought this form of advertisement added 'an unnecessary quota to the burden of noises that have to be endured'. Some witnesses had called it an indecency to use the sky for the benefit of the few. The committee recommended that no more aircraft should be licensed for banner-towing, and that the licences of aircraft so employed should not be renewed after 1 October 1941. By that date there were more urgent problems than the control of aerial advertising.

After the war no petrol was available for aerial publicity until 1950. Then banner-towing aircraft began to reappear over British towns and beaches. By 1955 outbreaks of sky-shouting were being reported, notably from Richmond Hill, where a Messianic voice from aloft gave advice on lipstick. Several municipal bodies protested to the Government.

It is now illegal in Britain to 'emit or display' any advertisement from an aircraft. The prohibition, contained in the Civil Aviation (Licensing) Act of 1960, became effective on 1 January 1962. In Parliament, Mr Graham Page objected to the killing of an industry by a last-minute amendment to a Bill which was primarily concerned with other matters; respectable business men, he said, were to be turned into criminals at the stroke of a pen. Mr Duncan Sandys pointed out that these respectable business men were being given time to redeploy their resources. Aerial advertising was not a nuisance, but 'we are trying to forestall a nuisance'. The public hardly noticed that aerial advertising had ceased.

In America the sky still belonged to the salesman. A specialist in 'electric spectaculars' bought up Navy blimps which would otherwise have been turned into raincoats, and sent them aloft bearing mobile electric letters twenty feet high. In 1949 came the invention of 'sky-typing', which, its originators claimed, was to skywriting as typewriting is to handwriting. It called for the services of seven aircraft flying in line abreast. At the appropriate moment the centre aircraft sent out radio impulses which caused the other aircraft to eject puffs of smoke so timed that letters were formed. Mr Sidney G. Pike, president of the Skywriting Corporation of America, told the *New Yorker* that in ideal conditions aircraft could type a thirteen-letter message ten miles long in two minutes; or 'we can have the whole coast scribbled up in two hours'. The system had the advantage that anyone who could fly an aircraft could engage in skytyping. Nobody was unduly dismayed because on one occasion the words 'Skytyping Test' had come out as 'Skytyping Pest'.

Skywriting easily survived this challenge. In 1950 it was announced that 'Pepsi-Cola' had been written in rainbow smokes by as many as six aircraft in formation over 5,000 communities from Canada to Venezuela. In some areas competition between skywriters was so fierce that when one pilot wrote his appeal to 'Buy So-and-So' a rival pilot went up to inscribe 'Don't' in front of it.

In 1960 the newspapers told of experiments with an ultra-powerful Swiss-designed projector capable of throwing advertisements on clouds, dams, mountain tops, or large buildings. An assurance was given that the message left absolutely no scar and that unsightly clutter would be avoided.

In 1962 an outbreak of sky-squirting was reported. The people of San Fernando Valley, California, were sprayed with £7,000 worth of French perfume to mark the opening of a new department store near Los Angeles. This, however, was not a new idea; it had been tried out in Paris some years before.

12   The Tortured Air

When G. K. Chesterton complained that man had vulgarized Infinity, he may have had in mind the words 'Daily Mail' traced in the firmament above the dome of St Paul's, or he may have been thinking of the thousand unseen advertisements bombinating in the void – the radio messages flashing from beyond the sunset to warn mankind against pink toothbrush and athlete's foot.

In America, advertising on the air began nervously, haphazardly, after the First World War. Now there is a long and impressive list of countries in which – to quote the tactful phrase of an advertising impresario – 'the spoken word is at the advertiser's service'. In Britain the advertiser was firmly excluded from sound radio, but in 1955 he was allowed access to television. Here it will be convenient to review first the growth of the American system.

At the outset, broadcasting was the sport of amateurs. Even before the First World War ended, enthusiasts in America had begun playing gramophone records over the air, with or without credit to their local retailers. In 1920 came the event which roused Americans to the potentialities of the new toy: the broadcasting by Station KDKA (Pittsburg) of the presidential election results. The boom began. Within a year some 500 licences to operate broadcasting stations were requested and granted. A large proportion of these licences went to operators whose chief concern was to sell radio sets; others were taken up by educational and religious bodies, newspapers, and department stores. Notable in the throng was Station WEAF, operated by the American Telephone and Telegraph Company, which was willing to hire out its transmitter to any firm or organization wanting to provide a programme.

By 1923 there was near-chaos, thanks to the multiplicity of transmitters. In the listener's earphones sounded a crude charivari, a tumult of shouting and counter-shouting, of name-calling and deliberate jamming. The public had been assured that broadcasting was an invention not less important than printing, but at least printers did not print their messages on top of each other's sheets. Eventually President Harding appointed Mr Herbert Hoover as arbiter of wavelengths, and some semblance of order was brought to the air. 'Wave jumping' continued, however, until in 1927 a Federal Radio Commission was set up to enforce order and decency.

From the beginning, there was much wrangling as to whether advertising should be allowed. Some listeners thought it blasphemy that the cry of the salesman should be allowed to beat against the very gates of heaven. Others were content to look on broadcasting as merely another amenity devised by science for man's amusement and advantage. It was only right, they argued, that a capitalist who met the heavy cost of a radio entertainment should be allowed to mention the product he manufactured. Opinions varied as to whether he should be allowed to give a sales talk about that product and mention its price. Some thought it permissible to include 'commercials' in daytime, but not in the evenings. Others were prepared to tolerate a sponsor lauding his product, but drew the line at the non-sponsoring advertiser who leapt in between changes in programme with an irritating one-minute harangue.

What stimulated the growth of advertising on the air was the formation of networks, the first of which began to take shape in 1923–4. Many station operators had found that the maintenance of day-to-day programmes was a heavier commitment than they had expected, and were only too anxious to be taken under the wing of a resourceful parent body. As the 'hook-up' idea caught on, those national advertisers who had been reluctant to buy time from impecunious stations with no discernible following realized that there was a new mass public for the exploiting. In 1926 the National Broadcasting Corporation's network was set up, and in the following year that of the Columbia Broadcasting System. Advertising agencies, which at first had displayed little interest in the possibilities of broadcasting, now began to recognize where the profits of the future lay. They realized, more-over, that the new medium gave them access to a big section of the public who rarely if ever looked at print.

One of the tasks of the Federal Radio Commission was to establish the principle that the air was not a lake in which any American had the right to fish at whim. The lake was the property of the community, and was to be fished in only by those holding a licence, and in accordance with strict rules. If any fisherman abused or did not take advantage of his privilege, his licence could be revoked. When it tried to enforce the decencies, the Federal Radio Commission soon found itself accused by the broadcasting interests of being harsh, meddlesome, and irresponsible; while those who still hoped to make an honest woman of broadcasting belaboured the Commission for irresolution and timidity in the face of vested interests. In its own time and in its own way the Commission began to tackle the seamier side of commercial broadcasting, in which it was assisted by the swindle-hunting Federal Trade Commission. The air at an early stage had become a happy hunting ground of the medicine men. Whereas the old-time quack had run the risk of being thrown into a horse trough if he overplayed his hand, his successor had merely to possess himself of a microphone and broadcast his humbug with impunity across a State. In 1930 the Federal Radio Commission was not the only official body to close in on John R. Brinkley the 'goat gland specialist', who for years had used his radio station at Milford, Kansas, to lure to his hospital persons willing to pay $750 for a 'rejuvenating' operation. In 1929 he began to prescribe treatments over the air for those who wrote in describing their symptoms. These patients were directed to druggists belonging to the Brinkley Pharmaceutical Association, an organization with 500 members in Kansas, Oklahoma, and Nebraska. Soon doctors began to lose their patients and Brinkley found himself under attack. His 'goat gland' operation was denounced as a fake. Brinkley was able to produce a long, indeed an endless string of witnesses – including prominent figures in banking and oil – to testify that they had had their money's worth from the operation. Reluc-tantly, the State Medical Board agreed to watch Brinkley conduct two operations – from goat to user – but they revoked his licence to practise medicine next day, without waiting to see the results of the operations. Then the Federal Radio Commission revoked his licence to operate a radio station. Brinkley, who had powerful supporters, announced that he would appeal to the public. To dramatize the issue, he decided to run as independent candidate for the governorship of Kansas, and it seemed probable that there would be a political upset of some magnitude. However, Brinkley eventually sold his station and crossed the Rio Grande into Mexico, where he continued to broadcast defiantly from a new station.

Another broadcaster to be disciplined by the Federal Radio Commission was one nicknamed 'the Oregon wildcat', who in 1930 was alleged to have used 'indecent, obscene, profane, and objectionable' language over station KVEP in the course of nightly attacks on the chain stores. The Federal Radio Commission also attacked lottery organizers, fortune tellers, tipsters, and matrimonial racketeers. In 1934 the commission was reorganized and renamed the Federal Communications Commission, but still continued to draw abuse from both sides.

By the late twenties there were many and bitter complaints about the importunities of advertisers on the radio; but sponsors had begun to find new formulae of light entertainment which beguiled the masses to the extent that they were prepared to tolerate a certain measure of salesmanship in order to continue receiving it. The element of aggressive salesmanship was introduced by Albert Lasker, now the *enfant terrible* of radio. His agency hired talent scouts, built up stars like Bob Hope, produced shows, and became a powerful branch of show business. One of his pioneer programmes, for Pepsodent, featured Amos 'n Andy, who became a national obsession. Then came amateur talent shows, quizzes, and give-away programmes, all of which caught the public imagination. The 'plugs' might be irritating, but at least these entertainments were brought to the home at no cost, whereas listeners in Britain were forced to pay a licence fee for programmes of notorious dullness. More serious-minded Americans, watching the give-away programmes grow into a popular frenzy, suspected by now that they had been cheated. The radio industry was firmly in the hands of advertisers, and advertisers were concerned only to reach the largest mass audiences. It followed therefore that the great bulk of programmes would be light, popular, and unlikely to inspire thought or controversy. Radio, in short, was only a time-filling interval between bouts of salesmanship. True, the Columbia Broadcasting System could point to its New York Philharmonic Orchestra, and the National Broadcasting Corporation could boast its Toscanini, but these were only the show pieces.

Llewellyn White, in *The American Radio*, sums up what happened as follows:

Like the beleaguered Czechs of ancient Bohemia, the broadcasters had cried out for succour. Like the Hapsburgs, the advertising men who came to rescue remained to rule. And like many a philosophical Slav, the broadcasters accepted the conqueror's tongue.

When the 1929 crash came, the grip of the advertiser on the radio networks began to tighten. There were goods to be moved, and they *had* to be moved – even if it meant driving a coach and four through one code of ethics after another. Sales talk became still brisker and brasher and highly supercharged. To save their audiences from becoming punch-drunk under this kind of attack, some networks began to limit the number of words which could be spoken in a minute. A contrasting technique was to hire a voice which was lush, leisured, plummy, and avuncular, seemingly steeped in worldly wisdom.

Ingenious attempts were made to dramatize the 'commercial', to make it forceful or amusing in itself. Listeners heard the sound of a girl sobbing over a cancelled date, and a motherly voice tactfully counselling a change of face powder. Now, in all its horror, was heard the conversation at that blighted dinner party when the wife offered a cheap table napkin to her husband's boss. One excursion into dramatization was discouraged by the networks, however: the broadcasting of an after-dinner 'burp' to point the need for taking somebody's cure for indigestion.

The trail-blazers began to show increasing effrontery in tying in the 'commercial' with the subject-matter of the programme – the 'integrated plug', as it was called. Sometimes the 'plug' itself was guyed, as in this excerpt from a comedy programme (quoted, with apparent approval, in *Advertising Copywriting*).[1]

1. By Philip Ward Burton, Bowman Kreer, and John B. Gray.

'Messieurs, ze duel shall begin now and shall end when you hear "*touché*".'

'What do you mean, *touché*?'

'I mean to shay that Swift's Premier Ham is the ham that's brown-sugar cured to give it a fine flavour. . . .'

From making a joke of the 'plug' it was only a short step to making a joke of the product. But 'ribbing the product' had its perils. Not every sponsor was a Henry Ford, willing to listen to a joke against himself, day in, day out.

In the early days the 'commercials' had been delivered by the sponsor's own hireling. Now the performers themselves were called upon to praise the product. Even stars like Bing Crosby and Gene Autry had to be ready and willing to sandwich in their patter items like this (again from *Advertising Copywriting*):

AUTRY: I won't interrupt you again.

CROSBY: Good! Because what I am going to say now is too important to interrupt. So listen closely. Friends, there is only one genuine Wrigley's Spearmint Gum, and it always has the name Wrigley's clearly printed on the package. Look for it!

AUTRY: For my taste there's nothing else that can match the refreshin' Doublemint Flavour. It always gives me a welcome lift. And I get a lot of enjoyment out of Doublemint's pleasant, smooth chewin', too.

In 'tear-jerking' plays, characters who suffered ruin or sudden death would sometimes return to life a few moments later to take part in a commercial charade; which was as disruptive of mood as the lining-up of the corpses to take a bow at the close of *Hamlet*. And not only popular entertainers were called upon to endorse the product; so were news announcers, military commentators, members of brains trusts, and counsellors on human problems.

The attitude of many performers seemed to be: 'The show must go on, and we know it's a good show, so let's get the "plug" over as painlessly and entertainingly as possible.' Some artists found difficulty in delivering the more fatuous blurbs convincingly, and the impression – in the words of one critic – was that 'of a school bully reciting Mary's Little Lamb'. The surprising thing was that so many top-ranking performers contrived to say their lines as if they believed them.

The 'integrated plug' was not infrequently used in the 'soap operas' which became a rage in the nineteen-thirties. These day-time serials, on which James Thurber wrote long and devastatingly, were directed by the soap firms at the less intelligent house-wife, who would listen to three or four of them daily as she went about her domestic chores. Churned out by relays of cynics, the serials were designed to give frustrated wives the maximum opportunities for self-identification with the sorely tried heroines. Some listeners could not distinguish romance from reality and would send telegrams and bunches of grapes to a fictional character involved in a traffic accident. To the soap sellers it seemed a fair certainty that if the heroine of a soap opera were made to endorse a certain soap, the listeners would carry self-identification to the point of imitation. Which they did.

Criticism of soap operas came from 'sophisticated urban elements', but the soap firms could afford to ignore it; just as the manufacturers of 'yummy' or explosive breakfast foods could afford to ignore the criticism that their gift schemes were corrupting the child listener and filling a million homes with 'box-top jitters'.

At the end of the thirties the networks surrendered unconditionally to the 'singing commercial'. A two-man team launched the craze with a verse in praise of Pepsi-Cola, fitted to a swing version of John Peel. This verse –

> Pepsi-Cola hits the spot,
> Two full bottles, that's a lot.
> Twice as much, and better, too–
> Pepsi-Cola is the drink for you!

– was soon the scourge of the continent. In 1941 it was played 296,426 times over 469 stations. The public were even willing to put nickels into 'juke boxes' in order to hear it. Soon the air was full of maddening jingles, many of them composed by the same pair of writers. Few were so simple and catchy as Pepsi-Cola's. But the nation which had obstinately revelled in the 'singing telegram' had no intention of lightly forsaking the 'singing commercial'.

Another popular fashion was to give 'commercials' the Sono-vox treatment. This curious invention made birds, beasts, foghorns, and locomotives *talk*, or sing. On behalf of Lifebuoy, a foghorn achieved the noteworthy feat of enunciating 'Beeee Ooooh'. The manufacturers of Bromo-Seltzer, having been persuaded that the name of their product repeated over and over was the sort of noise a locomotive makes when it gathers speed, were further persuaded to allow the Sonovox experts a free hand. The result was a talking locomotive, which puffed into the programme to the delight of all small boys (who were the least likely, however, to be interested in the product itself).

Since the big advertiser likes to be confronted with charts and graphs showing that his appropriations are being scientifically spent, the most strenuous efforts were made to measure 'listener reaction' to programmes. Fan mail was too easily manufactured to be a reliable index. In the mid thirties the firm of C. E. Hooper, Inc., organized a system whereby snap checks were made by telephone on listeners selected at random from the directory. John Doe would be called to the telephone and asked whether he had been listening in, if so to what programme, and over which network, and finally: 'Who sponsored the programme?' Having satisfied the inquisition, he would be at liberty to return to his radio; though it was always possible that he might be called to the telephone again by a Hooper supervisor anxious to check that the firm's interviewers had been doing their job conscientiously.

Much importance began to be attached by radio advertisers to their 'Hooperatings'. But in due course other methods were devised of assessing the pull of radio advertising. The A. C. Nielsen Company fitted 'audimeters' to receiving sets in listeners' homes, and by this means obtained a traced record of all those periods when the radio was in use. Another idea was to instal an 'ear' which could transmit the sound from a receiving set by telephone wire to a central switchboard, where monitors could check which programme was in most demand. Critics of these devices pointed out that there was no proof that anyone was *listening* to or enjoying the radio when it was switched on. Possibly Junior was revelling in the programme, while the rest of the family were writhing.

It was one thing to check on the popularity of the programme after it had been broadcast. To some, the smart thing seemed to be to check on its merits *before* it was broadcast. Methods of pre-testing advertising copy have been described earlier (p. 222). Radio advertisers also seated their guinea-pigs before buttons labelled 'like' and 'dislike' and played over the programme to them, afterwards analysing the synchronous record of pleasures and aversions. Not surprisingly this method of producing predigested entertainment has been a subject for satire, but it is not likely to be abandoned so long as there are sponsors – and there are many – whose chief consideration is that no programme shall cause offence to anybody.

Those research organizations whose function was to amass facts about the consumers' tastes and habits were now given such tasks as discovering what percentage of housewives in the Eastern Time Zone were engaged in ironing, washing-up, tending children, or performing toilet at any time between 8 a.m. and 5 p.m. Figures were produced to show that mystery stories were more popular than serials among listeners in big cities, and the lesson was:

> Consider how much more effective the mystery story would be for decaffeinated coffee (a big city product), and how much more efficient the serial would be for baking powder (a small town product).

There was a period when advertisers feared that intrusive 'commercials' might defeat their purpose by antagonizing listeners. Nowadays they worry no more. Expert after expert has assured them that there is nothing to be lost and much to be gained by annoying the listener. 'Some of the most effective radio selling has been and is being done by commercials that seem to get the most negative comment,' say the authors of *Advertising Copywriting*. In *Modern Radio Advertising* Charles Hull Wolfe says: 'Make your announcement either intensely liked or intensely disliked.' There is no need to worry, he says, when 'people repeat your commercial in slightly derisive mimicry'. In any case, irritation over 'commercials' is 'largely momentary'. Aesop Glim, in *Copy – The Core of Advertising*, warns that the technique of irritation should be employed only in a programme of high merit. 'The show creates its goodwill – and a corresponding degree of tolerance in the hearts of its audience. Then the droning commercials go to work – like drills. They are geared to eat up seventy per cent to ninety per cent of that tolerance, but are not supposed to pass 100 per cent.'

Be this as it may, there would appear to be a sufficient number of individuals with a dislike of 'commercials' to encourage inventors in the production of gadgets designed to tune out 'plugs', or to switch off the sound by remote control. The advertiser can afford to overlook these perverse inventions, for he can produce evidence to show that some listeners, not necessarily children, prefer the 'commercials' to the programmes – just as thousands of persons prefer the advertisements in a magazine to the editorial contents. He can also produce statistics of polls showing that only a very small proportion of the American public would be willing to pay a licence fee rather than tolerate 'commercials'.

BRITANNIA DEFENSIVE

How did Britain contrive to thwart commercialism on the air? There are some who believe that only the intransigence of Mr J. C. W. (later Lord) Reith kept the advertiser at bay in those early days at Savoy Hill. Others prefer to think that it was the innate decency and good sense of the British public that prevented the profanation of a new cultural medium. Captain P. P. Eckersley, one-time Chief Engineer of the BBC, has another theory: 'Commercial broadcasting would undoubtedly have been instituted in Britain had it not been for the wavelength shortage.'[1]

In the aftermath of the First World War broadcasting seems to have been regarded by the Government as a tiresome child which kept making exasperating noises while its elders were trying to speak. It had to be held sternly in check, and the Postmaster-General was the man answerable for its good behaviour. On sufferance, the Marconi Company was allowed to broadcast an amateur service, which amused the broadcasters as much as it did its audience. When, on a summer's day in 1920, the company broadcast the voice of Melba, the Postmaster-General's department is said to have complained that wireless telegraphy was being used for frivolous ends. Soon many requests began to be made for permission to set up broadcasting stations, notably

1. *The Power Behind the Microphone.*

from big stores and national newspapers. These requests were flatly turned down.

The precocious infant could not be held back indefinitely, however, and eventually the decision was taken to allow the radio manufacturers, as being those most interested, to form a single broadcasting company, and to transmit programmes likely to encourage the public to buy receiving sets. The question of advertising had been anxiously considered. Sir Henry Norman, who was chairman of the Wireless Sub-Committee of the Imperial Communications Committee, wrote in *The Times* of 8 May 1922: 'Of course every big retail house would like to shout the merits and low prices of its taffetas and tulles, its shirts and shoes. There is no room for this.' The British Broadcasting Company was set up later in the year, and J. C. W. Reith became its general manager in December.

In the following year the Sykes Committee on Broadcasting heard evidence on the desirability or otherwise of allowing advertising. The newspaper proprietors had worked themselves up to a tense pitch on this topic. Lord Riddell, their spokesman, said that it was difficult to imagine anything more dreadful than that the atmosphere should be filled day and night with announcements of the merits of Beecham's or any other pills. If a firm gave a concert every night, and its name were mentioned each time, said Lord Riddell, that would be a valuable advertisement. 'The Press thinks that means should be devised to prevent this sort of thing. . . . If traders wish to advertise they should confine themselves to the existing methods.' Lord Riddell even suggested that radio advertising would be an infringement of 'newspaper rights', whatever those might be.

The Committee in their Report said:

In newspaper advertising the small advertiser as well as the big gets his chance, but this would not be the case in broadcasting. The time which could be devoted to advertising would in any case be very limited, and therefore exceedingly valuable; and the operating authorities who would want revenue would naturally prefer the big advertiser who was ready to pay highly, with the result that only he would get a chance of advertising. This would be too high a privilege to give to a few big advertisers at the risk of lowering the general standard of advertising.

The Committee thought there would be no objection to the broadcasting company being allowed to accept the gift of a concert and to name the donor; to broadcast the names of song publishers and the prices of their songs; or even to transmit commercial information in code, if it was necessary to augment revenue.

Contrary to the belief of many, sponsored broadcasts did take place in Britain occasionally in the early days of broadcasting. One of the first was by Harrod's, in 1923. One of the last was a fashion talk organized by Selfridges from the Eiffel Tower in 1925. Code advertising was never tried; but great liberties were given and taken in the naming of plays and theatres, cinemas and films, on the slenderest of pretexts – as they still are.

The British Broadcasting Company became the British Broadcasting Corporation in 1927. Sponsored programmes were still permitted under the terms of its charter, but few if any were broadcast. This was a cause of much satisfaction to the newspaper proprietors, who had scotched, as they thought, a dangerous threat to their well-being. In the entertainment world there had been some apprehension that broadcast programmes of lively quality might keep people at home; but as private enterprise was discouraged from sponsoring programmes, it did not seem that much was to be feared from a sober-minded monopoly sworn to give the public only what was good for them. The public at large worried little over the advertising issue. They had heard that broadcasting in America was constantly and ludicrously interrupted by sales talk. Perhaps it was better to leave British broadcasting in the hands of a benevolent despot.

Would-be advertisers were restless, however; and soon they got their chance. In 1930 Captain L. F. Plugge founded his International Broadcasting Company, which began to transmit commercial programmes in English from Radio Normandie. Three years later the Duchy of Luxembourg granted a concession to a French company to broadcast sponsored shows in such languages as it might wish. The Lucerne Convention offered Luxembourg a wavelength which was adequate for its internal needs, but the station 'pirated' a long wavelength which was lying idle. Both stations achieved quick popularity among those who found the BBC's programmes unduly heavy. 'Pirate' stations began to multiply', and soon Britain was being bombarded with recorded programmes from a wide radius – from Athlone, Madrid, Hilversum, Toulouse, and elsewhere. Many of the programmes were sponsored by well-known American firms, others by American religious bodies.

At first the BBC pretended that no one listened to programmes from the Continent, but by 1935 it was vigorously complaining to the Ullswater Committee about unfair competition. The Committee agreed that these foreign broadcasts were undesirable. So did the Postmaster-General; so, finally, did the Government. Then how, asked the critics in Parliament, did the Government propose to prevent the broadcasts? It was clear that the Government could do little or nothing.

In the newspapers, by common agreement, Continental broadcasts were never mentioned. When the *Sunday Referee* broke the vow of silence and began printing programmes of these stations, it suffered excommunication by the Newspaper Proprietors Association. This was a fate not lightly to be suffered (it meant, among other things, distributing editions by motor-cycle), and on promising to fall in line the newspaper was readmitted. The British public continued to tune in Luxembourg and to hum such jingles as 'We are the Ovalteenies'.

The Second World War was hardly over before the controversy flared up anew. A Socialist Government took even graver exception to the broadcasts of the pirate stations. 'Sheer naked exploitation' was a phrase used in July 1946 by Mr Herbert (later Lord) Morrison to describe the activities of Radio Luxembourg. 'We will do our best not to have commercial broadcasting directed at this country'. This was one of the many topics on which Mr Morrison clashed with Mr (later Sir) Winston Churchill.

When the Beveridge Committee on Broadcasting was set up in 1949, several big firms, notably Horlicks, Lever Brothers, Unilever, and Rowntree, submitted that it was essential for British advertisers to be able to go into radio if export markets were to be developed. They contended that the manufacturer was 'working with one hand tied behind his back'. These firms did not want to see the BBC displaced as such; all they wanted was a separate commercial network. The Institute of Incorporated Practioners in Advertising thought that Britain should be in the van of those who create new techniques in distribution and selling, and that the introduction of sponsored radio 'would enable us to compete in the vitally important entertainment industry, which through film and radio has become a great international force and in which our present weakness is a national danger'.

The BBC also submitted a memorandum to the Committee, pleading that

because competition in broadcasting must in the long run descend to a fight for the greatest possible number of listeners, it would be the lower forms of mass appetite which would more and more be catered for in programmes.

The Committee, in its Report published in 1951, turned down – though not unanimously – the idea that broadcasting should 'become financially dependent on sponsoring, as it is wholly in the United States and largely in Canada and Australia'. In the end this would only put control into the hands of those 'whose interest is not broadcasting but the selling of some other goods or services or the propagation of particular ideas. If the people of any country want broadcasting for its own sake they must be prepared to pay for it as listeners or viewers; they must not ask for it for nothing as an accompaniment of advertising some other commodity.'

To the general surprise, three members of the Committee – Lord Beveridge, Lady Megan Lloyd George, and Mrs Mary Stocks – proposed a compromise course of allowing advertisements on the air at specified hours. 'Is there any decisive reason why the most pervasive of all means of communication should not be used at all for this legitimate purpose? ... We believe that such advertising programmes at named hours, so far from causing offence to the public, would be welcomed by many of them'. There was another minority report, that of Mr Selwyn Lloyd, who was in favour of commercial programmes competing against the existing ones.

As for commercial broadcasts from abroad, the Committee thought 'the choice may come to lie between jamming them and making bargains to keep them under control'. The likelihood of a British Government jamming Radio Luxembourg, however, has never been very strong. In the 1960s several European states, notably Belgium, Holland, and Sweden, were beset by pirate ships beaming commercial entertainment from beyond the three-mile limit. Many obstacles were put in the way of British attempts to operate advertising ships, but by 1964 Radio Caroline and other maritime stations (including some based on abandoned forts) were bombarding Britain with light music. In 1967 new legislation drove all but Radio Caroline out of business.

TV – THE 'SALESMAN'S DREAM'

Television had not long been invented before it was being hailed, in America, as the 'vacuum cleaner salesman's dream' and 'advertising's third dimension'. It was one thing to make the public read about a product; it was another to make them listen to the recited virtues of a product; but how much, how infinitely, better if they could be made to *see* the product, to watch it being demonstrated in the comfort of their own homes. Moreover, a television audience would be one with superior 'buying power'.

On 1 March 1940, the Federal Communications Commission agreed to allow limited commercial operation of television from 1 September of that year, with a rider that 'emphasis on the commercial aspects of the operation at the expense of programme research is to be avoided'. Development was held up by the war, and when the fighting ended America had only half a dozen television stations. The subsequent pace of expansion, though uncommonly rapid, was not fast enough for the American Television Manufacturers' Association, which sought to expedite the avalanche by inserting, in more than a thousand newspapers, advertisements designed to shame parents into buying television sets for their children. A big illustration showed a tearful little girl and her sulky older brother. 'There are some things a son or daughter won't tell you', ran the text (a curious echo of 'Even your best friends . . .'). The boy and girl were ashamed to be with the rest of the gang, because they had no opportunity of seeing the television shows the others saw. Too proud to tell their parents, they bore with what fortitude they could the 'bruise deep inside'. There was an old-fashioned, nineteen-thirties ring about this advertisement, which as it turned out raised a widespread outcry. Some newspapers refused to publish it. The mistake, according to professional critics, was that the appeal was 'negative'. Soon afterwards a 'positive' advertisement depicting happy children cried: 'You'd give them the world if you could – this Christmas you can.' And they did.

The cost of running a television show was soon seen to be formidable, and one thing became rapidly obvious: there would have to be 'commercials' at painfully frequent intervals if the cost were to be covered. Though writers on advertising adjured demonstrators to remember 'You're in a living-room, not an auction-room', much high-pressure selling was to be seen. Many housewives, it must be conceded, took a keen pleasure in watching the latest household gadgets demonstrated. Television offered a lucrative new scope for the suave-mannered professional 'pitchmen' who ordinarily performed at exhibitions and fairs; it also gave employment to hundreds of minor actors and actresses, models, cartoonists, and animators. Filming of the 'commercial' saved much time and trouble and also eliminated the risk of a flustered performer spoonerizing a phrase like 'Always demand the best in bread' (which once happened). But if an 'integrated plug' was required – like interrupting a film about Lady Hamilton to suggest that she would have been a happier woman if she had used a deodorant (which also happened) – a live performer was necessary.

Those who prophesied that the public would rise in anger at the image, as well as the voice, of the salesman in their homes now had to explain away such phenomena as Arthur Godfrey, whose idiosyncratic delivery of 'commercials' earned him the sort of following accorded as a rule only to top-flight professional entertainers – and an income, from all quarters, estimated at $1,000,000 a year. Godfrey succeeded because he worked at low pressure; he was relaxed and gave the impression of being on the side of the consumer. According to *Time*, which on 13 February 1950 devoted its front cover and four pages to this untidy young man with the 'warty' voice, he was 'the embodiment of the homespun debunker'; he had 'found the medium bristling with split-second efficiency and slowed a portion of it down to a comfortable walk'. Godfrey had no inhibitions about 'ribbing the product' or mentioning other sponsors' wares. He liked to fool about with a ukulele, and in so doing revived the moribund ukulele industry.

The distinction between entertainment and advertising was hopelessly blurred in a spate of give-away programmes, in which mink coats, cars and refrigerators were awarded to persons who could find approximate answers to elementary questions, or who were prepared to compete in imbecile games before the cameras. One programme was especially designed for persons with hard-luck stories to tell. A pathetic-looking woman whose family had been ravaged by death and polio would be handed a package of the product and asked: 'How many yards in a mile?' If she was lucky she would win not only the sponsor's prize but hundreds of dollars promised over the telephone by sympathizers watching the programme. The camera would focus impartially on the twitching hands of the aspirant and on the commodity whose soaring sales made such largesse possible.

The crowning give-away programme, as many thought, was the television wedding. One such ceremony watched by the writer began with a cake being made with the aid of somebody's cake mixture. Then a master of ceremonies introduced a very sub-dued bride and groom, and in an effort to jolly them into life asked them how many children they wanted. A ring was presented to the best man, and the party moved into the studio chapel for a quick service, followed immediately by a grand distribution of presents – steamship tickets and hotel reservations for the honeymoon, refrigerator, washing machine, gas range, cutlery, and so on. The groom looked as if he would have been happy to forget the whole thing, but he was promised a motion picture of the ceremony to keep it green in his memory. The occasion was concluded by a spiel about enriched flour.

The Federal Trade Commission often inspired amused head-lines by its efforts to discipline the makers of 'commercials'. It ruled that if actors were to be dressed in doctors' white coats in order to sell drugs, then it must be clearly stated that a drama-tization was in progress. This drove many of the white-coated 'doctors' from the screen. If it was necessary to show ice-cream, the Commission said, then ice-cream must be shown, not mashed potatoes or creamed cheese, even though these were more photo-genic. Salt was not to be added to beer to improve the froth; red wine brought to the boil was not to be used to simulate coffee; compressed air must not be employed to make cakes fluffy. Male models who shaved before the camera were required to put a blade in the razor, whatever facial dilapidations might ensue from looking at a lens instead of a mirror. A firm which claimed that its shaving cream softened sandpaper so that it could be shaved clean with a razor had to scrap its commercial; it had been using plexiglass coated with heavy sand.

In enforcing these restrictions, the Commission was sometimes criticized for an obsession with the letter of the law. Many of the tricks were used merely to overcome technical difficulties of photography. Defending itself, the Commission adapted the words of Isaiah. Advertising, it said, must be so clear that 'wayfaring men, though fools, shall not err therein'.

In some quarters it had been urged that the choice of television programmes for children ought not to be left in advertisers' hands. Early in 1952 the Federal Communications Commission published the results of a check by a group of San Francisco mothers on children's hour entertainment. In four hours they logged (according to *Time*) 'thirteen murders and assorted killings, four sluggings, six kidnappings, five hold-ups, three explosions, three instances of blackmail and extortion, three thefts, two armed robberies, two cases of arson, one lynching, one torture scene, and one miscarriage. One mother clocked 104 gun shootings during a half-hour serial, and another found sudden death shudderingly described fourteen times in twenty minutes'.

In Britain, post-war television was operated on such a tight purse that many voices were heard calling for sponsored entertainment. Only in this way, it was argued, could better programmes be mounted.

The Committee on Broadcasting, reporting in 1951, held that television advertising would be a backward step. In their minority report, however, Lord Beveridge and his two associates thought that the public ought to have an opportunity at some stage of saying whether they would rather pay large fees in order to keep advertisements off the screen, or whether they would prefer to see some extra revenue raised by advertisements.

The issue was strenuously debated in Parliament and Press in the early part of 1952. A Conservative Party 'pressure group' had let it be known that they would strike as hard as they knew for the liberty of the advertiser. To the loudly expressed chagrin of the socialists (and the dismay of some of their own supporters), the Churchill government announced, in a White Paper issued in May, that they approved the principle of sponsored television – with reservations. Advertisers would have to build their own stations; there would be no 'commercials' over the BBC network. Moreover, no commercial television would be allowed until the BBC had completed its regional transmitters, and until much more research had been carried out in very high frequency broadcasting. The socialists lost little time in announcing that if returned to office they would not tolerate advertising on television.

When the House of Lords debated this White Paper, no one was greatly surprised to hear Lord Reith class commercial television with smallpox and the Black Death. In the Commons, defenders of the proposal argued that Britain need not copy the worst excesses of American television. 'We are a much more mature and sophisticated people', said Sir David Maxwell-Fyfe (Lord Kilmuir).

At first the Government inclined to the idea of sponsored programmes on the American pattern, but was persuaded this would be a mistake. Instead it proposed to set up an Independent Television Authority which would appoint programme contractors, and these companies would recoup their expenses by selling time to advertisers. In order that advertisers should have no control over programme material, advertising agents would be barred from joining programme companies. The Independent Television Authority would ensure that no excesses were committed by producers of programmes or by advertisers.

The Television Bill of 1954, which at long last broke the BBC monopoly, secured its second reading in the Commons by a modest majority – 296 to 269. Mr Herbert Morrison (Lord Morrison) discerned in the measure a Tory plot on behalf of big business to harm the small business man, who would be unable to afford television advertising. Lord Reith described the Bill as a maggot sunk into the body politic of England, and Lord Hailsham called it 'evil, mischievous, and ill-considered'; but there were several speakers who denounced as unthinkable the notion that Britain's great commercial corporations would demand degraded programmes before they would consent to advertise. *The Times*, edited by a former Director-General of the BBC, Sir William Haley, said: 'There are enough influences degrading public taste to forbid adding another'. Several newspapers thought that the diversion of advertising revenue to television would mean a shutdown of newspapers, thus constituting a threat to free speech. Economists said commercial television would encourage the public to spend on consumer goods when the Government was begging them to save.

The first commercial programmes were screened on 22 September 1955. To guide it, the Independent Television Authority had an extensive Code of Practice. Everything was to be honest and above reproach. All advertisements were to be reserved for 'natural breaks' in the programme and were not to occupy more than ten per cent of the total viewing time. No 'commercial' would be tolerated during a religious service or a royal ceremony. There were to be no advertisements the objects of which were wholly political or religious, or which related to industrial disputes. It was conceded that in certain circumstances substitute materials might be used by makers of 'commercials' in order to overcome technical difficulties of reproduction, but these must not lead to any exaggeration of the virtues of the product.

Special rules governed advertising to children. It was forbidden to take advantage of their 'natural credulity and sense of loyalty'; to encourage them to enter strange places or talk to strangers in search of coupons; to suggest that if they failed to buy some product or to encourage others to buy it, they were failing in some duty or lacking in some loyalty; to make them think they would be inferior to other children, or would be held in contempt or ridicule, if they did not possess a certain product; to encourage them to make themselves a nuisance to others, including their parents, in the interests of any product or service; and to allow children in advertisements to show bad manners.

The rest of the story is familiar. Independent television *did* screen a great many cheap, nasty, and trivial programmes, with a surfeit of sex and violence; but it also had its shining successes, even if these tended to be screened at unpopular viewing times.

There were protests because advertisements were spatchcocked into programmes at unnatural breaks, and because they were concentrated on peak viewing hours, but at least there were no 'integrated plugs'. A godsend to parodists were the advertising magazines, in one of which, for example, a group of public-house regulars would enthuse over a succession of covetable objects conjured up on various pretexts, or on no pretext at all, for their inspection; mysteriously, these programmes did not count towards the total of advertising time. At one period, cigarettes were advertised before and after children's programmes. Children *did* show bad manners in commercials, and some parents may have felt more distress on this score than over scenes of hanging.

Sadly, the BBC watched its viewers desert to the commercial fold. There was much envy of the enormous profits made by programme contractors, after a disastrous start; and in 1961 the first tax to be imposed on advertising for more than a hundred years was clapped on television 'commercials' by Mr Selwyn Lloyd (who, it will be remembered, had signed a minority report in 1951 recommending the introduction of commercial radio and television).

Attempts were made, as in America, to assess the impact of 'commercials' on viewers. At a conference of the Market Research Society in 1962 tribute was paid to the 'enthusiastic young men and women engaged in field work [who] visit homes – by permission, of course – to watch the reactions of typical families to the television commercials. There they sit on several evenings a week, these devoted investigators, noting who give full attention to the commercials, who give half attention, and who (grim thought) pay no attention at all.' If advertising was doing nothing else, it was providing fascinating new fields of employment.

The controversial strictures on Independent Television voiced by the Pilkington Committee on Broadcasting, which reported in 1962, need only brief summary. The Committee recommended that the Independent Television Authority should plan all programmes and sell advertising time to contractors; these would be paid fees for furnishing the required programmes, and any surplus would go to the Exchequer. There was a recommendation that the Authority should exert stronger control not only over the programmes but over the advertisements, which tended to appeal to 'human weakness'. Advertising magazines, the Committee urged, should be abolished, as they were a form of sponsoring. To this last proposal the Government agreed, and the necessary order was given to end them.

Even before the Pilkington Committee reported, the BBC had begun to shake off its reputation for staidness, shocking many of its devotees in the process. Those who consider it has betrayed its heritage are free to blame the introduction of commercial television; those who think the result is an improvement must, however reluctantly, give credit to the same cause.

13   Subliminal

In the late 1950s no debate on the ethics of advertising, in Britain or America, was complete without shocked references to the new weapon of 'subliminal' advertising.

For many years there had been rumours that advertisers had found a way of bombarding the consumer without his conscious knowledge. In 1934 (according to Mr N. J. Lambert in *The Times* 18 May 1957) a British company concerned with film publicity had experimented by projecting brand names on a cinema screen too quickly to be consciously seen, and also by transmitting messages in sound beyond the range of human hearing. These, it was claimed, were received by a number of people who were unaware of having seen or heard anything. In 1951 Francis Williams's novel *The Richardson Story* had as its theme the popularization of a quack medicine in America by means of inaudible messages grafted on to film sound tracks and radio recordings; a device with interesting political possibilities.

The real fuss began, from 1956 onwards, when reports were published of the supposedly successful use of subliminal advertising in America. Much cited was the story of a New Jersey cinema in which messages reading 'Eat popcorn' and 'Drink Coca-Cola' were flashed for about one three-hundredth of a second on the screen, the claimed result being a marked increase in the consumption of those commodities. One advantage of this device, it was argued, was that radio programmes need be interrupted less often for the sponsor's announcements, and audiences would thus receive more entertainment to the hour.

Indignant voices were quickly raised. Hitherto, as a reader of *The Times* pointed out, the victim of advertising had always known that he was being got at and could close his mind to importunity if he wished. Was it not antisocial and immoral to deprive the consumer of free choice? Sceptics said that, like hypnotists, advertisers could never hope to do more than stimulate latent desires, and that only the weak-willed were likely to respond.

Anxious that such faith in advertising as existed should not be undermined, the Institute of Practitioners in Advertising carried out a detailed study of the subject. Reporting in 1958, the investigators said they could trace no significant measure of success in any of the numerous experiments made. Certain 'case histories' which had been talked about did not exist. If subliminal advertising had any effect, there was some reason for believing that it promoted resistance to the message. Whether such methods were feasible or not, the Institute thought that any attempts to influence the unconsciousness were wrong and 'professionally unacceptable'. It was essential for the good name of advertising that the public should have free choice to accept or reject. The Advertising Association concurred.

The Times congratulated the Institute on its report. It deplored the notions of 'hitting below the belt of consciousness' and 'psychological assault and battery', and asked: 'If, in a televisionary trance, we are induced to buy some commodity for which our waking self has no appetite, should an action lie for fraudulent misrepresentation?'

Public apprehension was slow to be allayed. In November 1958 a suggestion was made in Parliament that subliminal advertising was being used by South Wales Television, but the reply was that the 'Keep watching' sign which was instanced was in fact shown for a readable length of time.

It is quite clear that the threat of subliminal advertising was blown up into an absurd bogy. In America, where advertising was already under fire for using 'hidden persuaders', intense irritation was caused among those who were trying to give a face lift to Madison Avenue. In Britain the Pilkington Committee on Broadcasting, reporting in 1962, were careful to recommend a ban on any introduction of the practice.

LAST WORD

We have seen how the advertiser has adapted old wiles to new forms of communication. It is probable that the future history of advertising will be a record of similar adaptations, for it is hard to believe that there can be any new wiles for cozening humanity still left in the bag. If the reader protests that at this stage it is equally hard to think of any new media which could be profaned by commerce, let him remember that sixty years or so ago it did not seem likely that the advertiser would be in a position to intrude his voice into private houses, to demonstrate his wares at the family hearth, or even to scrawl his message across the heavens.

Any advertising man who has read this far may demand to know why he alone of those who exploit human nature should be expected to head the procession along the road to absolute truth and honesty. It is a point he is entitled to make; on the other hand he may be willing to accept the responsibility. He may point out, with some justice, that his copy often observes a more scrupulous code of ethics than is observed in the editorial columns.

The responsibility for raising the standards of advertising (as of the Press) lies partly with the public, but not, as many apologists pretend, wholly so. Human nature, though glacially slow to improve, *has* responded on occasions to a lead; and today the advertising man, with his self-imposed codes setting a standard higher than the law requires, can fairly claim to have given this lead. Wrily, the hard-bitten veterans of the game may complain that modern advertising is in peril of foundering in a slough of good taste from which it will be impossible to extract it. This seems a pessimistic view. Advertising, after all, is the mirror of man, and man has never been in serious danger of becoming bogged down in grace.

Index

More about Penguins

Penguin Book News, which appears every month, contains details of all the new books issued by Penguins as they are published. From time to time it is supplemented by *Penguins in Print*, which is a complete list of all books published by Penguins which are in print. (There are nearly three thousand of these.)

A specimen copy of *Penguin Book News* will be sent to you free on request, and you can become a subscriber for the price of the postage – 3s. for a year's issues (including the complete lists). Just write to Dept EP, Penguin Books Ltd, Harmondsworth, Middlesex, enclosing a cheque or postal order, and your name will be added to the mailing list.

Some other books published by Penguins are described on the following pages.

Note: *Penguin Book News* and *Penguins in Print* are not available in the U.S.A. or Canada